CASES OF CONFLICT

CASES OF CONFLICT

TRANSBOUNDARY DISPUTES AND
THE DEVELOPMENT OF
INTERNATIONAL ENVIRONMENTAL LAW

ALLEN L. SPRINGER

UNIVERSITY OF TORONTO PRESS

LIBRARY AND ARCHIVES CANADA CATALOGUING IN PUBLICATION

Springer, Allen L., author
Cases of conflict : transboundary disputes and the development of international environmental
law / Allen L. Springer.

Includes bibliographical references and index.

Issued in print and electronic formats.

ISBN 978-1-4426-3518-0 (bound).—ISBN 978-1-4426-3517-3 (paperback).—
ISBN 978-1-4426-3520-3 (pdf).—ISBN 978-1-4426-3519-7 (html).

1. Environmental law, International—Cases. 2. Boundary disputes—Cases. I. Title.

K3585.3.S67 2016   344.04'6   C2015-905540-7
                                            C2015-905541-5

We welcome comments and suggestions regarding any aspect of our publications—please feel free to
contact us at news@utphighereducation.com or visit our Internet site at www.utppublishing.com.

North America
5201 Dufferin Street
North York, Ontario, Canada, M3H 5T8

2250 Military Road
Tonawanda, New York, USA, 14150

ORDERS PHONE: 1-800-565-9523
ORDERS FAX: 1-800-221-9985
ORDERS E-MAIL: utpbooks@utpress.utoronto.ca

UK, Ireland, and continental Europe
NBN International
Estover Road, Plymouth, PL6 7PY, UK
ORDERS PHONE: 44 (0) 1752 202301
ORDERS FAX: 44 (0) 1752 202333
ORDERS E-MAIL: enquiries@nbninternational.com

Every effort has been made to contact copyright holders; in the event of an error or omission,
please notify the publisher.

This book is printed on paper containing 100% post-consumer fibre.

The University of Toronto Press acknowledges the financial support for its publishing activities of
the Government of Canada through the Canada Book Fund.

Printed in the United States of America.

To

Anne

Sophie Jake

Seneca Buck Tess

&

Jackson

Contents

Preface

THE ORIGINS OF THIS BOOK LIE IN A MEETING IN VIENNA in 1990 focusing on the development of customary international environmental law.[1] I was among those defending the position that states have a legal obligation to prevent activities on their territory or under their effective control from causing environmental damage to neighboring states. Should serious transboundary damage be done, compensation is required. Yet squaring this alleged rule with the reality of state behavior was not easy. Those at the conference were all too aware of the Chernobyl nuclear accident, which had occurred just four years earlier. Not only had the Soviet Union failed to take any of the "reasonable measures" international law seemed to require, but there had been no formal claims from downwind states suggesting that Russia had a responsibility to do so or should bear liability for the damage that had resulted. To our skeptical colleagues, the rules we claimed to see were a mirage, the product of a unique North American experience or simply idealistic rhetoric, standards so distant from actual state behavior as to be essentially meaningless.

In nearly 40 years of exploring issues of international environmental policy with Bowdoin College undergraduates, one of the greatest challenges has been to help them come to grips with a body of law that seems so often ignored. The problem is hardly unique to the world of environmental protection. When confronted by such obvious inconsistencies as the nearly universal condemnation of torture and yet its common use by governments around the world, students have an understandable reluctance to embrace anything like "state practice" as playing a constructive role in promoting the goals of justice many presume that any system of law should uphold. However, in the environmental arena, there is a particular suspicion of rules created by states whose territorial divisions seem to defy basic ecological principles and whose past policies have often contributed to the environmental problems we face.

This volume is part of a larger project exploring how international law in all its various forms, from treaty law to customary state practice and general principles of law, is used and developed during transboundary environmental disputes. A series of case studies examines the relevance of international law by analyzing how it is invoked by the increasingly complex array of governmental and non-governmental actors typically engaged in them. The focus is not simply on what people say the rules are, but how they actually behave.

The goal of *Cases of Conflict* is not to prove the relevance of international environmental law, or to suggest that that a cohesive and effective body of substantive and procedural rules is necessarily emerging. Indeed, as at least several of the case studies make clear, the gap between what states and others say the law is and what they actually do is often quite significant. There can also be honest differences about the content of the rules and how they apply not in abstract discussions of broad legal principle, but in concrete situations where real problems are faced and differences must be resolved. Recognizing and understanding the broader implications of this reality is crucial for anyone hoping to see the progressive development of international environmental law.

Many people deserve my sincere thanks for all they have contributed to the project. Robin Trangsrud, who worked with me as a Surdna Fellow, did extensive work on South American river disputes and was a valued colleague in helping choose and define the format of the case studies. Liz McCaffrey helped research the Baia Mare and Sellafield case studies, and other research assistants in Bowdoin's Department of Government and Legal Studies, including Charley Allen, Stevie Lane, and Chase Taylor, assisted in updating all six of them. They are among hundreds of students who have contributed to the project, sharpening its analytical focus with their probing questions and their refusal to accept too easily assumptions about the content of international environmental law or how it is developed.

I owe special thanks to Tyler DeAngelis who, with advice from Eileen Johnson in Bowdoin's Environmental Studies Program and help from Sierra Frisbie and Emi Gaal, produced the maps for each of the disputes. Without Lynne Atkinson, the Government Department coordinator, nothing important gets done. Like all of my colleagues, I am in her debt. I am also very grateful to Bowdoin College and the Faculty Research Fund for providing funding for background research and the time needed to complete the book. As long as this project has been in its development, it is also ongoing, and the help and support of my colleagues continue is much appreciated.

I also want to thank everyone at the University of Toronto Press for all their assistance in turning a rough manuscript into a finished book: Mark Thompson; Beate Schwirtlich; Ashley Rayner; freelance copy editors Beth McAuley, Chris Cameron, and Barbara Kamienski of The Editing Company; proofreader Judith Earnshaw; and indexer François Trahan.

Note

1   Papers prepared for the conference may be found in Hanspeter Neuhold, Winfried Lang, and Karl Zemanek, *Environmental Protection and International Law* (Boston: Graham & Trotman, 1991).

1
Constructive Conflicts

For all their caprice and impermanence, the
boundaries that mark the diplomats' world . . .
are no less to be reckoned with than carbon.
—*Christopher Stone*[1]

Introduction

Territorial boundaries endure. While the common environmental dangers
we face are increasingly evident, the political lines that divide nations remain
stubbornly real. Finding ways to work together across these human-imposed
boundaries is crucial to the development of stronger, more effective environmental regimes.

Much of the current literature on international environmental policy
focuses on cooperation: deliberate, proactive collaboration by states and
other international actors. Scholars have analyzed the conditions promoting
cooperation and the ways in which international regimes can be structured
and managed to achieve shared environmental goals. When environmental disputes are studied, the goal is to prevent, manage, or end them. This
emphasis is understandable because some of the most important environmental successes have indeed been the product of conscious international
efforts to deal with problems ranging from marine dumping to stratospheric
ozone depletion.

Yet conflict over resources and their protection is as much a part of the
international landscape as cooperation and will only intensify, given growing resource scarcity and the dislocations caused by changing global climate
patterns. *Cases of Conflict* focuses directly on times of dispute as important
moments in the development of international environmental law. Conflict
tests international law; both its content and its relevance become clearer
in times of controversy. How states and other international actors actually
behave when real interests are at stake reveals more about existing state practice than do the early stages of environmental regime formation, when it
may be all too easy for states to agree on broad cooperative principles with
no immediate impact. The rules that are most effective are those with the
resilience to withstand the pressure of real-world disputes.

Conflict can also help shape the law, as national governments work to
manage their immediate differences and create new rules and procedures to

I

prevent future disputes. That specific events can have a significant catalytic effect on international environmental regimes has long been evident. Major tanker accidents, such as the *Torrey Canyon*, *Exxon Valdez*, and *Prestige* oil spills, brought higher liability limits and tougher structural standards for oil tankers. The nuclear meltdown at Chernobyl prompted the International Atomic Energy Agency to promulgate new notification and assistance agreements. Well-publicized incidents involving the dumping of hazardous waste at sea and in developing countries led directly to the negotiation of the Basel Convention on the Control of Transboundary Movements of Hazardous Wastes and Their Disposal (hereafter referred to as the Basel Convention). However, the development of law takes place not only in response to major catastrophes but also through a process of environmental dispute management that occurs on a regular basis across complex international boundaries.

Cases of Conflict focuses on six transboundary environmental disputes. It examines critically the relationship between the rules and processes of international environmental law and international behavior—how states and other international actors actually respond to the environmental problems they face. It does not attempt to confront directly the largely unanswerable question of the extent to which international law actually shapes state behavior. Instead, it explores ways in which legal norms are employed in the course of international environmental disputes, and how, in the process, those norms are developed.

Architectural Engineers?

Cases of Conflict is located at the intersection of several bodies of international relations scholarship. It builds on important work being done to bridge the gap between scholars of political science and those of international law, who have traditionally inhabited distinct and unconnected worlds. Although interested in similar issues, their approaches reflect different disciplinary perspectives. Working in separate academic departments, publishing in different journals, and attending their own professional meetings, lawyers and political scientists rarely interacted. Michael Cardozo has suggested that the differences between them reflect not an inherent gap, but differences in training and perspective more akin to those separating architects and engineers. Political scientists (architects) tend to examine broadly how political systems are designed, while lawyers (engineers) focus on the narrower task of building them, applying legal norms to particular international problems to help make the systems work.[2] Historically, these groups have also disagreed about the importance of international law in shaping international behavior.

Hans Morgenthau was a central figure in the realist approach to international politics that dominated the political science literature of the 1950s and 1960s. Challenging the utopian visions of those who had placed such apparently misguided hopes on the ability of institutions like the League of Nations and United Nations to promote international cooperation through the "rule of law," realists linked state behavior to the pursuit of power designed to defend and promote individual state interests. In such a world, international law would play only the most limited role and certainly not one to constrain state action. In Morgenthau's words, "International law owes its existence and operation to two factors . . . : identical or complementary interests of individual states and the distribution of power among them. Where there is neither community of interest nor balance of power, there is no international law."[3]

In contrast, traditional international lawyers, particularly those influenced by the neopositivist writings of Hans Kelsen,[4] placed limited emphasis on the political context in which international law was developed and applied. For Kelsen, international law was a body of normative standards, enforceable at least in theory by a decentralized process of state-imposed sanctions. The content of the law, the rules themselves, could be derived through careful scientific analysis of state practice. Kelsen had little interest in either the forces shaping the behavior of states or the circumstances likely to promote either state self-adherence to the rules or external efforts to punish violations.

In the 1950s and 1960s, Myres McDougal[5] and his associates at Yale challenged Kelsen's neopositivism, arguing against its preoccupation with formal rules, which they felt overemphasized the role of the state and encouraged a technical, legalistic approach to international law. Instead, the New Haven school described international law in terms of a complex "world constitutive process of authoritative decision," which took place among a wide range of state and non-state actors, and in multiple arenas with varying degrees of institutionalization.[6] Individual decision makers promoted views of what was right, derived from their individual political, economic, and social perspectives. For the legal scholar, the challenge was to identify the core values on which these decisions were based and to construct a theory of international law using these common values, such as the "advancement of human dignity," as its foundation.

Political values and processes played an important role for McDougal, occupying so central a place that critics could find little that was "legal" in his analysis. Richard Falk worried that McDougal's approach denied international law any "guidance function" and was open to "self-serving manipulation, thereby giving credence to the view that international law is little more than a repository of legal rationalizations."[7] In the short run, the challenge posed by the New Haven school seems only to have reinforced the neopositivists' determination to maintain a clear line between law and politics, with their focus trained clearly on the former. McDougal's work did encourage international lawyers to recognize the broader political context in which legal norms were shaped and applied, but it did not lead many to reach across the disciplinary barriers between themselves and political scientists.

There were notable exceptions. Important work published in the 1960s and 1970s on the relationship between politics and international law provided a useful foundation for more recent initiatives from within the international legal community. In 1959, Canadian legal scholar Percy Corbett published *Law in Diplomacy*,[8] which analyzed the ways in which international law had been invoked and shaped by British, American, and Soviet diplomats as they engaged over issues ranging from maritime jurisdiction to human rights. Two years later, colleagues at the University of Chicago, political scientist Morton Kaplan and international lawyer (later to serve as US Attorney General) Nicholas Katzenbach teamed up to produce their seminal book *The Political Foundations of International Law*.[9] Building on Kaplan's work in systems theory, they argued that rules of international law, both their content and their effectiveness, were closely linked to the structure of the political systems in which they operate. William Coplin's *The Functions of International Law*,[10] published in 1966, brought a sociological perspective to the issue of the relationship between international law and politics, suggesting that the lack of a strong "international political culture" was a serious impediment to the development of a robust system of international law. Of perhaps the greatest impact, at least on scholars of international relations, was Louis Henkin's *How Nations Behave: Law and Foreign Policy*,[11] which came out in 1968. Explicitly criticizing international lawyers and diplomats for failing to communicate with each other, Henkin analyzed case studies ranging from the 1956 Suez crisis to the 1962 Cuban quarantine to show the ways in which international law, though typically "submerged" rather than actively directing state behavior,[12] had affected what political leaders actually did. He also examined the political factors, both international and domestic, that helped determine whether international law, "primitive" as it still was, would actually be observed.[13]

By the time a new generation of international legal scholars began to connect with colleagues in political science in the mid-1980s, much had changed in the world of international relations scholarship. The rise of regime theory in the 1970s brought to the field of political science researchers who were keenly interested in forces promoting patterns of international cooperation that did not seem adequately explained by realist and neorealist models.

However, the work of people like Robert Keohane and Joseph Nye[14] did little immediately to breach the divide between political science and international law. Regime theory, like its functionalist and neofunctionalist predecessors, placed a premium on process in explaining why states cooperate. Rules had a place, including formal legal rules found in the treaties and conventions that formed the institutional core of many regimes. Yet their role was clearly secondary, and regime theorists tended to blur the line between law and other normative standards in ways that would be difficult for traditional international lawyers to accept, given the debate that had been taking place within the legal community during the previous decade. However, many regime theorists were drawn to the world of international environmental policy, since the years immediately after the 1972 United Nations Conference on the Human Environment (held in Stockholm and hereafter referred to as the Stockholm Conference) were a time of significant environmental institution-building. This provided empirical material for testing new theories of regime development, as the subfield adopted the new label "institutionalism" to more clearly reflect its central concern. This interest in the environment would later provide a substantive focus that institutionalists would share with those members of the legal community who were drawn to the environmental field.

The emergence of constructivist theories in the early 1990s brought additional opportunities for collaboration with international lawyers. Led by Nicholas Onuf,[15] Friedrich Kratochwil and John Ruggie,[16] and Alexander Wendt,[17] constructivists emphasized the central place of ideas in affecting the behavior of states and other international actors, rather than the material forces that both neorealists and their neoliberal colleagues considered dominant. Norms began to occupy a more important place in this wing of international relations scholarship, and Kratochwil argued that the character of certain norms as "legal" should be more fully appreciated by regime theorists.[18] More recently, constructivists have focused attention on the concept of diffusion, which attempts to analyze how ideas, norms, and policy instruments that are developed in one country travel across international boundaries and influence behavior even in the absence of strong centralized international institutions.[19]

Interdisciplinary initiatives beginning in the 1990s have brought international lawyers and international relations scholars closer together. Some of this is the result of changes taking place within their respective disciplines. Perhaps more important is that they "seem increasingly to see the same world outside their office windows."[20] Shared is an awareness of the growing importance of formal, increasingly "legalized" international institutions, the emergence of subnational and non-state actors as key players on the international stage, and the development of patterns of international governance where soft and hard law can intersect and reinforce each other. The question of compliance, when and why states obey international law, continues to be of genuine interest to scholars in both camps.[21]

Emerging is a body of interdisciplinary international law/international relations (IL/IR) research that has allowed legal scholars to make creative use of theoretical insights generated from all four major schools of international relations theory: institutionalism, constructivism, liberalism, and even realism. Indeed, among the most significant works emerging in recent years is *The Limits of International Law.* Written by Jack Goldsmith and Eric Posner,[22] it offers a critical assessment of the ability of international law to provide the degree of constraint on state behavior suggested by more optimistic scholars and political leaders. A very different perspective is presented in Jutta Brunné and Stephen Toope's *Legality and Legitimacy in International Law: An Interactional Account,*[23] which applies insights from constructivist analysis to explore the forces that shape the sense of obligation underlying effective standards of international law.

With such competing viewpoints emerging in the IL/IR literature, Jeffrey L. Dunoff and Mark A. Pollack make a compelling case for researchers to avoid an "ism" war and to embrace "pragmatic, eclectic theoretical approaches to . . . problem-driven research."[24] Despite the potential danger of "conceptual muddiness," Peter Katzenstein and Rudra Sil have reinforced this call for an "analytical eclecticism" that would attack "substantive problems in original, creative ways." Empirical reality should drive the research process "by recognizing the complexity of real-world problems and the practical consequences of different strategies for addressing these problems."[25] In a similar vein, Robert Beck has suggested that the key to overcoming the "two cultures" problem may be to identify "specific substantive areas of mutual scholarly interest."[26]

Two fields of international policy that have attracted the attention of interdisciplinary research are human/humanitarian rights and environmental protection, both areas of active regime development, but ones in which the shape of emerging regimes has been quite different. Since the early 1990s, the field of human rights has seen an unusual degree of centralization with the creation of new rule-based institutions and a dramatic expansion in the role played by international courts ranging from the European Court of Human Rights to the International Criminal Court. Scholarship has thus naturally been drawn to the impact of adjudicative bodies in promoting important human values.[27] Far greater fragmentation has been evident in the development of international environmental policy, which has nonetheless attracted significant engagement by both political scientists and international lawyers.

On the international relations side, much of the recent empirical work done by institutionalist and constructivist researchers has focused on the environment. Interest in diffusion emerged just as people began to acknowledge the weakness of global responses to problems such as climate change and, thus, the practical need to develop other mechanisms through which international cooperation can take place and rules can develop. International environmental lawyers, many of whom represent NGOs, multinational corporations, and other non-state and substate actors, now have a direct appreciation of the complexity of the emerging process of multilevel environmental governance that international relations scholars have been studying for some time. The rules are now being written in many arenas, including private ones, and international lawyers are very much involved in the process.

Transboundary Environmental Disputes

Cases of Conflict builds on this research but from the ground up. It is first and foremost a study of six interesting and very different transboundary environmental disputes, part of the messy real world these new research efforts attempt to understand. It embraces an eclectic research process, avoiding the lure of isms, although hoping to use their insight to understand more clearly what these disputes can tell us about the nature and development of international environmental law. It also attempts to understand more clearly the challenges faced in making this complex body of law more effective.

The six disputes are summarized in Table 1.1 below.

Why the focus on *disputes*? Daniel Bodansky has suggested that this "classic" approach to international environmental law is outdated, offering too narrow a perspective on problems that require a more complex process of environmental management.[28] In one sense, Bodansky is certainly right.

Table 1.1   Transboundary Environmental Disputes

Date	Name	Principal parties	Environmental effect
1997–1998	Indonesian Haze	Indonesia/ Malaysia/Singapore	Transboundary air pollution
2000	Baia Mare Cyanide Spill	Romania/Hungary	River pollution
2001–2005	MOX at Sellafield	UK/Ireland	Nuclear waste, air/ water pollution
1995–1996	Turbot War	Canada/EU	Overfishing
2005–2006	Voyage of the Clemenceau	France/India	Toxic waste
2003–2010	Uruguayan Pulp Mills	Uruguay/Argentina	Air/water pollution

Law created only in response to disputes would indeed be reactive and fragmented, and there is obvious appeal to law developed within the framework of robust, forward-looking institutional frameworks. Unfortunately, as the next chapter explains, political and economic factors and the complexity of the problems themselves have inhibited the development of strong environmental institutions, at least on a global level. The argument put forth here is that there are other ways to develop international environmental law, particularly in situations lacking the consensus required to create new institutions or where political differences make it difficult for states to act decisively within existing ones.

Adopting this approach does not imply that disputes dominate international environmental relations.[29] The focus on disputes seems appropriate because, when they do arise, they can reflect much about the reality of international environmental law. Disputes can also have a catalytic effect by making clear the need for more effective institutional development and by helping sharpen the normative framework in which these regimes are designed.

A working definition of "dispute" helps clarify the focus of *Cases of Conflict*. In the 1924 Mavrommatis Palestine Concessions case, the Permanent Court of International Justice (PCIJ) offered this definition: "A dispute is a disagreement on a point of law or fact, a conflict of legal views or of interests between two parties."[30] This formulation works well for our purposes, because it identifies important aspects of the conflicts being analyzed. While it suggests that a dispute can be primarily a disagreement over facts, not law, this may oversimplify the situation. Whether a proposed factory will actually pollute a transboundary river would appear to be a question that should be answered by scientists, not lawyers, and the dispute may be resolved simply by finding an objective, or at least an agreed-upon, basis on which to determine whether pollution is occurring. However, while law might seem likely to play a minimal role in the process, standards for what constitutes pollution may reflect a judgment in which legal standards are at least as important as scientific ones.[31]

The Mavrommatis definition also recognizes that conflicting interests, as well as views of law, can be the underlying cause of disagreement, something that is very much the case in the disputes analyzed here. This does not suggest that the law is irrelevant. Whatever their true motivations, few dispute participants, whether states or private parties, are willing to argue simply in terms of protecting their interests. Normally, at least one party argues that existing rules of international law support its position and that a state's legal rights are being violated or threatened. This can trigger what may be a contentious dialogue among many different actors about what standards should govern state behavior, both directly and in terms of how the state exercises control over its territory, corporations, and private citizens. While this book does not attempt to weigh the impact of law on state behavior, the fact that dispute participants feel the need to justify their positions in legal terms suggests that the law is generally perceived to be important and something that should be followed.[32]

Finally, there is the question of identifying the relevant disputants. In 1924, the PCIJ clearly meant two states when it referred to two parties, since only states could appear before the Court in contentious cases. Contemporary environmental disputes commonly involve many state and non-state actors, but this implied formulation is useful because it suggests at least the formal centrality of the state, legally if not politically, in the dispute process. While there are transboundary disputes in which national governments deliberately choose not to get involved, all of the disputes analyzed here ultimately engage states, whether or not they end up as the most important participants.

Why focus on *transboundary* disputes when climate change and its potential to disrupt basic planetary systems would seem to dwarf all other environmental problems? Beyond the general point that transboundary environmental issues have not received the attention they deserve, there are at least three justifications for this approach.

First, transboundary environmental problems can be intrinsically important, even if their effects are not on the scale of global warming. States seldom engage each other on minor matters, and the stakes involved can be significant, affecting the lives and interests of real people on a very large scale. For all the impact of globalization, territorial boundaries continue to matter and boundary regions are becoming increasingly busy, complex areas. While the primary focus here is not on dispute settlement per se, developing rules and procedures to manage transboundary disputes has genuine value.

Second, many local problems are directly linked to broader global concerns. Efforts to regulate pollution on the transboundary level may be easier and more immediately effective than attempting to reach broad international agreement on a complex problem such as climate change. European efforts to deal with acid rain in a transboundary context through the Long-Range Transboundary Air Pollution Convention (LRTAP)[33] have led to regulatory action that has helped reduce the production of at least some greenhouse gasses. Alternatively, if Southeast Asian nations fail to control local burning practices that they may view as a regional concern, the broader global interest in controlling carbon dioxide emissions will be compromised. The point is that multilevel governance is increasingly necessary in the environmental field, and managing transboundary problems is part of that process.

Third, even if there is no direct connection between problems at the local and global levels, bilateral initiatives provide a laboratory in which to develop legal norms and policy instruments that can later be applied elsewhere. The creation of a market for sulfur dioxide allowances in the United States, the product of efforts by Canada and the United States to respond to transboundary air pollution, played a key role in promoting the inclusion of an emissions trading program in the Kyoto Protocol. Recent literature on the nature of norm diffusion suggests how complex this process can be in practice,[34] but the recognition that norms can travel both vertically and horizontally makes efforts at all levels, including transboundary ones, worthy of analysis. It is true that transboundary problems can raise issues specific to their context, and there may be duties owed by states to each other in a bilateral context that may be different from those owed more broadly to the international community. Yet rules of broad relevance, such as the precautionary principle and the standards that should govern environmental impact assessment, can be given clearer meaning through their practical application at the local level.

In its most traditional form, transboundary pollution involves a situation in which the source of pollution is separated physically from the place of impact by an international boundary, and the problem is bilateral. The Trail Smelter dispute, discussed in the next chapter, is literally a textbook example involving damage occurring in the United States caused by sulfur dioxide being emitted by a smelter operating just across the Canadian border. The tribunal that heard the case held Canada responsible because it had failed to take adequate measures within Canada to prevent the pollution of US territory. The 1991 Convention on Environmental Impact Assessment in a Transboundary Context adopts this traditional approach, defining "transboundary impact" as "any impact, not exclusively of a global nature, within an area under the jurisdiction of a Party caused by a proposed activity the physical origin of which is situated wholly or in part within the area under the jurisdiction of another Party."[35] The duties of the regulating state are thus linked to the potential damage done directly to one or more neighboring states by activities taking place within its boundaries. Several of the cases analyzed here do fit this traditional definition of "transboundary."

Yet the forms of environmentally damaging behavior that produce relevant transboundary effects need not be seen so narrowly. As Xue Hanqin has argued, "Transboundary damage does not solely refer to bilateral cases or claims among a few States. . . . It also comprises damages to the commons arising from national activities or emanating from sources on national territory."[36] It is perhaps best understood in relationship to Principle 21 of the Declaration of the United Nations Conference on the Human Environment (hereafter referred to as the Stockholm Declaration), which asserts, "States have, in accordance with the Charter of the United Nations and the principles of international law, the sovereign right to exploit their own resources pursuant to their own environmental policies, and the responsibility to ensure that activities within their jurisdiction or control do not cause damage to the environment of other States or of areas beyond the limits of national jurisdiction."[37]

From this perspective, an environmental dispute could be labeled transboundary whenever effects are felt within another state or in areas of the commons as a result of the state's failure to control activities taking place on its territory or "within [its] jurisdiction or control." This could extend to the overseas activities of its nationals, human or corporate, which is a more extensive approach to defining the state's extraterritorial responsibilities that is by no means uncontroversial. International environmental law has almost certainly not moved as far in this direction as some might wish, as is evident in the Baia Mare dispute. The purpose here is to provide a sufficiently expansive definition of transboundary to permit a discussion of important issues raised by the crossing of boundaries not just by physical pollutants, but by corporate actors, technology, and capital as well. The term "transboundary" is used to separate the disputes covered here from issues largely internal to a single nation and from those that take place within global environmental regimes. While there are transboundary dimensions to the controversy within the Convention on International Trade in Endangered Species (CITES) over trade in elephant ivory, that dispute would not fall easily into the framework outlined here.

A similar breadth is implied by the term "environmental" to describe the nature of the disputes themselves. This book deliberately focuses on disputes that cover many types of environmental problems. The study of international environmental policy has all too often exhibited an ad hockery mirroring the decentralized nature of the international environmental policy-making process that has led scholars to treat issues such as river pollution, marine resource protection, and transboundary air pollution as inhabiting separate legal realms. Yet the case should also be made that principles are emerging that transcend these divisions and can help develop a more cohesive body of international environmental law, even if their application in different policy sectors may vary.

In labeling these disputes environmental there is the presumption that either the threat or reality of detrimental physical impact on the environment is a significant issue between the parties. In these cases, the detrimental impacts range from increased air pollution levels, which threaten human health, to overfishing, which leads to reduced availability of fish stocks and has potentially broader effects on the marine ecology. In reality, concern for the environment may not be the sole or even a principal factor motivating the disputants. All of these disputes also involve a complex mix of economic, social, and political factors, and the key issue may be perceived very differently by the various participants. What one state considers a crucial economic development project may seem the source of an unacceptable environmental risk to people located a short distance away. Nowhere is this more evident than in the case study of the Uruguayan pulp mills project.

There is also a presumption that detrimental impacts are a direct product of human action. Thus, damage caused by natural disasters, such as earthquakes and hurricanes, would not normally be considered relevant in this context. The fact that increased incidence of violent weather may be the result of human-induced climate change would not provide a sufficient link to bring such problems within this framework.[38] However, even here the line may not be so clear. Consider the example of the 2011 tsunami that wreaked such havoc in Japan and badly damaged the Fukushima nuclear plant. Any transboundary damage resulting directly from the tsunami would hardly be something for which Japan would be held legally responsible. Yet, if transboundary effects are felt later, either from radiation leaking from the damaged plant into areas beyond Japanese waters or from debris crossing the Pacific and landing on Californian beaches, questions of liability could arise. This is particularly true if the damage is perceived to be at least partly due to poor Japanese land-use decisions, construction standards, plant supervision, or post-accident responses.

The Argument

Three key assumptions underlie the central argument in *Cases of Conflict*; they have driven the basic approach taken, the selection of cases, and the questions asked. All three also raise issues that have been the focus of much scholarly debate.

The first is that norms play an important role in the process of international environmental governance; within the range of relevant norms, legal norms, often referred to as hard law, have a distinctive place. States and other actors normally treat these rules differently. Even if there is disagreement about their content, few are willing to disregard legal norms openly. As international adjudicative bodies have come to play an increasingly active role in environmental disputes, the law/non-law line has become even more significant than in the past. The increased relevance of hard law is not necessarily a good thing. As more actors become involved in transboundary disputes and use international law to justify their positions, there is a real danger that the political uses of international law will only produce more disagreement about what the rules actually mean. In addition, when key actors frame their positions in legal terms, there may be less room for negotiated settlement.

Second, relevant legal norms include not only treaty law but also rules of customary state practice and general principles of law. There has been a common tendency to focus almost exclusively on the development of environmental norms within the framework of treaty-based regimes. Treaty law is certainly important, since it allows states to design rules that respond directly to emerging problems and to build regimes with the flexibility to evolve as our understanding of the problems changes. However, it would be a mistake to ignore the place of customary state practice and general principles of law in the fabric of international environmental law.[39] These rules frame the legal context in which treaties are negotiated, interpreted, and applied, and they can help fill in the gaps where treaties do not exist. Again, the fact that these principles are relevant may actually make the resolution of transboundary disputes more difficult. The standards they reflect are seldom precise, and disagreement over what they require and the tests to prove their existence often make their application not a basis for settlement but a focus of debate.[40] Complicating matters is the fact that very few of the participants in these disputes are trained in international law. Even those who are seldom speak with the precision of lawyers meeting in formal courtroom proceedings. They are people caught up in the middle of heated disagreements, often talking through the media to important constituencies, where their language is one of advocacy rather than careful legal analysis. Still, the arguments they put forward become part of the broader political context in which international law is understood and developed. When courts do become involved, as during the Uruguayan pulp mills dispute, there is an opportunity to give concepts such as the precautionary principle greater precision.

Third, in part because the hardness of law does matter, states and the governments that represent them play a unique role in shaping the legal and political landscape in which international environmental policy is set. Governments provide formal regulatory authority, crucial in wielding certain types of policy instruments, and possess an accountability often lacking at other levels of environmental governance.[41] State sovereignty remains an important concept, although what it implies in a modern, increasingly complex global setting is changing in response to a variety of political, economic, and social forces.[42] This is not to suggest that national governments are the sole, or even the central focus in the disputes analyzed here. Subnational and non-state actors are often the driving force behind the disputes, actively invoking international environmental law and bringing about changes in it.

Cases of Conflict poses two central questions. First, how is international law employed in the context of transboundary environmental disputes? The concerns here are how key players in the dispute process perceive the legal issues at stake and how they attempt to use the law to advance their positions. To the extent that law affects the final settlement, it is important to know how and why this is true. Second, what is the broader impact of the dispute on the law itself? This question is more difficult to answer, since it is seldom possible to draw clear lines of causation between a particular set of events and any changes in law or policy that emerge later. Where a connection can be made, the goal is to examine the form that changes take, as well as to better understand the mechanisms that helped transform what might otherwise have been a singular episode into something with broader legal impact.

It is important to make clear what this book does not attempt to do. No effort is made to measure or assess in any rigorous way the extent to which international law affected either the behavior of key actors during the disputes or their actual outcomes. Nor does it try to evaluate the effectiveness of the processes by which these disputes were settled, if indeed they were. There is a rich literature on environmental dispute settlement, but the interest here is less on that process and more on the broader implications of the disputes themselves for the development of international environmental law. Finally, no judgment is made about the rightness of the positions adopted by any of the disputants, the outcome of the disputes themselves, or even the changes in international environmental law they may have helped promote. One of the realities that these disputes may reveal is the continuing distance between the legal standards many would like to see and the "living law" reflected in the way states and others actually behave. To the extent that this is true, it is a tension that needs to be recognized and explored more fully.

What *Cases of Conflict* does offer is an analysis of how international environmental law can emerge even during periods of serious international disagreement. The impact of these six disputes on the development of the law varies. In some cases, they directly encourage governmental efforts to codify the law, as through the development of clearer rules of civil liability for environmental damage or agreed-upon procedures for conducting environmental impact assessments. In others, the impact is less obvious, as disputes may simply reinforce the general sense that rules like the precautionary principle do apply, and help narrow the differences between the disputants about what they mean in practice. In still other situations, disputes may bring into sharper relief international disagreement about the content of the rules and the ways in which they should be applied, and the immediate effect of the law may be more divisive than productive. One should not expect the development of international environmental law to be an inevitably progressive process, given the important and often competing values these disputes reveal. Yet even significant short-term friction can provide the political impetus to lead governments to develop a more effective body of law.

The Cases

A case-study approach has limitations. While focusing on six disputes permits analytical depth, it does make it more difficult to link that analysis to broader patterns of international behavior. Each situation has unique characteristics that need to be acknowledged, and it is important to avoid overgeneralizing from a limited number of cases. However, this reflects the very complexity of the international environmental challenge that those studying global environmental governance have come to recognize.

Selecting the cases was, unavoidably, a subjective process. The main objective was to focus on cases that raised intrinsically important questions of international environmental law, whether or not what emerged from the dispute offered clear answers. Individual disputes were selected with an eye to avoiding those, such as the Chernobyl nuclear accident, that have already been explored in depth. Still, it was important that the cases present interesting stories, to help readers gain an appreciation of the increasing complexity and significance of transboundary environmental disputes. While most are fairly recent, and in many cases ongoing, enough time has passed since each began to make possible at least a preliminary assessment of its impact.

Collectively, the cases offer the opportunity to examine different types of environmental problems involving different media (atmosphere, rivers, oceans) and different types of environmentally degrading activities (pollution, overfishing). The disputes include situations where serious pollution has already taken place and others where there is simply the risk that it might occur. They also span different geographical regions and involve disputants with varying levels of political and economic power. One of the critical questions being posed, most directly in the Indonesian haze case, is whether the rules of international law so often invoked by North American and European legal scholars reflect a law that really does extend to all areas of the globe. The cases also differ in the forms of dispute settlement mechanisms involved, ranging from bilateral diplomacy to international adjudication, and include situations where international law seemed to play a decisive role and others where its impact appeared marginal.

An Overview

Chapter 2, "Trail Smelter and Beyond: Evolving Regimes, Emerging Principles," offers a broad historical perspective on the framework of international environmental law in which these disputes are set. After a brief review of important forms of state practice dating back to the nineteenth century, it focuses on the 1941 Trail Smelter arbitration, certainly the most cited and influential court ruling in the field of international environmental law. The point is not to rehash a case already studied exhaustively but to identify through it issues of state responsibility that remain central to contemporary disputes. Chapter 2 then traces important changes that have taken place in the construction of treaty-based regimes, explaining why such a complex maze of institutions has evolved in an area of international policy that would seem to cry out for greater centralization. It also focuses on broader concepts of environmental responsibility, offering a critical analysis of emerging principles of customary international law, such as the precautionary principle, whose meaning and application are commonly key points of contention in transboundary disputes.

Chapters 3 to 8 present the six disputes, the political context in which each occurred, the key events, the processes by which some form of resolution was achieved, and subsequent developments. Each chapter focuses on an issue that not only relates to the broader development of international environmental law but is also central to the dispute. The first three cases examine key normative questions, the basic rules that are said to govern state behavior: state environmental responsibility, liability for environmental damage, and the assessment of environmental risk. The second three address issues of process: how international law can be shaped through unilateral action, the processes by which new rules evolve in a decentralized environmental framework, and the enhanced role of international courts in transboundary environmental disputes.

Chapter 3, "Indonesian Haze," analyzes the dispute that arose in 1997–98, when smoke from Indonesian land-clearing operations spread across East Asia, causing serious health effects and economic losses. A key issue is why Indonesia's most directly affected neighbors, Malaysia and Singapore, did not make direct legal claims about Indonesia's responsibility to control the fires and to pay compensation to those who had been injured. This might seem to call into question the global relevance of the Trail Smelter principles so often cited as being among the foundations of international environmental law. However, a closer look at what happened both during and after the dispute can actually be seen as supporting an emerging view of state environmental responsibility—emphasizing procedural obligations that complement Trail Smelter and reinforce the duty to prevent environmental damage.

Chapter 4, "Baia Mare Cyanide Spill," explores the narrower question of the role of liability and compensation regimes in responding to transboundary pollution. In 2000, cyanide from a Romanian gold mine did extensive damage in Hungary and forced local governments to take costly remedial measures, yet no compensation was ever paid. Indeed, despite clear indications that Hungary felt compensation was due from either the Romanian state or the companies involved, no international claims for damage were ever filed by Hungary, suggesting a broader concern about the limitations of liability as a tool for responding to environmental damage. Steps were taken after the dispute to improve liability rules, at least in a European context. However, the question of who should bear responsibility for transboundary damage was left unresolved. This could have included Australia, the state in which the mine's primary investor was incorporated.

Chapter 5, "MOX at Sellafield," focuses on the important issue of how environmental risk is assessed and managed in a transboundary context, particularly when that risk involves something as potentially dangerous as exposure to ionizing radiation. The case involves the controversy triggered by the United Kingdom's 2001 authorization of a nuclear reprocessing facility, which Ireland believed posed both a direct threat from the plant's operations and an indirect threat through the transit of ships carrying nuclear materials through the Irish Sea. While the United Kingdom ultimately refused to allow Irish concerns to prevent the MOX plant from opening, the British never challenged the need for their consultation and environmental impact assessment procedures to conform to international standards, and took concrete steps during and after the dispute to strengthen both.

Chapter 6, "Turbot War," adds maritime and resource depletion dimensions to the analysis, focusing on the 1995 dispute triggered when Canada seized the Spanish fishing trawler *Estai* in waters seemingly beyond Canada's lawful enforcement jurisdiction. Given the timing of the Canadian action, just before a United Nations meeting called to discuss the straddling stocks issue, the dispute offers an opportunity to discuss efforts by states to bring about changes in international environmental law through unilateral action that might appear to violate existing legal standards. The chapter focuses on factors surrounding the Canadian action that help explain how the dispute was instrumental in promoting changes in the regulation of straddling stocks, both in the Northeast Atlantic and globally.

Chapter 7, "Voyage of the *Clemenceau*," analyzes the debate concerning French efforts to dispose of the aging aircraft carrier *Clemenceau* at ship-breaking yards in Alang, India. The plan generated widespread protest because of the hazardous materials believed to still be on board the ship and because of the working and environmental conditions at Alang. France's decision to repatriate the vessel and have it broken in the United Kingdom came as the international community was engaged in a serious debate about how to deal with end-of-life ships, with states and non-governmental organizations divided on the basic question of what international regime should govern ship breaking. The French decision reinforced the view of ship-breaking opponents that rules of the Basel Convention should apply, while others argued that it demonstrated the need to create a new convention within the general framework of the International Maritime Organization. The issue remains unresolved, and the dispute underscores the challenges faced in confronting environmental problems that do not fit neatly into established international regimes.

Chapter 8, "Uruguayan Pulp Mills," focuses on the role of adjudication in contributing to the management and ultimate resolution of a bilateral dispute over Uruguay's 2003 decision to authorize construction of a large cellulose plant at Fray Bentos, on the River Uruguay across from Argentina. Although the project was to be developed by a Finnish company using modern technology, Argentina objected to its potential transboundary impact, as well as to the procedures Uruguay had used to approve it. Both the arbitral process of a regional free-trade organization and the International Court of Justice became directly involved in the dispute, making modest but valuable contributions to its resolution. The pulp mills dispute thus provides an opportunity to explore the benefits and potential drawbacks of the increased presence of adjudicative bodies in transboundary environmental disputes.

The final chapter examines the broader implications of these six disputes. While all are different and generalities are dangerous, it is clear just how complex, multidimensional, and persistent transboundary environmental disputes have become. National governments remain in regulatory control, but non-governmental actors from private corporations to environmental NGOs often dictate both the nature of the dispute and the extent to which amicable resolution is possible. Also clear is that international environmental law is very much a part of these disputes, helping frame the arguments of the participants and, at least in some cases, providing the basis for settlement. What emerges is the sense of a body of law, still very much in the process of development, where states increasingly agree on the basic principles that should direct their behavior, even if these principles do not yet have the clarity and depth of international support needed to provide an effective response to the environmental challenges we face.

Notes

1   Christopher D. Stone, *The Gnat Is Older Than Man: Global Environment and Human Agenda* (Princeton, NJ: Princeton University Press, 1993), 34.

2   Michael Cardozo, "Bridging the Gap between Political Scientists and Lawyers," *Proceedings of the Annual Meeting-American Society of International Law* 81 (1987): 392.

3   Hans J. Morgenthau and Kenneth W. Thompson, *Politics among Nations: The Struggle for Power and Peace*, 6th ed. (New York: Knopf, 1985), 296.

4   Hans Kelsen, *Pure Theory of Law*, 2nd ed. (Berkeley: University of California Press, 1970).

5   See, generally, Myres S. McDougal, *Studies in World Public Order* (New Haven, CT: Yale University Press, 1960).

6   Myres S. McDougal, Harold D. Lasswell, and W. Michael Reisman, "The World Constitutive Process of Authoritative Decision," in *The Future of the International Legal Order*, ed. Cyril Edwin Black and Richard A. Falk (Princeton, NJ: Princeton University Press, 1969), 73–154.

7   Richard A. Falk, *The Status of Law in International Society* (Princeton, NJ: Princeton University Press, 1970), 45.

8   Percy Ellwood Corbett, *Law in Diplomacy* (Princeton, NJ: Princeton University Press, 1959).

9   Morton A. Kaplan and Nicholas Katzenbach, *The Political Foundations of International Law* (New York: John Wiley and Sons, 1961).

10   William D. Coplin, *The Functions of International Law: An Introduction to the Role of International Law in the Contemporary World* (Chicago: Rand McNally, 1966).

11   Louis Henkin, *How Nations Behave: Law and Foreign Policy* (1968; repr., New York: Columbia University Press, 1979).

12   Ibid., 21.

13   Ibid., 39–87.

14   Robert O. Keohane and Joseph S. Nye, *Power and Interdependence: World Politics in Transition* (Boston: Little, Brown and Co., 1977).

15   Nicholas Greenwood Onuf, *World of Our Making: Rules and Rule in Social Theory and International Relations* (Columbia: University of South Carolina Press, 1989).

16   Friedrich Kratochwil and John Gerard Ruggie, "International Organization: A State of the Art on an Art of the State," *International Organization* 40, no. 4 (1986): 753–75.

17   Alexander Wendt, "Anarchy Is What States Make of It: The Social Construction of Power Politics," *International Organization* 46, no. 2 (1992): 391–425.

18   Friedrich Kratochwil, "Thrasymmachos Revisited: On the Relevance of Norms and the Study of Law for International Relations," *Journal of International Affairs* 37, no. 2 (1984): 343–56.

19   Fabrizio Gilardi, "Transnational Diffusion: Norms, Ideas, and Policies," in *Handbook of International Relations*, ed. Walter Carlsnaes, Thomas Risse, and Beth Simmonds (Thousand Oaks, CA: Sage Publications, 2012), 453–77.

20   Anne-Marie Slaughter, Andrew S. Tulumello, and Stepan Wood, "International Law and International Relations Theory: A New Generation of Interdisciplinary Scholarship," *American Journal of International Law* 92, no. 3 (1998): 370.

21   Ibid., 370–1.

22   Jack L. Goldsmith and Eric A. Posner, *The Limits of International Law* (Oxford: Oxford University Press, 2005).

23   Jutta Brunné and Stephen J. Troope, *Legality and Legitimacy in International Law: An Interactional Account* (Cambridge: Cambridge University Press, 2010).

24 Jeffrey L. Dunoff and Mark A. Pollack, "Reviewing Two Decades of IL/IR Scholarship: What We've Learned, What's Next," in *Interdisciplinary Perspectives on International Law and International Relations: The State of the Art*, ed. Jeffrey L. Dunoff and Mark A. Pollack (New York: Cambridge University Press, 2012), 648.

25 Peter Katzenstein and Rudra Sil, "Eclectic Theorizing in the Study and Practice of International Relations," in *The Oxford Handbook of International Relations*, ed. Christian Reus-Smit and Duncan Snidal (New York: Oxford University Press, 2008), 101–39.

26 Robert J. Beck, "International Law and International Relations: Prospects for Interdisciplinary Collaboration," in *International Rules: Approaches from International Law and International Relations*, ed. Robert J. Beck, Anthony C. Arend, and Robert D. VanderLugt (New York: Oxford University Press, 1996), 17.

27 See, for example, Michael D. Goldhaber, *A People's History of the European Court of Human Rights* (New Brunswick, NJ: Rutgers University Press, 2007); and Laurence R. Helfer and Erik Voeten, "International Courts as Evidence of Legal Change: Evidence from LGBT Rights in Europe," *International Organization* 68, no. 1 (2014): 77–110.

28 Daniel Bodansky, *The Art and Craft of International Environmental Law* (Cambridge, MA: Harvard University Press, 2010), 21–22.

29 Louis Henkin had a similar concern about the danger that his own case studies of disputes where international law was not followed would obscure the broader patterns of cooperation made possible by the "submerged" rules of law that states commonly follow. See Henkin, *How Nations Behave*, 242–43.

30 Permanent Court of International Justice (PCIJ), "The Mavrommatis Palestine Concessions (Judgment of August 30, 1924)," *PCIJ*, Series A, no. 2 (1924): 11.

31 See, generally, Allen L. Springer, "Towards a Meaningful Concept of Pollution in International Law," *International and Comparative Law Quarterly* 26 (1977): 531–57.

32 A similar argument, in this case concerning the role of morality as a "language of justification," is found in Michael Walzer, *Just and Unjust Wars*, 4th ed. (New York: Basic Books, 2006), 13–20.

33 United Nations Economic Commission for Europe (UNECE), "Convention on Long-Range Transboundary Air Pollution," Geneva, signed 13 November 1979 (in force 16 March 1983), *International Legal Materials* 18 (1979): 1442 [hereafter cited as "LRTAP"].http://www.unece.org/fileadmin/DAM/env/lrtap/full%20text/1979.CLRTAP.e.pdf.

34 See generally, Alexander Ovodenko and Robert O. Keohane, "Institutional Diffusion in International Environmental Affairs," *International Affairs* 88, no. 3 (2012): 523–41.

35 United Nations Economic Commission for Europe (UNECE), "Convention on Environmental Impact Assessment in a Transboundary Context," Espoo, Finland, signed 25 February 1991 (in force 10 September 1997), *International Legal Materials* 30 (1991): Art. 1 (viii), 800. http://www.unece.org/fileadmin/DAM/env/eia/documents/legaltexts/Espoo_Convention_authentic_ENG.pdf.

36 Hanqin Xue, *Transboundary Damage in International Law* (New York: Cambridge University Press, 2003), 7.

37   United Nations, "Declaration of the United Nations Conference on the Human Environment," in *Report of the United Nations Conference on the Human Environment, Stockholm, 5–16 June 1972* (Doc. A/Conf. 48/14), *International Legal Materials* 11 (1972): 1420. http://www.unep.org/Documents.Multilingual/Default.asp?documentid=97&articleid=1503.

38   On the issue of "human causality," see Xue, *Transboundary Damage in International Law*, 6–7.

39   Bodansky, *The Art and Craft of International Environmental Law*, 96–102, 191–204.

40   On the challenges posed in proving the existence of a rule of customary international law, see Anthea Elizabeth Roberts, "Traditional and Modern Approaches to Customary International Law: A Reconciliation," *American Journal of International Law* 95 (2001): 757–91.

41   Liliana B. Andonova and Ronald B. Mitchell, "The Rescaling of Global Environmental Politics," *Annual Review of Environment and Resources* 35, no. 1 (2010): 274.

42   Karen T. Litfin, "Sovereignty in World Ecopolitics," *Mershon International Studies Review* 51, no. 2 (1996): 161–204.

2

Trail Smelter and Beyond: Evolving Regimes, Emerging Principles

Introduction

International environmental policy is too often seen as a modern development, emerging only after 1972 when the United Nations held its first
global Conference on the Human Environment in Stockholm. Decennial
celebrations of the Stockholm meeting have only reinforced its legacy as
the moment the international community acknowledged the need to work
collectively to protect the environment. Although the conference was important symbolically and created an institutional home for environmental issues
within the United Nations, what was accomplished at Stockholm did not
take place in a vacuum. The way the international community viewed and
responded to newly recognized environmental problems was conditioned by
past experience.

This chapter begins with an overview of early initiatives that set the stage
for the Stockholm conference. It analyzes the ruling of the Trail Smelter
tribunal to highlight the challenges posed by traditional rules of state responsibility for the development of international environmental law. It then
examines important institutional and legal changes that have occurred since
Stockholm in order to better understand the world in which the six disputes
studied here have taken place and which they, in turn, have helped shape.

Historical Perspectives

What are now considered environmental issues have been the subject of
international regulation since the mid-nineteenth century, even if the motivation for acting was less environmental than economic. The goal was to
protect resources of direct value to the state and its nationals in ways that
would prevent issues generally of secondary priority from affecting important
diplomatic relationships.

European waterways were an early focus. Agreements covering the
Rhine (1868) and Danube (1878) rivers created commissions that had
the power to directly supervise riparian activities. Technical experts were
appointed to try to keep politics out of the regulatory process. As environmental concerns became more prominent, the roles of these experts would

be expanded to incorporate efforts to control pollution. In North America, the United States and the United Kingdom (for Canada) approved the 1909 Boundary Waters Treaty, creating a comprehensive regime to resolve the disputes that would inevitably arise within the extensive network of rivers and lakes that define and cross the lengthy Canadian–American boundary. The treaty established a binational International Joint Commission (IJC) to supervise the agreement, and gave it an explicitly environmental responsibility when Article 4 declared that boundary waters "shall not be polluted on either side to the injury of health and property on the other."[1] Beyond the intrinsic importance of their work, these commissions became models for institutions that now manage international rivers ranging from the Niger and Senegal in Africa to the Mekong in Southeast Asia and the Uruguay in South America. Their work also provided an empirical foundation for state practice later codified in documents like the International Law Association's (ILA) Helsinki Rules on the Uses of the Waters of International Rivers.[2] Central to the ILA's assessment of the rules that have emerged from these organizations is the concept of "equitable utilization," a principle reflecting the emphasis that states have traditionally placed on the economic value and utility of international waterways rather than their ecological significance. Article 10 of the Helsinki Rules makes clear that there is no presumed "hierarchy of uses," no particular priority to be accorded environmental interests. In context, the need to dispose of raw sewage could take precedence over preserving the capacity of a river to provide clean drinking water or to support fish habitat.

Early efforts to protect migratory species reflected a similar utilitarian perspective. Birds received international protection in Europe as early as 1902, but the title of the relevant agreement, the European Convention Concerning the Conservation of Birds Useful to Agriculture, made clear the driving motivation behind the pact. Living marine resources have also received international attention dating back to the 1911 Fur Seal Convention and the 1931 Convention for the Regulation of Whaling. In both cases the goal was to ensure the health of populations to make possible continued harvesting of economically valuable mammals. A number of agreements were also signed to protect marine fish stocks, particularly species like tuna and salmon, which range widely and could not be protected effectively on a national level. Others, like the 1949 International Convention for North Atlantic Fisheries (ICNAF), were designed to manage interrelated species of fish, something that had to be done regionally because of the narrow limits of coastal state jurisdiction existing at the time.

This early history of environmental cooperation, though important, provides little evidence that a cohesive body of international environmental law was emerging in the early twentieth century. The law being developed was created within the framework of specific treaty-based regimes. Broader principles of customary international law, such as the state's exclusive jurisdiction over its territory and freedom of the high seas, seemed only to shield many environmentally destructive policies from international purview. However, the Trail Smelter case would suggest another important dimension to traditional international law that would provide a stronger normative foundation for later environmental protection efforts.

The Trail Smelter Legacy

The decision of the arbitral tribunal in the Trail Smelter case[3] remains the focus of heated scholarly debate nearly 75 years after it was issued. Applauded on the one hand as a "courageous and creative" ruling by judges working to resolve an intractable transboundary dispute,[4] the verdict has also been attacked for faulty legal reasoning,[5] indeed the entire case the product of the "wrong tribunal, the wrong parties and the wrong law."[6] Some who consider the decision progressive in 1941 view it as now reflecting an outmoded view of international environmental law. Compared to most modern disputes, it emerged from an environmental issue that was relatively simple. Moreover, the disputing states were two unusually cooperative neighbors operating in a state-controlled system that may seem to no longer exist.[7]

Whatever the criticism, the Trail Smelter decision has had significant influence on the development of international environmental law. Its central holding became the basis for Principle 21 of the Stockholm Declaration and Article 2 of the Rio Declaration on Environment and Development, and the ruling has been cited extensively by the International Court of Justice and the International Law Commission. The Trail Smelter case also raised issues of state responsibility that remain crucial to the development of international environmental law.

The smelter that triggered the controversy was constructed in 1896 by US nationals at Trail, British Columbia, along the banks of the Columbia River, 11 miles from the US border. In 1906, it was sold to a private Canadian firm, the Consolidated Mining and Smelting Company, and the smelter soon became part of a major industrial complex important to the economy of British Columbia. Designed to refine low-grade zinc ores, the smelter produced thick smoke with high concentrations of sulfur dioxide. Canadian farmers close to the smelter were the first to object, and claims were litigated in Canada that led to compensation and a decision by Consolidated Mining to erect a tall smokestack designed to project the emissions beyond the immediate vicinity of the plant. The smoke was now transmitted downwind across the border into the state of Washington, where US farmers began to complain of the damage being done to crops and livestock.

What might have remained a local problem was transformed into an international dispute in part because the law in both British Columbia and Washington made a local resolution impossible. Farmers in Washington could not bring effective claims against the smelter in British Columbia, because the courts there did not have jurisdiction over damage caused in the United States. In Washington, foreigners were not allowed to hold title to real estate, and thus Consolidated Mining was unable to purchase smoke easements that could have compensated farmers while permitting the smelter to continue operations. The US government took up the claims of American farmers in 1927; a year later, Canada and the United States agreed in a joint reference to send the dispute to the International Joint Commission. In 1931, after extensive investigation, the IJC found that damage was being caused in the United States by the smelter. It recommended changes in the smelter designed to limit its emissions and a Canadian payment to the United States of $350,000 as compensation for damage caused through the end of 1931. While Canada accepted the IJC's recommendations, the United States did not, considering the amount of compensation too low for the range and extent of damage it felt the smelter had caused.

In 1935, Canada and the United States signed a convention to send the matter to international arbitration.[8] As part of the *compromis* establishing the tribunal, the United States agreed to accept from the Canadian government the money previously awarded by the IJC as payment for the damage inflicted before 1932. The three-member tribunal was asked to determine whether damage had been done by the smelter since then and, if so, what the consequences should be. The crucial question it was not required to answer directly was whether, as a matter of international law, Canada was responsible for whatever harm the smelter was causing, since Canada had implicitly agreed to accept responsibility by agreeing to pay the $350,000. This was perhaps the most important legal question posed in the dispute. Determining when actions by private players can be attributed to states is a critical issue in international environmental law since so much environmental degradation results from private rather than governmental action. Canada's concession on this key point might seem to limit the potential significance of the Trail Smelter ruling, however the tribunal would go farther than was strictly required and discuss directly the nature of Canadian responsibility for the smelter.

Another aspect of the case that could undermine its broader relevance is the law the tribunal was empowered to apply. Negotiators for both countries were aware of how little international practice existed in the field of air pollution and were determined to avoid a situation where the tribunal would be unable to reach a decision. After reviewing cases decided by the US Supreme Court involving interstate pollution, both sides felt that the rulings offered sufficient support for their respective positions to allow US law to be used by the tribunal. The parties authorized the tribunal to "apply the law practice followed in dealing with cognate questions in the United States of America as well as international law and practice, and . . . [to] give consideration to the desire of the high contracting parties to reach a solution just to all parties concerned."[9] The call for a "just" decision was also a clear signal that both sides sought a reasonable and balanced solution to the Trail Smelter problem, one that would not require the closure of the smelter. Such a ruling would pose as much potential danger to the United States as it would to Canada given the former's extensive industrial operations in the Midwest, close to the Canadian border.[10]

On the surface, the final decision offered a strong assertion of Canadian responsibility for the damage the tribunal concluded had continued since the end of 1931. The tribunal stated, "Under the principles of international law . . . no State has the right to use or permit the use of its territory in such a manner as to cause injury by fumes in or to the territory of another or to the properties or persons therein, when the case is of serious consequence and the injury is established by clear and convincing evidence."[11] It is difficult to read this statement, generally seen as the central holding in the Trail Smelter case, as anything other than an affirmation that Canada was strictly responsible for the damage caused by the smelter. The United States had never alleged and the tribunal did not rule that the Canadian government was somehow at fault for what had happened. Canada did not own or operate the smelter, and there was no suggestion that Canadian regulation and supervision of the plant had been inadequate. Crucial to the case's broader impact, the tribunal held that Canadian liability was required by customary international law. It was not simply the result of Canada's willingness to pay compensation under the terms of the *compromis* or derived from US legal standards Canada had agreed could be applied. "*Apart from the undertakings in the Convention*, it is . . . the duty of . . . Canada to see to it that this conduct should be in conformity with the obligations of the Dominion under international law" [emphasis added].[12] The tribunal was convinced that the US principles cited extensively in its decision were a reasonable reflection of general international law, even though its members found no relevant international court decisions to support this conclusion.[13]

The next question concerned what Canadian responsibility entailed. The tribunal required Canada to pay additional compensation for the damage done since 1931, although the amount ($78,000) was far less than the nearly

$1.9 million the United States had sought. More important, the tribunal held that Canada had an obligation not simply to compensate victims but to prevent future pollution, at least above some level of seriousness. Changes were ordered in the operation of the smelter that would cost Consolidated Mining roughly $20 million, although this cost was later recouped by the company from the sale of recycled products. The tribunal also provided a small amount of funding to the United States to pay for ongoing monitoring to ensure that further damage was not done.[14]

Other aspects of the Trail Smelter decision were less positive from an environmental perspective. First, the tribunal required that damage be done before any international claim could be brought. This has obvious appeal to states with a shared desire to avoid unnecessary disputes. However, it increases the likelihood that damage will occur that might have been prevented through a less restrictive process of objection. From a practical perspective, the types of structural changes required of Consolidated Mining are normally more expensive to implement once a facility is built than when they can be incorporated into its original construction. As a political matter, it may also be far more difficult to get polluting states to reduce pollution, as Canada did voluntarily here, once there are real costs to impose and immediate jobs at stake. Second, the damage felt had to be "serious," a standard that raises the question of how high a threshold of injury is required and to what interests legally significant damage can be done. The fact that the tribunal provided compensation only for damages that could be given clear economic value could have an impact not simply on levels of compensation, but even on the types of injury considered sufficiently important to allow victim states the right to complain. Third, injury had to be proven by clear and convincing evidence, a standard relatively easy to meet in 1941 in the comparatively undeveloped world of the Pacific Northwest, with substantial IJC research to support it. Proving a clear cause-and-effect relationship between specific pollution sources and environmental damage in a congested border area like the Detroit–Windsor region would be virtually impossible. Finally, the tribunal held that Canada's duty was one it owed to the United States, which had the sovereign right to protect its territory from environmental degradation. This focus on reciprocal duties was reasonable given the nature of the dispute the tribunal was asked to resolve. But what about damage to areas of the high seas, where no state could claim specific territorial rights, or to other shared areas like the stratospheric ozone layer? Would Canada bear a similar responsibility to control activities within its territory that damaged collective interests?

The Trail Smelter decision can be challenged as overly optimistic about the nature of the responsibility that states would generally be willing to accept, and it articulated standards that would be difficult to apply to the complex environmental challenges that would emerge later in the century. However, the ruling provided a solid foundation for the argument that the state has a central and legally necessary role to play in protecting the environment.

Evolving Regimes

By the time the international community recognized the importance of environmental problems in the late 1960s, the basic institutional framework through which it would respond was already constructed. In the last days of World War II, the Allied powers agreed to create a set of global organizations designed to provide both a more effective political deterrent to a potential aggressor and cooperative mechanisms to deal with underlying economic and social sources of conflict. Committed to universal participation, the founders of the United Nations also attempted to learn from the checkered experience of the League of Nations. While a strengthened Security Council would focus on security issues, the General Assembly would be responsible for a broad range of non-security concerns, operating through a one-state, one-vote process of decision making. The 1939 report of the Bruce Committee, formed to assess the League in its declining days, had argued that it was possible for states to cooperate in economic and social arenas, even in the face of serious political differences between them, if these issues could be housed in separate institutional structures to insulate them from political pressures. A system of Specialized Agencies, each with its own founding agreement and separate institutional structure, was created to deal with problems ranging from world health to agricultural development. Within the UN, the Economic and Social Council (ECOSOC) was established to coordinate these efforts.

It was in the Specialized Agencies that much of the work on international environmental issues took place during the 1950s and 1960s. The International Maritime Consultative Organization (now the International Maritime Organization—IMO), originally established to regulate and promote international maritime commerce, took on questions of maritime safety and marine pollution. The Food and Agriculture Organization (FAO) began to address problems of overfishing, soil erosion, deforestation, and the protection of wildlife. Other organizations that became active in the environmental field included the International Labor Organization (ILO), concerned with workplace safety, the World Health Organization (WHO), focusing on issues such as safe levels of exposure to toxic chemicals, and the United Nations Educational, Social and Cultural Organization (UNESCO), whose

1968 Man and the Biosphere Conference helped provide an intellectual foundation for the Stockholm Conference. The independent International Atomic Energy Agency (IAEA) added nuclear reactor safety to its work promoting the peaceful use of nuclear power, a role that acquired particular significance after the 1986 Chernobyl accident. The World Meteorological Organization (WMO) would become the primary organization focusing on stratospheric ozone depletion and global climate change. Other important Specialized Agencies, like the World Bank and the International Monetary Fund (IMF), had less direct interest in the environment. However, because they help fund major development projects, bringing them into international environmental protection initiatives would become a top priority after Stockholm. Similarly, efforts to liberalize international trade within the framework of the General Agreement on Tariffs and Trade (GATT), later strengthened by the creation of the World Trade Organization (WTO), had important implications for the use of tools such as trade sanctions to enforce international environmental policies.

Specialized Agencies brought to the table experience and technical expertise. They also had an interest in maintaining a role in the development of future institutional structures. Some were viewed with suspicion by environmentalists, since their areas of responsibility extended far beyond environmental concerns. The IMO, for example, had a decision-making process that gave special representation to major maritime states; it was unclear how high a priority would be attached to environmental values by an organization where major shipping interests played such a prominent role. As independent institutions, these organizations varied tremendously in the breadth of issues they addressed and in their ability to make and enforce international standards. Each also had developed a unique political culture that would challenge efforts to integrate them into a cohesive system of international environmental governance.

The United Nations Conference on the Human Environment

The immediate impetus for the Stockholm Conference was concern in developed nations about the deteriorating quality of life, as patterns of largely unchecked industrialization had created serious problems of air and water pollution with direct effects on local populations. While there was growing awareness of the impact of pollution on the oceans and the broader global ecology, the goal was as much to coordinate and rationalize national policies as it was to develop a broad international response. Some environmentalists did hope to see the establishment of a strong global watchdog organization, perhaps modeled on the newly created US Environmental Protection

Agency. However several factors worked against taking such a dramatic institutional leap at Stockholm.

First, liberalizing international trade was also a major concern of developed states. There were fears that new environmental policies being developed on a national level could impose costs on industries that would make them uncompetitive unless efforts were made internationally to "level the playing field." This concern, which would help promote the development of the "polluter pays principle" by the Organisation for Economic Co-operation and Development (OECD), was clearly on the minds of US negotiators as they headed off to Stockholm.[15]

Second, tensions remained among developed states of the East and West. There had been optimism that the détente emerging between the United States and the Soviet Union would provide an opportunity to build on areas of shared concern. In 1968, President Johnson's proposal that the United States and Russia spearhead the creation of an International Council on the Human Environment was soon followed by an essay by Russian dissident Andrei Sakharov, who called for enhanced cooperation by the two nations on a range of issues, including environmental protection.[16] However, hopes that the environment might be one policy area into which East/West politics would not intrude were dashed when the Soviet Union and its Eastern European allies boycotted the Stockholm meeting after East Germany was not allowed to participate. While their absence smoothed the process of reaching agreement at Stockholm, it also undermined chances for significant institutional development.

Third, the Stockholm Conference came at a time when the UN agenda was already crowded with a number of difficult diplomatic initiatives, some of which intersected with environmental issues. Perhaps the most important was the effort to negotiate a new regime to govern the oceans. While the Third UN Conference on the Law of the Sea (UNCLOS III) would not formally convene until 1973, preparatory meetings had been underway for several years. Through a complex, multidimensional process, a draft agreement was emerging that would grow to over 300 articles and 9 Annexes covering subjects ranging from maritime passage through international straits to deep seabed mining. What had originally been proposed as a strong institutional framework to manage an extensive "common heritage of mankind" was giving way during the negotiations to a system of nationally managed, 200-mile exclusive economic zones (EEZs), where many of the most important marine resources were located. This initially suggested the possibility that coastal states would have the authority to take more effective action to protect the marine environment. Yet, as the area to be managed collectively shrank, maritime powers gained concessions from coastal states to limit the extent of control they would have over ships operating within their waters. The agreement that began to emerge, providing limited coastal state enforcement of rules agreed upon by existing international bodies like the IMO, would not enhance the prospects for any strong new environmental institution to emerge from Stockholm.

Finally, developed and developing countries were at odds over whether the UN should even undertake a major environmental initiative. A global North-South divide had permeated most UN negotiations since the early 1960s when developing countries led by China and India began to argue for fundamental changes in the global economic system. What they sought, later termed a New International Economic Order, was a system not simply left to the vagaries of free-market capitalism but one consciously designed to promote Third World development. Among its central principles was "permanent sovereignty over natural resources,"[17] which held that states have a fundamental right to develop resources within their territories as they choose. While the early focus of this often-contentious debate was the right of developing countries to nationalize the assets of foreign-owned companies, it raised a more fundamental question about whether any external limitations, including environmental ones, could be placed by the international community on the way individual countries choose to develop.

Sweden's proposal to convene a conference on the human environment was greeted skeptically by developing countries. For many in the Third World, the pollution of concern to Northern environmentalists was the byproduct of a modernization process that they had yet to experience. On the one hand, the issue could be seen as simply irrelevant to them, and the primary danger was that an emphasis on the environment would divert attention from the development objectives they felt should be the United Nations' top priority. More worrisome was the possibility that Northern states, which had managed to industrialize using environmentally damaging technologies, would now deny the South the same opportunity. Access to Northern markets was a crucial component of the development plans of most Southern countries. There was fear that, in the name of environmental protection, markets might be closed to Less-developed Countries' (LDC) imports that had not been produced according to new Northern production standards. Even if that did not happen, aid might be diverted or "tied" to development projects considered more environmentally responsible. On the most fundamental level, Southern nations risked losing even more control over key national development decisions, a result in direct conflict with the permanent sovereignty they felt they should be able to exercise.

Attempting to address these concerns, Maurice Strong, the Secretary-General of the Stockholm Conference, convened a group of experts in June

1971 at Founex, Switzerland, to discuss the relationship between environmental protection and economic development. What emerged from these
discussions was the Founex Report,[18] which acknowledged and responded
to much of what LDC representatives had been saying. The report made clear
that LDCs had an agenda that, while different from that of many Northern
countries, was at least as important and deserved Northern respect. "The
major environmental problems of developing countries are of essentially a
different kind. They are predominantly problems that reflect the poverty and
very lack of development in their societies. . . . In their context, development
becomes essentially a cure for their major environmental problems. For these
reasons, concern for the environment must not and cannot detract from
the commitment of the world community—developing and more industrial nations alike—to the overriding task of development of the developing regions of the world."[19] While developing countries should attempt to
avoid the "mistakes and distortions that have characterized the patterns of
development in industrial societies,"[20] resource use decisions were still theirs
to make and each nation had to decide how best to balance environmental
and development values. This included the right to allow companies facing
tough environmental restrictions at home to relocate on their territories.
"[I]ndustries which may be regarded as pollutive in some advanced countries because of their more limited environmental carrying capacity may
well not be pollutive, or much less so, in the context of the developing
countries with much less environmental pollution at present."[21] To do all of
this wisely would require national planning and additional economic and
technical assistance from the North. [22]

The Founex Report helped promote the active participation of developing countries at Stockholm, but it also set the stage for a package of
conference outcomes quite different from what some of those planning
the conference had originally envisioned. The Stockholm Declaration, later
adopted by the General Assembly, reflected the tenuous compromise that
was reached. Principle 21 was a particular focus of negotiation, since it was
designed to articulate the basic rule of state responsibility for environmental protection. The final wording represented an interesting fusion of the
permanent sovereignty and Trail Smelter principles. Principle 21 states,

> States have, in accordance with the Charter of the United Nations and
> the principles of international law, the sovereign right to exploit their own
> resources pursuant to their own environmental policies and the responsibil-
> ity to ensure that activities within their jurisdiction or control do not cause
> damage to the environment of other States or of areas beyond the limits of
> national jurisdiction.[23]

Environmentalists could be pleased that the language of Principle 21 did remove the thresholds of seriousness and clarity of proof required by Trail Smelter and recognized that damage to communal areas and resources could also trigger state responsibility.[24] Moreover, the statement that states had a responsibility over "activities within their jurisdiction or control" could suggest an international duty to regulate the overseas activities of private corporations, an issue that would be an important aspect of several of the disputes studied here.

Compromise was also evident in the nature of the institution created at Stockholm and the mandate it was given. The United Nations Environment Program (UNEP) was designed to play a far less dynamic role than some environmentalists had hoped. Reporting to the General Assembly through ECOSOC, UNEP was thus two steps away from a body which itself had only the power to make recommendations. UNEP's job would be to convene and coordinate, rather than to act. It would start by monitoring global environmental conditions through the Earthwatch program, attempting to identify threats that required an international response. UNEP would then try to leverage a small Environment Fund, initially set at $100 million coming from voluntary contributions, to coordinate the environmental activities of the Specialized Agencies where much of the actual programmatic work would take place. Coordination would not be made easier by the decision to establish UNEP's headquarters in Nairobi, far from the European and North American cities where all of the Specialized Agencies were located. While the goal was to help build LDC support for the organization and encourage UNEP to take seriously the environmental concerns of developing countries, it also had the effect of emphasizing UNEP's peripheral position in actually responding to environmental problems. UNEP's head bureaucrat was given the title of Executive Director, a designation not conducive to leadership in a world of independent international organizations, many of which were led by a Secretary-General.

The Action Plan adopted at Stockholm included eight specific recommendations on the relationship between development and the environment, and many of UNEP's early efforts would be in response to problems like desertification. This was certainly an important issue but one quite different from the sources of environmental degradation in the developed world that had first prompted calls for international cooperation. While initially a source of disappointment among some environmentalists, the recognition of the importance of developing countries and their legitimate development needs did provide a foundation for later North-South cooperation in responding to problems like ozone depletion and global climate change.

Stockholm to Rio

The first years of UNEP's existence were a time of frustration. Funding was a continuous challenge, and UNEP developed a reputation as a weak, catalytic organization, rather than a source of environmental leadership.[25] The challenges facing UNEP were only compounded by the election of Ronald Reagan as US President in 1980. Reagan had campaigned on a platform of reducing government interference in the marketplace and brought to Washington advisers highly critical of a number of international policies associated with the New International Economic Order and multilateral initiatives more generally. Soon after taking office, Reagan ordered a review of US policy on the law of the sea; in 1982, the United States became one of four nations to refuse to sign the now completed United Nations Convention on the Law of the Sea. With regard to UNEP, Reagan administration officials attempted to cut by 70 per cent the United States' $10 million contribution to its annual budget and successfully resisted efforts to expand UNEP's role, urging it instead to focus on more technical ventures like the development of the Global Environmental Monitoring system and to leave action-oriented initiatives to Specialized Agencies like the FAO or bilateral assistance programs. By the time UNEP convened in Nairobi in 1982 on the 10th anniversary of the Stockholm Conference, it was representatives from the South who were now arguing that the North needed to take environmental issues more seriously.[26]

Nonetheless, UNEP did make·progress in its first decade, particularly in identifying environmental problems requiring action, generally by other institutions. The IMO was particularly active in the area of marine pollution, and UNEP supported efforts to draft and bring into force the 1972 London Dumping Convention[27] and the International Convention on the Prevention of Pollution from Ships (MARPOL).[28] UNEP played a more direct role in the creation of two new treaty-based regimes. The Convention on International Trade in Endangered Species (CITES)[29] was signed in 1973. Modeled on the US Endangered Species Act, CITES was able to use the impact of international trade on species loss to bring international attention to a problem normally controlled by sovereign states. Similarly, the 1979 Convention on Migratory Species (CMS),[30] for which UNEP serves as secretariat, created a system that has permitted the international community to promote efforts to control habitat loss by bringing together the range states through which birds and animals migrate. UNEP also sponsored global conferences on topics ranging from human settlements (Vancouver, 1976) to water problems (Mar del Plata, 1977).

Among the most successful early ventures were those taking place on a regional level. Evident since Stockholm was the difficulty of reaching consensus within a large and diverse global community on anything other than broad statements of principle. Moreover, complex environmental problems do vary by region, something UNEP recognized early on in developing a Regional Seas Program that would become one of its most effective initiatives. In the case of the Mediterranean Sea, UNEP was able to bring 16 states together in 1976, including such long-time adversaries as Greece and Turkey, Israel, Libya, and Syria, to develop a common environmental action plan.

Outside of the UNEP framework, the UN's Economic Commission for Europe (UNECE), which includes countries of Eastern and Western Europe as well as Canada and the United States, had an interest in the environment dating back to the 1950s. In 1979, the UNECE developed the Convention on Long-Range Transboundary Air Pollution (LRTAP)[31] designed to respond to problems of acid rain then being identified in both Europe and North America. LRTAP became an early example of the framework or umbrella convention that has since become so prevalent in international environmental policy. The approach was to begin with a treaty that demanded little more of signatories than recognition of the problem and a willingness to exchange scientific data and cooperate with other parties to address it. Article 2 requires parties to "endeavor to limit, and as far as possible, gradually reduce and prevent air pollution," hardly a demanding obligation. Through periodic contact between the parties and the work of an ongoing Executive Body, eight protocols have been adopted, which incorporate specific obligations to reduce sulfur dioxide and nitrogen oxide emissions.

In the mid-1980s, UNEP began working with the United States and the IMO to address the problem of stratospheric ozone depletion. The United States, which had taken steps in the 1970s to control chlorofluorocarbons, played an important leadership role since US industry again wanted to stop what it considered unfair competition coming from less-regulated European industries. In 1985, 45 nations, including only 16 developing countries, signed the Vienna Convention for the Protection of the Ozone Layer,[32] a framework convention that identified the nature of the problem and set up a procedure to examine the science surrounding it and facilitate a response strategy. Awareness within the chemical industry that alternatives to ozone-depleting chemicals could be developed made the prospect of regulation less daunting—indeed perhaps necessary to create the market conditions required to spur innovation—and companies like Dow Chemical saw an opportunity to profit when a shift to less dangerous chemicals was mandated.[33] Aided by media interest in a problem dramatized by the discovery of a rapidly expanding "ozone hole" over Antarctica, the parties agreed in a remarkably short period to adopt the 1987 Montreal Protocol on Substances that Deplete the Ozone Layer,[34] which established targets and timetables for the reduction of both the use and production of ozone depleting chemicals. Subsequent amendments and adjustments of the Protocol expanded dramatically the number of substances covered and the speed of the phaseouts.

The pace with which regulatory changes could be made and the apparent effectiveness of the agreement in helping contain the problem of ozone depletion made the Montreal regime a genuine success story. Developing countries, originally reluctant to become involved in controlling a problem they viewed as a Northern creation, were motivated to join the regime both by their own dependence on the chemicals being phased out, since trade sanctions would be imposed on non-members, and by the promise of additional economic assistance. The Montreal experience created new hope about the ability of the international community to respond to emerging environmental problems.

Rio and Beyond

The 1992 United Nations Conference on Environment and Development in Rio de Janeiro was intended to celebrate 20 years of progress under UNEP and to begin addressing what had become the central focus of concern: global climate change. Reasons for optimism went beyond Montreal. The reunification of Germany and the breakup of the Soviet Union suggested new opportunities for global cooperation through a United Nations no longer divided between East and West. *Our Common Future*,[35] the 1987 report of the Brundtland Commission, emphasized how the concept of "sustainable development" could be used to balance the goals of developing countries and the need for environmental protection. While the report could not bridge the divide between North and South, it did provide a basis for a more productive dialogue. In the United States, George H. W. Bush had been elected president in 1988. Bush had campaigned in New Hampshire against acid rain, declaring that he would be the "environmental president." Prospects for progress in US federal environmental policy brightened further when William Reilly, a professional conservationist, was named to head the Environmental Protection Agency and Maine's George Mitchell replaced coal-state representative Robert Byrd as Senate Majority leader. In 1990, President Bush signed into law amendments to the Clean Air Act to significantly reduce US sulfur dioxide emissions. The United States subsequently ratified a bilateral Air Quality Agreement with Canada, which helped solidify its commitment to reduce acid rain. The international leadership many felt had been missing on environmental issues seemed to be emerging.

The goals for Rio were perhaps overly ambitious and, as with other meetings driven by an anniversary calendar, difficult to achieve in the time available.

An Earth Charter was being drafted to expand the principles of the Stockholm Declaration and to make them legally binding. A Convention on Biological Diversity would provide a more holistic approach to governing animals, plants, and the world's genetic resources than had been possible in past species-focused regimes. The goal was to strike a reasonable balance between the state's sovereign control over its resources and the legitimate interests of the international community, which ranged from environmentalists hoping to conserve valuable habitat to pharmaceutical companies seeking access to rare plants. However, for many the top objective was to reach agreement on a convention that would commit states to binding targets and timetables for capping and reducing carbon dioxide emissions. Controlling global climate change meant doing more to protect carbon sinks, and a legally binding forestry agreement was also being drafted. A meeting at the level of heads of state, surrounded by over 1,400 NGOs, and with the full glare of media attention, the "Earth Summit" was intended to provide a solid foundation for global environmental governance for the next decade and beyond.

The politics of Rio were complex, and North-South divisions remained very real. A key issue was funding: how much the North was prepared to provide and what form it would take. This alone would have made a comprehensive agreement difficult. However, the most important source of discord was US policy as it played out in the days just before and during the Rio conference, and the United States took much of the blame for the failure of the conference to accomplish more. Domestic forces in the United States, particularly in the Republican Party, had begun to challenge the science behind climate change. Vice President Dan Quayle's White House Council on Competitiveness, working to limit the effect of federal regulation on private business, became an important source of opposition to several of the documents being negotiated.

In the end, the Earth Charter was replaced with a non-binding Rio Declaration on Environment and Development.[36] Key language in the Biodiversity Treaty was watered down at the insistence of the US delegation, which, even then, refused to sign the agreement. The forestry negotiations produced not a binding agreement but a set of "forestry principles" that reflected continued disagreement about the extent to which the tropical forests of the South were a global resource deserving not only protection but also financial support from the North. The participants did adopt the UN Framework Convention on Climate Change (UNFCCC),[37] arguably misnamed because it departed in several respects from the "framework" model. Voluntary targets and timetables for developed countries were included in the agreement and a critical decision was made to create three groups of countries defined in the Convention Annexes, with differential obligations for each. This would set the stage for bitter disagreement later as the United States would insist that China and India and other major developing country emitters of carbon dioxide agree to limit their own emissions as the price for US ratification of the 1997 Kyoto Protocol, something the UNFCCC had not required. Agenda 21 offered an ambitious work plan for the future, embracing a number of new program initiatives. In addition, a Commission on Sustainable Development (CSD) was created in the hope that it would be able to set priorities and provide leadership, something very much needed given the breadth of Agenda 21 and the limited funding available to implement it. However, most delegations left Rio with the sense that an important opportunity had been missed.

Emerging Principles

Although the past 40 years has produced few significant changes in the formal institutional framework in which international environmental policy is made, it has been a period in which the normative landscape has become much more complex and varied. In some areas of international law, states have managed to agree on a reasonably clear set of fundamental rules. International humanitarian law has developed standards governing the conduct of armed conflict based on multilateral conventions dating back to 1899. In 1998, states signed the Rome Statute establishing an International Criminal Court to enforce them.

This degree of consensus has simply not been evident in the environmental arena. Without a binding Earth Charter or the equivalent of an international environmental court, international environmental law has seen an explosion of normative claims of varying degrees of specificity and persuasiveness. Some of these principles have achieved widespread recognition and others, though perhaps reflecting reasonable approaches to environmental protection, are still the subject of substantial debate, at least in terms of their application. Some have sufficient grounding in empirical state behavior to be legal standards that can reasonably become the basis of decisions by an international tribunal. The rules of state responsibility and liability fall into that category. Others, like the principle of subsidiarity, which suggests that environmental governance should take place at the lowest level where effective regulation is possible, serve more as directives to political institutions than as enforceable rules. Still others, like sustainable development, straddle the line between law and politics.

This section discusses seven principles that have been the focus of disagreement in a number of international environmental disputes. How they have been applied and developed in practice is a central concern of the case studies that follow.

State Responsibility/Liability

International law remains a state-centered system and the most important principles of international environmental law are designed to govern state behavior. This is true despite the fact that much of the activity requiring regulation is undertaken by private parties and that many of those most ready to challenge environmentally destructive behavior are non-state actors.

International law has traditionally focused on the duties states owe to each other. Basic concepts of sovereignty begin with the assumption that the state has exclusive jurisdiction over all activity taking place on its territory, a fundamental rule that has been re-emphasized by developing nations in the debate surrounding permanent sovereignty over natural resources. Yet sovereignty also presumes the state's right to protect its territory from unwanted interference. Principles like "good neighborliness" provide guidelines for state behavior when activities within the state's territory threaten or cause transboundary damage, the issue at the heart of the Trail Smelter case.

In its work to codify the general rules of state responsibility, the International Law Commission (ILC) raised a conceptual issue about how issues of transboundary damage, including environmental damage, should be approached. State responsibility is traditionally seen as something that results when the state violates a rule of international law, a primary norm that indicates how it should and should not behave. When a primary norm is violated, the secondary rules of state responsibility apply, indicating the legal consequences that should follow as a result of the breach. These normally include a duty to make reparation, which in the case of environmental damage might well include financial compensation, and steps taken to prevent further violations. However, unless one applies a doctrine of strict state responsibility, it is seldom clear that the state has violated international law simply by permitting an otherwise lawful activity, such as the operation of an industrial plant, to take place on its territory. In this situation, the ILC suggests that it is better to approach the problem as "international liability" for the damaging effects of otherwise lawful activity.[38]

Why does the distinction matter? Primarily, because this recognizes the way that states have actually behaved in recent years, which is not to accept or even assert against others the type of strict liability the Trail Smelter decision seemed to suggest. An exception is the 1972 Space Liability Convention,[39] which imposes strict liability on states for any damage caused to the surface of the Earth from space objects launched from their territories.

However, this is a very special case given the particularly hazardous nature of space activity and the central role played by national governments in conducting space activities at the time the agreement was signed.

An alternative has been to channel whatever liability might come from activities that threaten or cause transboundary damage to the private actors who engage in them, thus creating regimes of civil liability to respond to transboundary damage. This approach is consistent with the polluter pays principle discussed below and has an obvious appeal for states. Examples can be found in treaties governing damage caused by oil spills from oceangoing tankers and by the operation of nuclear facilities. While several of the treaties impose strict liability, this is normally accompanied by overall liability limits designed to make it economically feasible for operators to conduct what is risky—but still lawful—activity. Besides provisions requiring insurance to guarantee that compensation can be paid, it is also common to create a fund supported by multiple operators to distribute the risk associated with the activity. The role of the state is chiefly to make sure that these civil liability regimes are implemented effectively, although it also may help administer the fund and, in the case of the Paris Convention on Third Party Liability in the Field of Nuclear Energy,[40] actually contribute money to supplement what the fund provides.

However, even developing civil liability regimes can be a highly charged political process and many treaty regimes do not include them. Most of those that have been developed are for activities considered highly risky, often where well-publicized accidents have helped focus public attention on the need to compensate victims. Parties to the Basel Convention on the Transboundary Movement of Hazardous Wastes and their Disposal[41] took ten years to negotiate a complex Liability Protocol,[42] and that agreement, signed in 1999, has yet to come into force. Given the difficulty of reaching agreement on civil liability provisions within the framework of a specific agreement, it would be difficult to suggest that customary law requires such an approach as a general rule in transboundary disputes, and there is no indication that states commonly accept liability where no civil liability regime exists. The issue of who should bear liability for the transboundary consequences of a serious environmental accident is an issue at the center of the Baia Mare dispute, analyzed in Chapter 4.

Mitigating Risk

An important development in international environmental law has been the effort to limit the need for after-the-fact liability by focusing on steps that can be taken to reduce the chances that serious environmental harm will occur. With this has come an emphasis on developing procedural rules governing state behavior before transboundary damage is done. The concern for prevention is not new. In its 1949 ruling in the Corfu Channel case,[43] the International Court of Justice found Albania responsible for the loss of life on two British destroyers sunk by mines in its territorial sea, because it had failed to warn the United Kingdom of hazards to navigation of which it should have been aware. This suggested a duty both to monitor and to publicize hazardous conditions, even if it did not require states to prevent them from occurring. In the 1957 Lake Lanoux arbitration,[44] Spain challenged France's attempts to divert waters of a transboundary water system arguing that it would violate Spanish rights as the lower riparian. The tribunal held that France could proceed without Spanish prior approval, but only because it had acted responsibly in engaging Spanish officials extensively about the project and had taken concrete steps to take Spanish interests into account in the final plans.

Emerging from state practice dating back to the work of the Danube and Rhine commissions are procedural duties that now arguably extend to transboundary airsheds and other areas of transboundary impact. These include the duty to inform, the duty to consult, the duty to evaluate or assess (taking into account the potential impact on other states), and the duty to take reasonable measures to limit transboundary damage. As the Lake Lanoux tribunal had held, this does not require the approval of the potentially affected state, since this would amount to unjustifiable interference in the right of a state to control what happens on its territory.

While most states agree that these procedural duties exist, there can be significant disagreement about how they should be applied in a given situation. At what point in the planning process should the state begin to engage with potentially affected states, and how serious must the potential impact be? To whom is information given and with whom must the state consult? In the days of the Lake Lanoux dispute, contact between government officials, perhaps at the technical level, might well have been sufficient. However, the very active roles now played by members of civil society suggest the need for a much broader consultative process. If some form of environmental impact assessment must be conducted, what standards, particularly in assessing and weighing potential transboundary impact, ought to apply? When these issues are considered sufficiently important, states can set up guidelines and standards by treaty, as they have in the UNECE's Espoo Convention on the Environmental Impact Assessment in a Transboundary Context,[45] but how extensive the assessment obligations of non-signatories are is a matter of continuing disagreement.

Taken together, these duties amount to a broader state obligation of what has come to be known as "due diligence," a concept at the heart of

Argentina's case against Uruguay in the Pulp Mills case. Central to the dispute was disagreement over what due diligence required of Uruguay, whether the government had demonstrated it, and if not, what the legal consequences should be.

Common Heritage

Although international environmental law is generally based on state sovereign control over territory, the common heritage principle asserts that there are areas beyond the territorial jurisdiction of states, as well as resources and historic sites of general interest, that should be seen as held jointly, whether by states collectively or by the global community defined more broadly. Malta's Ambassador Avi Pardo is credited with having introduced the concept to the United Nations in a 1967 speech calling for the seabed beyond the limits of national jurisdiction to be considered the "common heritage of mankind" to be managed and protected collectively for the benefit of all. The common heritage concept has since been extended by treaty to cover the moon and other celestial bodies, and asserted over Antarctica by the General Assembly. UNESCO has also used it as the basis for designating places of particular historical and cultural interest "world heritage sites" to help build political and financial support for their preservation, although the fact that they remain located within the territory of individual states limits the extent to which they can actually be managed collectively. More controversial have been attempts to designate the Earth's genetic resources as a common heritage, given the potential interference with the right of states to develop those resources according to national priorities.

Beyond the question of what areas and resources deserve common heritage status, the most important issue is what this implies legally. Principle 21 of the Stockholm Declaration asserts that states have a duty not to damage "areas beyond the limits of national jurisdiction," but who has the right to invoke that obligation? This issue was raised in the 1973 Nuclear Tests case,[46] when New Zealand and Australia challenged the legality of the French program of atmospheric nuclear testing in the South Pacific and asked the International Court of Justice to order interim measures of protection to stop the tests while the case could be heard. One basis of their complaint was the damage they felt would be done to high seas resources. Invoking the principle of actio popularis, they claimed the right to speak on behalf of the international community's collective interest in protecting the high seas. The Court issued the interim order, but never formally ruled on the merits of the case, as it was declared moot when France later announced plans to end the tests. However, the dispute highlighted the challenge to international environmental law of providing a mechanism to permit claims to be brought against a state whose actions threaten common heritage resources.

Common but Differentiated Responsibilities

Related to the common heritage concept is the principle of common but differentiated responsibilities (CDR). While all states share an obligation to protect the environment, CDR suggests that they have different legal duties in the ways they are expected to behave. While this may seem to violate the principle of sovereign equality of states, the UN Charter already gives special rights to its five permanent members in the form of the veto, and treaties negotiated between states of unequal power commonly reflect these power relationships in the rights the parties actually acquire. What makes the CDR principle unusual and potentially more problematic is the range of possible claims states may make to differential treatment, particularly outside of a treaty regime where the implications of applying CDR can be defined more precisely.

CDR is both a principle of equity and a political necessity. In dealing with environmental problems to which states have made such different contributions and have such different capacities to respond, expecting all to bear the same costs would be unfair and usually non-negotiable. The logic behind this principle was evident in the Founex Report, but it was not clearly integrated into an environmental regime until the Montreal Protocol adopted a provision to allow "low-consuming developing countries" the right to increase their use of ozone-depleting chemicals, even as more developed states were being required to reduce theirs. Principle 7 of the Rio Declaration explicitly recognizes the CDR principle and links differential state duties to "different contributions to global environmental degradation." The UNFCCC is even clearer in endorsing the CDR principle and making it operational. Article 3 lists a series of equitable criteria that should be taken into account, including the particular vulnerability of some developing countries to the effects of climate change and the "disproportionate or abnormal burden" some would have to bear under the convention. More practically, states are divided into three different groups including those expected to implement carbon dioxide reduction strategies, those required to provide additional aid to developing countries, and implicitly all the rest, whose obligations are far more vaguely defined.

The experience with the UNFCCC also reveals one of the most serious challenges posed by the CDR principle. Even when integrated into a treaty-based regime, it can be very difficult to alter the special status some states enjoy if conditions change. It has become evident that any comprehensive response to the problem of climate change will require China and India, now two of the chief emitters of carbon dioxide, to accept cutbacks they are now not required to make and have a principled basis to reject. Perhaps more problematic is the potential impact of the CDR principle and the rationale behind it when invoked outside a treaty framework, since it can permit virtually any developing state to deflect responsibility for environmental damage. In several of the disputes studied here, the rationale behind CDR seems to be used to justify the actions of key states, even if the principle itself is not invoked directly.

Polluter Pays Principle

The polluter pays principle (PPP) argues that those who damage the environment should be required to pay the costs arising from their actions. In a world where environmental damage could be reasonably anticipated, it would be possible to force those engaged in damaging activities to internalize those costs, which would then be reflected in the price of goods and services produced. The OECD was an early proponent of the PPP, since it was seen as a way to protect the environment that was both economically efficient and less likely to produce competing national anti-pollution measures that would distort international trade. In adopting the principle in 1972, the OECD understood that taking this approach, designed "to ensure that the environment is in an acceptable state," did not in any way clarify what an "acceptable state" would be and merely provided what the Council felt was an appropriate general approach to achieve it.[47] There are also many different policy tools that can be used to make polluters pay, ranging from command and control regulations to user taxes to the imposition of civil liability once damage occurs. Thus adopting the principle only provides a general orientation toward the process of regulation, and does not clarify either the environmental goals sought or the means to be used. The European Union has made the PPP one of the cornerstones of its environmental policy, integrating it in 1987 into what became Article 191(2) of the Treaty on the Functioning of the European Union (TFEU).[48] However, it was not until 2004, in the aftermath of the Baia Mare cyanide spill and other serious accidents, that it was given clearer definition with the adoption of the Environmental Liability Directive.[49]

Developed within Northern institutions, the PPP has received less support in developing countries, where there is often concern that the costs it might impose on private business would make development too difficult and deter foreign investment. One alternative would be to transfer whatever environmental costs states are willing to accept onto the state itself.[50]

Principle 16 of the Rio Declaration does offer support for the polluter pays principle, stating "National authorities should endeavor to promote the internalization of environmental costs and the use of economic instruments, taking into account the approach that the polluter should, in principle, bear the cost of pollution." However, that language is followed by the phrase "with due regard to the public interest," which suggests the flexibility that national governments retain if they fear the potential effects of the principle's strict application.

Environmentalists have also viewed the PPP with suspicion, in part because of its political origins in the work of the growth-oriented OECD. One issue is the challenge of assigning monetary value to at least some forms of environmental damage, a concern that goes back to the US objection to the compensation award of the Trail Smelter tribunal. While our understanding of environmental damage and our ability to quantify it have improved since Trail Smelter, fear remains that effects on endangered species and important habitats would never receive the recognition they deserve. Moreover, the principle seems to accept the existence of pollution, as long as it is paid for; to think of the problem in this way could undercut efforts to prevent at least certain kinds and levels of pollution from occurring at all.

Precautionary Principle

The precautionary principle was a response, in part, to the debate of the early 1980s over acid rain. Officials in the United States and the United Kingdom, two of the chief producers of the sulfur dioxide believed to cause it, challenged the science behind proposed regulatory efforts. Claiming that there was insufficient proof that the alleged damage was linked to the sources targeted by environmentalists, they opposed the costly remedial measures being considered. Calls for more study angered critics, who felt this would only delay action and make response strategies more expensive. The precautionary principle reflects a broader concern that the science behind environmental degradation will almost never be so certain as to meet Trail Smelter's "clear and convincing evidence" standard. The result of inaction in the case of problems like global climate change could be catastrophic and irreversible environmental damage.

An excellent example of the practical application of the precautionary principle is found in changes made to the regime of the London Convention (formerly the London Dumping Convention). The 1972 Convention regulated the deliberate discharge of hazardous waste into the ocean by placing hazardous substances on one of two lists, a black list for those for which dumping was prohibited and a gray list for those requiring regulation.

A 1996 protocol shifted this process to a "reverse list" approach, whereby the presumption is that no substance can be dumped at sea unless it has been added to one of the annexes and the operator secures a permit indicating that it can be disposed of safely.[51] The EU has also embraced the precautionary principle, including it in the TFEU along with the polluter pays principle. Yet, like the PPP, it was adopted without being defined more specifically.

Although the value of precautionary action has been widely embraced rhetorically, its acceptance as an enforceable legal principle has been less than wholehearted. Principle 15 of the Rio Declaration states,

> In order to protect the environment, the precautionary approach shall be widely applied by States according to their capabilities. Where there are threats of serious or irreversible damage, lack of full scientific certainty shall not be used as a reason for postponing cost-effective measures to prevent environmental degradation.

Note the keywords. The level of potential damage must be very high, "serious or irreversible," and the phrase "lack of full scientific certainty," though framed in the negative, clearly implies that there should be a substantial body of scientific evidence before action must be taken. "According to their capabilities," brings the CDR principle back into play. Moreover, the action required is termed "cost-effective." All of this suggests room for disagreement, even among those who are generally supportive of the need for precautionary action. At least as significant was the decision to endorse precaution not as a "principle," but as an "approach," the same term used in the London Protocol. This reflects the concern felt by some states, most notably the United States, that precaution is less fully integrated into international law than many in the European Union would like to believe. The implications of the precautionary principle were an important dimension of Ireland's argument in the Sellafield MOX dispute and Argentina's ICJ challenge against Uruguay.

Sustainable Development

Sustainable development, the product of a determined effort to balance the goals of environmental protection and economic development, is largely self-defining. It seeks, in words of the Brundtland Commission, "development that meets the needs of the present without compromising the ability of future generations to meet their own needs."[52] The first five principles of the Rio Declaration all refer to it directly, and the major institutional change proposed at Rio was to create the Commission on Sustainable Development, suggesting the extent to which the phrase had achieved general acceptance.

In 1997, issues of sustainable development were raised before the International Court of Justice in the Gabčíkovo-Nagymaros dispute between Hungary and Slovakia.[53] Hungary had justified its decision to terminate a bilateral 1977 treaty to jointly develop the Danube River arguing, in part, that that the envisioned project would violate evolving norms of international environmental law, most notably the principle of sustainable development. Slovakia never challenged the existence of the principle, just the way it was being used by Hungary. In the end, the Court felt it unnecessary to address the issue directly, since not even Hungary had claimed that sustainable development had the *jus cogens* status that would permit it to be used to terminate a treaty. The Court acknowledged the importance of emerging international environmental law standards and instructed the two states to incorporate them into revisions of the Danube project, including "the need to reconcile economic development with protection of the environment . . . aptly expressed in the concept of sustainable development."[54] In a separate opinion, Judge Weeramantry went further, arguing that sustainable development is a "principle with normative value." It has achieved its status as a general principle of international law as a result of both its "inescapable logical necessity," in providing a way to reconcile the competing needs of development and environmental protection, and "its wide and general acceptance by the global community." Moreover, it did have practical application, and should have "a significant role to play in the resolution of environmentally related disputes."[55]

Sustainable development does have broad political appeal, and Judge Weeramantry may be correct in stating that it has sufficient general support to deserve recognition as a principle of international law. However, what it actually means remains a source of substantial practical disagreement, as much a basis for disputes as a principle useful in resolving them. This is evident in at least four of the cases studied here, where striking an appropriate balance between development and environmental interests is at the center of the controversy.

The Broader Setting

When the first of the disputes analyzed here began in the mid-1990s, the context in which they took place was complex and fragmented, institutionally, legally, and politically.

On an institutional level, Rio had failed to provide the greater centralization many felt was needed if the United Nations was to lead the response to problems like climate change. The Commission on Sustainable Development had yet to prove that it could provide any real leadership in promoting Agenda 21, and UNEP remained a weak, coordinating body, still with limited authority and funding. New organizations were being proposed, ranging from a World Environment Organization to an International Environment Court, but missing was the sense of direction and political momentum required to support significant institutional change. Emerging more out of necessity than design was a system of multilevel environmental governance, a complex web of international agreements and regimes often intersecting with related areas of international concern, like trade, security, and human rights.

Globally, the goal in the 1990s was not to create new organizations but to develop creative and cost-effective synergies between existing ones. Regional organizations were taking on a more prominent role in responding to environmental problems and would be actively involved in transboundary disputes arising among their members. Reflecting different political cultures and institutional priorities, organizations like the European Union and the Association of Southeast Asian Nations (ASEAN) approached these disputes very differently. New connections with varying degrees of institutionalization were also being made across state boundaries at lower levels of governance. Local officials, closest to where the effects of pollution were felt, often took the lead, especially in the absence of effective national and international action. Many became key players in the transboundary disputes analyzed here.

From a legal perspective, multilevel governance offered new arenas for confrontation, and battles over competing normative standards were common. Environmental diplomacy of the 1970s and 1980s had produced new concepts like sustainable development and common but differentiated responsibilities, but their malleable definitions created room for serious principle-based disagreement, particularly in the increasing number of regimes where third-party dispute settlement was possible or in states where national courts were willing to take on international environmental issues. While the "judicialization" of transboundary disputes offered hope that judges could give these fuzzy norms clearer definition, it did not remove their potentially divisive effect.

Finally, the dynamic political environment of the 1990s reflected a world where even the division between North and South that had so dominated past discussions of environmental policy was no longer the same. Within the North, the breakup of the Soviet Union and the political changes taking place in Eastern Europe had created a new group of countries in "economic transition." Though not "developing" in the old sense of that term, they required a different kind of assistance in responding to problems left by years of inefficient and highly polluting state-run industries. The diversity of the South was also apparent, as nations like China, India, and Brazil, increasingly affluent countries of East Asia, and major oil producers took on more prominent roles in international environmental policy arenas. At the other end of the spectrum were the poorest developing countries, whose vulnerability to problems of desertification, soil erosion, and sea-level rise now led to fears of environmental refugees and the possible displacement of whole populations as a result of deteriorating environmental conditions.

Non-state actors continued to proliferate, increased NGO influence both a product of multilevel governance and a force helping shape it. Representing a broad spectrum of environmental interests, and now with access to the internet and new communication technologies, the impact of NGOs on international environmental policy was dramatically enhanced. Transnational coalitions were forming to respond to issues like ship-breaking that cut across national and functional boundaries. For many governments the challenge became to keep up with the pace of policy change being demanded by civil society. Yet, while environmental NGOs would play a major role in many of the transboundary disputes analyzed here, they seldom behaved as a monolithic force, having different priorities and using different tools to try to influence policy.

A similar diversity was evident among the private actors whose polluting behavior was often the target of environmentalists. Some would fit the popular image of self-interested corporate polluters. However, others were firms that had been encouraged by governments to invest because they offered the prospect of jobs and economic growth while employing advanced technologies felt likely to improve environmental conditions, thus providing the opportunity for genuinely sustainable development.

Notes

1   United Kingdom and the United States, "Treaty Relating to Boundary Waters and Questions Arising Along the Boundary between Canada and the United States," Washington, 11 January 1909 (in force 5 May 1910) in Charles Bevans, *Treaties and Other International Agreements of the United States* 1976–1949 12 (1949), Art. 4, 322 [hereafter cited as "Boundary Waters Treaty"]. http://www. ijc.org/en/BWT.
2   International Law Association, "Helsinki Rules on the Uses of the Waters of International Rivers," *Report of the Fifty-Fifth Conference* (1966): 477–533.
3   "Trail Smelter Arbitration: United States, Canada (Final Decision, 16 April 1938, and 11 March 1941)," *Reports of International Arbitral Awards* 3 (1949): 1905–1982 [hereafter cited as "Trail Smelter Decision"].
4   Stephen C. McCaffrey, "Of Paradoxes, Precedents and Progeny: The Trail Smelter Arbitration 65 Years Later," in *Transboundary Harm in International Law:*

Lessons from the Trail Smelter Arbitration, ed. Rebecca M. Bratspies and Russell A. Miller (Cambridge: Cambridge University Press, 2006), 45.

5   Alfred P. Rubin, "Pollution by Analogy: The Trail Smelter Arbitration," *Oregon Law Review* 50 (1971): 259–82.

6   John H. Knox, "The Flawed Trail Smelter Procedure: The Wrong Tribunal, the Wrong Parties, and the Wrong Law," in *Transboundary Harm in International Law: Lessons from the Trail Smelter Arbitration*, ed. Rebecca M. Bratspies and Russell A. Miller (Cambridge: Cambridge University Press, 2006), 66–78.

7   See, for example, Karen Michelson, "Rereading *Trail Smelter*," ibid., 79–84.

8   Canada and the United States, "Convention Relative to the Establishment of a Tribunal to Decide Questions of Indemnity and Future Regime Arising from the Operation of Smelter at Trail, British Columbia," Ottawa, 15 April 1935, *U.S. Treaty Series*, No. 893, in "Trail Smelter Decision," 1907–1910.

9   Ibid., Art. IV, 1908.

10   John E. Read, "The Trail Smelter Dispute," *Canadian Journal of International Law* 1 (1963): 223–25.

11   "Trail Smelter Decision," 1965.

12   Ibid., 1963–64.

13   See generally, Rubin, "Pollution by Analogy."

14   Read, "The Trail Smelter Dispute," 221.

15   See testimony before the House Committee on Foreign Affairs, in US Congress, House Committee on Foreign Affairs, Subcommittee on International Organizations and Movements, "International Cooperation in the Human Environment through the United Nations," 92nd Congress, 2nd session, 15–16 March 1972, 4–25.

16   Lynton Keith Caldwell, *International Environmental Policy: Emergence and Dimensions*, 2nd ed. (Durham, NC: Duke University Press, 1990), 47.

17   See United Nations, General Assembly, "Permanent Sovereignty over Natural Resources," Res. 1803 (XVIII), 14 December 1962. http://www.un.org/ga/search/view_doc.asp?symbol=A/RES/1803%28XVII%29.

18   "Founex Report on Development and Environment: A Report Submitted by a Panel of Experts Convened by the Secretary General of the United Nations Conference on the Human Environment," Founex, Switzerland, 4–12 June 1971, in *International Conciliation*, no. 586 (January 1972): 7–36.

19   Ibid., 10–11.

20   Ibid., 10.

21   Ibid., 32.

22   Ibid., 33.

23   United Nations, "Declaration of the United Nations Conference on the Human Environment," in *Report of the United Nations Conference on the Human Environment, Stockholm, June 5–16, 1972* (Doc. A/Conf. 48/14), *International Legal Materials* 11 (1972): 1420. http://www.unep.org/Documents.Multilingual/Default.asp?documentid=97&articleid=1503.

24   How that responsibility might be invoked would shortly become an issue in the Nuclear Tests case. See discussion below.

25   UNEP's relative institutional weakness would ironically be one of the reasons states like Indonesia would be willing to bring UNEP officials into discussions about sensitive environmental problems they faced.

26   See, generally, Allen L. Springer, "United States Environmental Policy and International Law: Stockholm Principle 21 Revisited," in *International Environmental Diplomacy: The Management and Resolution of Transfrontier Environmental Problems*, ed. John C. Carroll (Cambridge: Cambridge University Press, 1988), 45–66.

27   "Convention on the Prevention of Marine Pollution by Dumping of Wastes and Other Matter," London, signed 13 November 1972 (in force 30 August 1975), *United Nations Treaty Series* 1046 (1977): 138–218 [hereafter cited as "London Dumping Convention"]. https://treaties.un.org/doc/Publication/UNTS/Volume%201046/volume-1046-I-15749-English.pdf.

28   "International Convention for the Prevention of Pollution from Ships 73/78 (MARPOL)," London, signed 2 November 1973 (in force 12 October 1983). http://www.imo.org/en/KnowledgeCentre/ReferencesAndArchives/HistoryofMARPOL/Documents/MARPOL%201973%20-%20Final%20Act%20and%20Convention.pdf.

29   "Convention on International Trade in Endangered Species (CITES)," Washington, signed 3 March 1973 (in force 1 July 1975). https://www.cites.org/eng/disc/text.php.

30   "Convention on the Protection of Migratory Species of Wild Animals (CMS)," Bonn, signed 23 June 1979 (in force 1 November 1983), *International Legal Materials* 11 (1979): 15. http://www.cms.int/en/convention-text.

31   United Nations Economic Commission for Europe (UNECE), "Convention on Long-Range Transboundary Air Pollution," Geneva, signed 13 November 1979 (in force 16 March 1983), *International Legal Materials* 18 (1979): 1442 [hereafter cited as "LRTAP"]. http://www.unece.org/fileadmin/DAM/env/lrtap/full text/1979.CLRTAP.e.pdf.

32   "Vienna Convention for the Protection of the Ozone Layer," Vienna, signed 22 March 1985 (in force 22 September 1988), *United Nations Treaty Series* 1513: 323, *International Legal Materials* 26 (1987): 1529. http://www.unep.ch/ozone/pdfs/viennaconvention2002.pdf.

33   See, generally, Edward A. Parsons, *Protecting the Ozone Layer: Science and Strategy* (Oxford: Oxford University Press, 2003).

34   "Montreal Protocol on Substances that Deplete the Ozone Layer," Montreal, signed 16 September 1987 (in force 1 January 1989), *United Nations Treaty Series* 1522: 3, *International Legal Materials* 26 (1987): 1550. https://treaties.un.org/doc/Publication/UNTS/Volume%201522/volume-1522-I-26369-English.pdf.

35   World Commission on Environment and Development, *Report of the World Commission on Environment and Development: Our Common Future* (Oxford: Oxford University Press, 1987) [hereafter cited as "Our Common Future"].

36   United Nations, "Rio Declaration on Environment and Development," in *Report of the United Nations Conference on Environment and Development*, Rio de Janeiro, 3–14 June 1992 (Doc. A/Conf. 151/26 (Vol. I) Annex I), *International Legal Materials* 31 (1992): 874 [hereafter cited as "Rio Declaration"]. http://www.unep.org/Documents.Multilingual/Default.asp?DocumentID=78&ArticleID=1163.

37   United Nations, "United Nations Framework Convention on Climate Change," Rio de Janeiro, signed 9 May 1992 (in force 21 March 1994), *International Legal Materials* 31 (1992): 849 [hereafter cited as "UN Framework Convention"]. http://unfccc.int/files/essential_background/background_publications_htmlpdf/application/pdf/conveng.pdf.

38   Luis Barrioneuvo Arevalo, "The Work of the International Law Commission in the Field of International Environmental Law," *Boston College Environmental Affairs Law Review* 32, no. 3 (2005): 493–507.

39   "Convention on International Liability for Damage Caused by Space Objects," New York, signed 29 November 1971 (in force 1 September 1972), *International Legal Materials* 10 (1971): 965. https://www.faa.gov/about/office_org/headquarters_offices/ast/media/Conv_International_Liab_Damage.pdf.

40   "Convention on Third Party Liability in the Field of Nuclear Energy," Paris, signed 29 July 1960 (in force 10 April 1968), *United Nations Treaty Series* 956: 251, *International Legal Materials* 28 (1989): 657. http://www.ecolex.org/server2.php/libcat/docs/TRE/Full/En/TRE-000435.txt.

41   "Basel Convention on the Transboundary Movements of Hazardous Waste and their Disposal," Basel, signed 22 March 1989 (in force 5 May 1992), *United Nations Treaty Series* 1673: 126, *International Legal Materials* 28 (1989): 657. http://archive.basel.int/text/con-e-rev.pdf.

42   "Protocol on Liability and Compensation for Damage Resulting from Transboundary Movements of Hazardous Wastes and Their Disposal," Basel, signed 10 December 1999 (not in force), UN Doc. UNEP/CHW.1/WG/9/2. http://archive.basel.int/meetings/cop/cop5/docs/prot-e.pdf.

43   ICJ, "Corfu Channel Case (United Kingdom v. Albania) (Merits)," 9 April 1949, *ICJ Reports* (1949): 4, General List No. 1. http://www.icj-cij.org/docket/files/1/1645.pdf.

44   "Lake Lanoux Arbitration (France v. Spain)," 11 November 1957, *Reports of International Arbitral Awards* 12 (1957): 281. http://www.ecolex.org/server2.php/libcat/docs/COU/Full/En/COU-143747E.pdf.

45   United Nations Economic Commission for Europe (UNECE), "Convention on Environmental Impact Assessment in a Transboundary Context," Espoo, Finland, signed 25 February 1991 (in force 19 September 1997), *United Nations Treaty Series* 1989: 310. http://www.unece.org/fileadmin/DAM/env/eia/documents/legaltexts/Espoo_Convention_authentic_ENG.pdf.

46   ICJ, "Nuclear Tests Case (New Zealand v. France)," 20 December 1974, *ICJ Reports* (1974): 457, General List No. 59. http://www.icj-cij.org/docket/files/59/6159.pdf.

47   OECD, "Note on the Implementation of the Polluter Pays Principle," OECD Doc. Env. (73)32 (1974), reprinted in *International Legal Materials* 14 (1975): 239.

48   European Union, "Consolidated Version of the Treaty on the Functioning of the European Union," signed 13 December 2007 (in force 1 December 2009), *Official Journal of the European Union* 115 (9 May 2008): 47, Doc. 2008/C 115/01. http://www.refworld.org/docid/4b17a07e2.html.

49   European Union (EU), "Directive 2004/35/CE of the European Parliament and of the Council of 21 April 2004 on Environmental Liability with Regard to the Prevention and Remedying of Environmental Damage," 21 April 2004, *Official Journal L* 143 (30 April 2004): 0056–0075. http://eur-lex.europa.eu/legal-content/EN/TXT/?uri=CELEX:32004L0035. For more on the history of the EU's development of the polluter pays principle, see Nicolas de Sadeleer, "The Polluter-Pays Principle in EU Law: Bold Case Law and Poor Harmonisation," *Pro Natura: Festskrift Til H.C. Bugge, Oslo, Universitetsforlaget* (2012): 405–19.

50 See, generally, Barbara Luppi, Francesco Parisib, and Shruti Rajagopaland, "The Rise and Fall of the Polluter-Pays Principle in Developing Countries," *International Review of Law and Economics* 32, no. 1 (2012): 135–44.

51 IMO, "1996 Protocol to the Convention on the Prevention of Marine Pollution by Dumping of Wastes and Other Matter," London, signed 7 November 1996 (in force 24 March 2006), *International Legal Materials* 36 (1997): 1. http://www. admiraltylawguide.com/conven/protodumping1996.html.

52 "Our Common Future," 43.

53 ICJ, "Gabčíkovo-Nagymaros Project (Hungary/Slovakia) (Judgment), 25 September 1997," *ICJ Reports* (1997): 7, reprinted in *International Legal Materials* 37 (1998): 162 [hereafter cited as "Gabčíkovo-Nagymaros Decision"]. http://www.icj-cij.org/docket/files/92/7375.pdf.

54 Ibid., para. 140, 78.

55 ICJ, "Gabčíkovo-Nagymaros Project (Hungary/Slovakia) (Separate Opinion of Judge Weeramantry)," 25 September 1997, *ICJ Reports* (1997): 88, 95. http://www.icj-cij.org/docket/files/92/7383.pdf.

3
Indonesian Haze[1]

Introduction

During late 1997 and early 1998, much of northern Indonesia was enveloped in smoke. Fires deliberately set to burn brush in the provinces of Kalimantan and Sumatra spread to forests and peat bogs, destroying nearly 10 million hectares of land.[2] What governments euphemistically labeled a thick "haze" soon spread over much of Southeast Asia. Fearful of the health effects, public health officials in Singapore and Malaysia warned people to stay indoors, and the region's tourism industry was badly disrupted. The resulting damage was estimated at between $8 billion and $10 billion.[3] What had begun as a local environmental problem was transformed into one with regional and global implications.

The damage inflicted on Indonesia's neighbors was certainly not intentional, but the fires were not an accident. Fire is commonly used throughout Southeast Asia as a cheap way to clear land, and the government was well aware that the fires were burning on Indonesian territory. Indonesia's permissive land-use policies had allowed the fires to be set, and the government's limited capacity to oversee land-clearing operations had enhanced the chances that the fires would get out of control. Once the fires spread, Indonesia seemed unable to stop them.

Despite the serious damage being caused and the fact that this had happened before, the response of Indonesia's downwind neighbors was remarkably restrained. Understandably, their first priority was to get the fires extinguished. However, even later the governments of Singapore and Malaysia did little to suggest that Indonesia had a legal obligation to do more to prevent the fires or to provide compensation to those injured by the smoke. Their failure to speak out more decisively would seem to call into question some basic rules of state environmental responsibility discussed in Chapter 2. Principle 21 of the Stockholm Declaration, reaffirmed in Rio, declared that states have "the responsibility to ensure that activities within their jurisdiction or control do not cause damage to the environment of other States or of areas beyond the limits of national jurisdiction." Yet if the victims of transboundary damage did not even attempt to invoke this principle, what does it really mean in practice? Shortly after the fires, Simon Tay, Singapore law professor and environmental activist, stated bluntly,

Map 3.1 This map highlights the Indonesian provinces in which the major brush fires occurred in 1997–98 and shows the location of neighboring states affected by the haze.

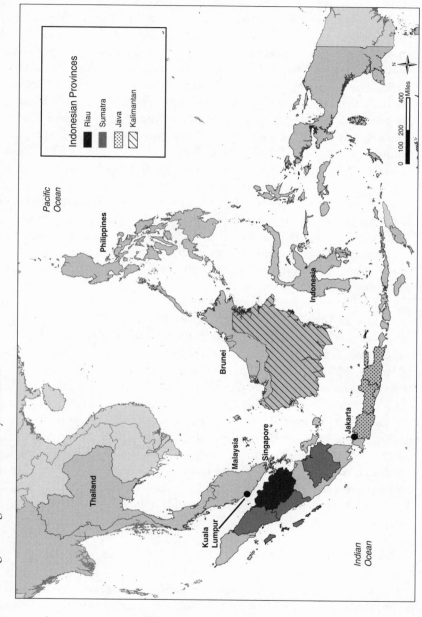

Indonesian Provinces
Riau
Sumatra
Java
Kalimantan

Pacific Ocean

Philippines

Indonesia

Brunei

Thailand

Malaysia

Singapore

Kuala Lumpur

Jakarta

Indian Ocean

N

0 100 200   400
Miles

"The fires . . . challenge the adequacy of international environmental law, both in practice and in principle."[4].

"Indonesian Haze" is the first of three case studies focusing on important substantive rules of international environmental law. The 1997–98 fires and international reactions to them provide an opportunity to examine the nature of state environmental responsibility, including the fundamental question of whether there really is a generally recognized body of law, beyond what states create by treaty, that imposes obligations on states when transboundary damage is done. A related issue is whether Indonesia had duties not only to the neighboring states most immediately affected but also to the larger international community. Other states and international organizations, worried about the effect of the fires on the region's rich biodiversity and the impact that the huge amounts of carbon being released would have on the global climate system, looked for ways to protect what they considered important shared environmental interests. Given the muted reaction by regional governments, it was the active and sustained involvement of these "outsiders" that helped make the Indonesian fires a genuine international dispute. However, the legal basis for external criticism of Indonesia's behavior was not at all clear, given the country's accepted legal authority over its domestic natural resources.

This chapter begins with an overview of the economic and political context in which this dispute took place, describes the sources of the fires and the damage they caused, and examines the reactions of those affected. Particular emphasis is placed on the role played by the Association of Southeast Asian Nations (ASEAN) and the United Nations Environment Program (UNEP) in managing what might have become a far more divisive dispute. It then describes how the legal claim against Indonesia that was never actually made might have been framed to get a clearer sense of the issues of state responsibility the fires raised, at least within the international legal community. The 1997–98 fires also led to reforms designed to prevent their repetition, as even Indonesia seemed to agree that the existing legal framework was inadequate. The chapter concludes with an analysis of those changes, including the 2002 ASEAN Agreement on Transboundary Haze Pollution (hereafter referred to as the Haze Agreement), and the challenges faced in implementing them.

The Context

The dispute began in 1997, during a period of profound economic crisis affecting virtually all of East Asia.[5] In July, Thailand, burdened by substantial foreign debt, had been forced to delink the Thai baht from the US dollar, a move that put tremendous pressure on neighboring countries, most notably Indonesia. Although Indonesia's economy had previously seemed strong, with healthy foreign reserves and a trade surplus of nearly $1 billion, many Indonesian corporations held substantial amounts of foreign debt denominated in US dollars. The value of the Indonesian rupiah compared to the dollar plummeted, and the Indonesian economy was broadly affected, in part because of a reduced regional demand for Indonesian timber and agricultural products. In 1998, Indonesia's GDP declined by over 14 per cent, real wages fell dramatically, and prices for key commodities soared, as the Indonesian government undertook significant domestic reforms to meet conditions imposed by the International Monetary Fund (IMF) in exchange for a substantial IMF bailout.[6] By the time rains put out the fires in June 1998, widespread and violent public protest had forced President Suharto from office, ending 31 years of military rule.

In 1997, Indonesia had a population of almost 210 million people, making it the world's fourth-largest country. An archipelagic state of over 730,000 square miles, Indonesia spans over 17,000 islands, 6,000 of them inhabited, presenting an enormous governance challenge simply from a geographic perspective. Its tropical climate, alternating between rainy and dry seasons, supports one of the world's richest areas of biodiversity, including habitat that is home to many endangered species. Protecting these internation-ally significant resources located on Indonesia's sovereign territory would become a major international concern and a key aspect of the haze dispute.

Suharto, who rose to power in 1967, had maintained his control over Indonesia for over three decades through a combination of authoritarian leadership and support from the West, which saw him as a stabilizing force in a region threatened by communist expansionism. Contributing to the longevity of Suharto's rule was a program of economic development that substantially reduced Indonesia's rate of poverty and brought an annual growth in per capita GDP of 5 per cent from 1967 to 1996. Much of this growth was made possible by the development of Indonesia's substantial oil and gas reserves in the 1970s, after the creation of the Organization of the Petroleum Export-ing Countries (OPEC) and the resulting dramatic increase in the price of oil. However, declines in oil prices in the early 1980s forced Indonesia to look for ways to diversify its economy, and it took advantage of its signifi-cant tropical acreage and large labor force to build a palm oil industry that would make it the world's largest exporter by 2006. In the 1990s, Indonesia actively encouraged outside investment, particularly from Malaysia. Malaysia was then the world's leading palm oil producer, but restrictive government policies and limited opportunities for expansion had encouraged Malaysian companies to look abroad for investment opportunities. Many of them had established strong ties with officials in the Malaysian government, who were quick to support their activities in Indonesia.[7] "Patronage politics" were also very much evident within Indonesia, where close connections had been forged between industry and government, particularly with members of the Suharto family. As observers later looked for explanations for the failure of Indonesian officials to do more to prevent the fires, a common explanation was that cronyism and corruption had led to a situation where palm oil companies could, in the words of Helen Varkkey, "act with impunity . . . where national laws against the use of fire are rendered useless in the face of powerful economic interests."[8]

Contributing to the regulatory challenge was the Indonesian government's limited institutional capacity to enforce the rules that were on the books. Poorly coordinated national agencies faced tight budgets and limited presence in the regions where the fires were being set. To some extent, this was the result of a policy of decentralization that the national government had implemented, recognizing the political and practical challenges of attempting to manage such a large area of disconnected islands from Jakarta. While a realistic general strategy, and one that would be continued by governments that succeeded Suharto, the effect was to make it even more difficult for the central government to police burning practices in regions under the effective control of 34 provincial and thousands of local governments.[9]

There were also direct environmental consequences from a government-supported policy of transmigration, originally begun by the Dutch when Indonesia was under colonial rule. Reinstituted under Suharto with support from international lenders, the program encouraged poor Indonesians to move from densely populated cities on the island of Java to cleared land in less settled areas. Although a reasonable development goal, the policy had the effect of creating one more reason to burn brush. Digging canals to make tropical soils appropriate for year-round agriculture also had the effect of draining peat bogs, making them more susceptible to fire during the dry season.[10]

Other than Indonesia itself, the states most directly affected by the fires were Malaysia and Singapore, both significantly smaller and less populous than Indonesia. With a geographical area roughly one-fifth the size of Indonesia, Malaysia had a population in 1997 of just over 20 million. Tiny Singapore's (250 square miles) population was approximately 3.5 million. Economically, however, Malaysia and Singapore were much better off than Indonesia, with levels of per capita GDP that were approximately 2.5 and 7.5 times greater, respectively, than Indonesia's. Companies from both countries had invested heavily in Indonesian plantations, and their contribution to the haze problem would become a complicating factor in the way both governments responded to the fires.

In the early 1990s, East Asian leaders had come under fire from Western governments and international human rights groups for authoritarian governance practices, as declining East-West tensions encouraged Western governments to look more closely at issues considered secondary when security concerns were paramount. This had triggered an international debate played out largely within the United Nations about whether Western human rights standards had universal application.[11] Leaders from Singapore and Malaysia had been outspoken proponents of what became known as "Asian values," which could prioritize the protection of sovereignty and the promotion of economic and cultural rights over individual human rights. Although the focus was not on the environment, this debate would contribute to regional skepticism about the broader relevance of what some saw as Western environmental norms. Critics responded that this was simply a self-serving argument intended to justify repressive internal policies.[12] It also suggested to Western environmentalists that the failure of the Malaysian and Singaporean governments to react more forcefully to transboundary haze could be attributed, in part, to a lack of responsiveness to domestic public opinion.

ASEAN was the international institution most directly involved in the dispute, serving initially as a forum for discussions between Indonesia and its neighbors and later as the framework in which legal reforms were developed. Formed in 1967, at the height of the Vietnam War, by Indonesia, Malaysia, the Philippines, Singapore, and Thailand, ASEAN was designed to promote political stability and economic development. The Treaty of Amity and Cooperation in Southeast Asia, 24 February 1976 (hereafter referred to as the Treaty of Amity) through which ASEAN was formalized embraced as key principles "mutual respect for the independence, sovereignty, equality, territorial integrity and national identity of all nations," and the "right of every State to lead its national existence free from external interference, subversion or coersion."[13] The organizational culture that emerged became known as the "ASEAN way," with members emphasizing cooperative problem-solving in areas of mutual concern. In the event unwanted disputes should arise, Article 17 of the treaty emphasized the use of "friendly negotiations" before any other forms of dispute settlement would be employed. With a consensus-based decision-making process and deliberately informal organizational structure, ASEAN generally avoided controversial issues and soon acquired a reputation as a reactive rather than proactive body.

Despite the fact that the Treaty of Amity was signed less than four years after the Stockholm Conference, it makes no mention of environmental issues. In 1978, ASEAN states did agree to create the ASEAN Environment Programme, but its focus was less on divisive transboundary issues and more on promoting cooperation between national agencies in areas of shared concern. At the 1992 Rio Conference, ASEAN was a strong proponent of the right of developing states to control the development of their own natural resources and strongly resisted efforts to treat tropical rain forests as part of a "global heritage."[14]

Given ASEAN's mixed environmental record, its 1985 Agreement on the Conservation of Nature and Natural Resources[15] would seem to have marked a shift toward a much more progressive environmental policy. Indonesia had recommended adoption of the agreement, which was actually drafted by Western environmental lawyers from the International Union for Conservation of Nature (IUCN). That it was to be a binding agreement was, in itself, an unusual step for an organization that had generally favored voluntary cooperation over treaty-making. It also explicitly embraced "sustainable development" even before this concept was adopted by the Brundtland Commission and emphasized the need to "preserve genetic diversity," something that would only later be incorporated into the Biodiversity Convention. Article 20 went beyond the basic rule of state responsibility embodied in Principle 20 of the Stockholm Declaration, explicitly stating that parties should "avoid to the maximum extent possible and reduce to the minimum extent possible adverse effects of activities under their jurisdiction or control," adverse effects that included those on "natural resources." It also asserted that this responsibility flowed not from the treaty alone, but from "generally accepted principles of international law." Article 20 acknowledged the procedural duties of environmental impact assessment, notification and consultation, and warning in situations of potential environmental damage and emphasized the responsibility of states to "refrain from actions which directly or indirectly adversely affect wildlife habitats situated beyond the limitations of national jurisdiction." Of special relevance to the Indonesian haze dispute, Article 6 made specific reference of the duty to "prevent bush and forest fires."

Missing in the agreement was any means of enforcement. States were required only to send reports to the secretariat, the content and timing to be determined later, and to meet at least every three years to review the implementation of the agreement. No mention was made of the need to develop any sort of liability mechanism, and the only reference to disputes was in Article 30, which stated that disputes would "be settled amicably by consultation or negotiation." However, stronger rules could be added later, since there were provisions permitting amendment of the convention and the adoption of additional protocols.

The most obvious limitation of the agreement was that it never received the six ratifications required to come into force, despite the fact that all six states who were members of ASEAN in 1985 were signatories. Interesting in the context of this dispute, Indonesia ratified the agreement, as did Thailand and the Philippines, but Brunei, Malaysia, and Singapore did not. Tay suggests that there is little chance the agreement will ever be formally approved, since its IUCN drafters "seem to have paid insufficient attention to both the ASEAN way and the ASEAN response to international and Western approaches to environmental protection."[16] However, the fact that Indonesia did back the development of the agreement and has both signed and ratified it would, at the very least, seem to undercut any possible argument asserting Indonesia's legal right to develop its resources without serious concern being given to the transboundary effect of those activities.

While the primary institutional focus of the dispute was within ASEAN, other international organizations would take on increasingly important roles as the fires continued to burn. UNEP took the lead on the global level, working under the direction of Klaus Töpfer, who became executive director early in 1998. Even better positioned to influence Indonesia's behavior were international financial institutions, notably the World Bank and the IMF and, on a regional level, the Asian Development Bank. IMF assistance was particularly important. A $43 billion package to support the struggling Indonesian economy was announced in January 1998. IMF officials spent much of that spring in difficult negotiations with the Indonesian government over the conditions of the loans, some of which involved reforms in agricultural sectors implicated in the fires. This heightened the Indonesian fear of unwanted outside pressure, an attitude that complicated the challenge facing UN officials responding to an environmental problem that intersected so directly with important economic concerns. Among non-governmental organizations, the World Wildlife Fund (WWF) was particularly active, given its focus on protecting endangered species and guarding against habitat loss. The WWF was in a position of unusual potential influence with Indonesian authorities, since it was assisting in the management of 17 Indonesian national parks and had helped draft important Indonesian biodiversity policies.[17]

The Dispute

The fires were first discovered by satellite in January 1997. In May, the World Meteorological Organization (WMO) confirmed the existence of "hot spots" in Riau province on the island of Sumatra. By late September, the WWF was warning of a potential "planetary disaster" and calling for international assistance to put out the fires in Sumatra and Kalimantan.[18] Contributing to the problem was the effect of El Niño. Unusually dry conditions encouraged the spread of the fires from Indonesian scrublands to tropical rainforests and peat bogs, where they were especially difficult to combat. Rain arrived in November and December, but the fires returned in February 1998, as El Niño conditions shortened the rainy season. The fires in East Kalimantan were now even worse than in the fall, although transboundary damage was reduced by a shift in the prevailing winds. Rains that began in May 1998 returned in June and July, finally putting an end to the immediate fire danger.

Estimates of the damage ranged widely, but the cost was clearly very high. One early study of the 1997 fires alone put the losses at roughly $4.4 billion, thus exceeding the assessed liability of the *Exxon Valdez* and Bhopal chemical accidents combined.[19] The Asian Development Bank later funded a more comprehensive analysis covering the entire 1997–98 period and came up with a damage estimate of $8 billion to $10 billion.[20] Most directly affected was Indonesia, with damage to agriculture and forestry production, but the smoke spread as far as Thailand, Singapore, Malaysia, Australia, and the Philippines. Officials ordered schools and factories closed, and people were urged to stay inside when air pollution reached dangerous levels. Hospitals were flooded with patients seeking treatment for acute respiratory infections, asthma, and conjunctivitis; tens of thousands of people were directly affected. The smoke apparently contributed to several accidents, including the crash of an Indonesian airbus, in which 234 people died; one study placed the number of Indonesians killed by the fires at 527.[21] Despite efforts by some government officials to play down the dangers posed by the smoke, the fires received extensive publicity worldwide. The effect on the region's $26-billion tourism industry, a major source of foreign exchange, was predictable and costly.

Beyond tourism, broader international interests were affected. The WWF actively publicized the impact on endangered species, most notably the orangutan, as the fires spread to their protected habitat. Less immediate, but part of the fires' global significance, was their contribution to global carbon emissions. This came directly from the release of carbon dioxide, especially from the carbon-rich peat swamps, and indirectly through the loss of the tropical forests, an important carbon sink for absorbing carbon dioxide. The World Bank later estimated that the 1997 fires alone "contributed about 30 percent of all man-made carbon emissions globally—more than the entire emissions from man-made sources from North America."[22]

Even as officials struggled to contain the fires, the question of blame arose. Given the El Niño weather pattern, Indonesian authorities were tempted to label the fires a natural disaster. However, the fires were not the result of lightning strikes and had been deliberately been set. Moreover, this was not the first time fires had gotten out of control. The "Great Kalimantan Fire" of 1982–83 had burned almost 3.2 million hectares, and fires in 1991 and 1994 had generated serious transboundary pollution.[23] Three general categories of potential culprits were identified: small-scale indigenous farmers and recent settlers, the timber industry, and palm oil plantations. Fire had been used by all three groups in the past, but the issue now took on new political and legal importance, given the scale of the damage. All were quick to blame each other. However, with the help of satellite imagery provided by the US National Oceanic and Atmospheric Administration, Indonesia's environment minister, Juwono Sudarsono, publicly accused the timber industry of responsibility for 65 per cent of the damage done by the East Kalimantan fires.[24]

The more fundamental question of what responsibility the Indonesian government might bear hung uncomfortably in the background. Only two years earlier, Indonesia had told its neighbors that steps were being taken to prevent a repetition of the 1994 fires.[25] Now the challenge was to convince them that Indonesia recognized the importance of the problem—but without offering to take more decisive action than it reasonably could or accepting any legal responsibility to pay for the damage. Indonesian officials were also well aware that their actions were being observed not only by Malaysia and Singapore but also by a broader international community whose support was critical in responding to both the fires and Indonesia's ongoing financial crisis.

What emerged was an Indonesian response with several distinguishable elements. First came a formal Indonesian apology. President Suharto used the opening of a meeting of ASEAN environment ministers on 17 September 1997, to state, "To the communities of neighboring countries who have been disturbed by the fires on our territory, Indonesia offers its most sincere apologies."[26] The gesture appeared sincere and was well received, even if the level of damage actually occurring seemed undervalued by the term "disturbed." What was unclear was the basis for Suharto's apology, since there was no indication of anything Indonesia had done or failed to do for which it might be blameworthy or of any tangible steps Indonesia was prepared to take to make up for the damage the fires had caused. Later comments by Indonesian officials blaming the fires on the weather or focusing only on the role played by small farmers left enough doubt about the sincerity of the Indonesian apology to force President Suharto to repeat it in early October.[27] Coupled with apologies came repeated statements of gratitude for the understanding Indonesia's neighbors were showing, given the difficult situation they all faced, one where Indonesia felt assigning blame was inappropriate. Indonesians were being more badly affected than anyone else and clearly wanted the fires extinguished. Moreover, the economic problems in Southeast Asia had been particularly devastating to Indonesia. This related to another aspect of Indonesia's public response: the country's limited capacity to do more and its need for outside help to put out the fires. "We have made whatever efforts we are capable of mobilizing to overcome this natural disaster," claimed

Suharto.[28] The challenges Indonesia faced in fighting the fires were real, given its very limited fire-fighting capacity and the extent of the acreage on which fires were burning. The economic crisis had only made matters worse. Responding to renewed complaints when the fires returned in February, Indonesia's environment minister indicated that Indonesia had only three aircraft capable of carrying water to the fires and would attempt cloud-seeding in an effort to stop the blazes.[29]

Indonesia did not ignore the fires' legal implications. First, the government recognized the need to identify and punish those responsible for setting them. There actually was a law on the books that made it illegal to use fire to clear land, although enforcement had been lax. After the 1997 fires began, efforts to prosecute violators intensified. A list of 176 companies believed to have used fire illegally was published by the forestry ministry, and in early October the government claimed to have revoked 151 wood-use permits of 29 of the accused companies and arrested 20 farmers in East Kalimantan for illegal burning.[30] At an ASEAN meeting in December, Indonesia's environment minister insisted that the government would continue enforcement efforts, even as he admitted the challenges faced in remote areas. It would also propose a complete moratorium on new investments by palm oil plantations.[31] Second, on 19 September the government took steps to tighten Indonesian environmental law when Suharto signed the Environmental Management Act of 1997 (EMA).[32] The EMA imposed strict liability on those responsible for pollution and provided for the imposition of fines, the confiscation of assets, and even the use of criminal sanctions against persons, including corporations, found in violation. Also included were procedures designed to improve enforcement, although the actual implementation of the law would remain challenging, given the territory to be covered, the limited resources available, and continuing ties between the government and key timber and oil plantation companies.[33]

The governments of Malaysia and Singapore responded to the fires with restraint, at least in public, although their criticism of Indonesian inaction did become more pointed when the fires returned in February 1998. Aware of the economic and political challenges Indonesia faced and somewhat complicit, given the role played by their own investors, they generally expressed concern about the impact of the fires and offered assistance. There was a tendency to play down the extent of the problem, in part to reassure potential tourists, and "haze" quickly became the accepted term to describe the problem. Yet serious damage was being done in both countries. Damage estimates from the 1997 fires alone suggested losses of $670 million to areas beyond Indonesia, with Malaysia suffering $310 million in quantifiable losses and Singapore $74 million.[34] In October, Malaysia's environment minister, Datuk

Law Hieng Ding, indicated that the government would be using a study by Japanese experts to compile information on the effects of the haze in Malaysia. However, in response to a direct question about whether Malaysia would bring a legal claim against Indonesia, Law said, "Now is not the time to talk about compensation. What is important is the people's health." When pressed about whether compensation would be sought later, Law replied somewhat vaguely, "We will see how other ASEAN countries . . . [react]."[35]

The public and the media were less forgiving, and there was pressure on governments to confront Indonesia more directly. At a rare public demonstration in Kuala Lumpur in late September 1997, protestors chanted "Immediate action! Immediate action!"[36] Singapore's *Straits Times* published satellite photos indicating where fires had been deliberately set. An editorial argued, "The cost of the haze is getting unacceptably high and it will get higher if not enough Indonesian officials act urgently, decisively."[37] The *Bangkok Post* was more direct: "If Indonesia refuses to address its deadly pollution seriously, its neighbors must force the issue."[38]

Yet civil society was a relatively undeveloped force in Southeast Asia, and governments were quick to rein in critics. Malaysia required academics to clear with the government any comments on the effects of the fires. Its education minister warned that bad publicity "could give a negative image of Malaysia, causing a scare among Malaysians and preventing foreigners from coming to the country."[39] Even the use of the relatively innocuous term "haze" was criticized, with Malaysia's information minister suggesting that "low-cloud, dew and smoke" was a more appropriate description.[40] Close ties between the government and the media, particularly in Singapore, helped ensure that media coverage would not overly dramatize the problem. However, criticism in editorials by papers such as the *Straits Times* may have provided an indirect means for government officials to signal displeasure without challenging Indonesia directly.

ASEAN became the natural focus of the regional response to the fires, its non-confrontational approach creating an institutional atmosphere in which Indonesia apparently felt comfortable. ASEAN had become involved with the haze issue after the 1994 fires. In 1995, the organization established a Cooperation Plan on Transboundary Pollution,[41] designed to respond to transboundary problems ranging from atmospheric pollution to the international shipment of hazardous waste through a series of voluntary "strategies" implemented primarily on a national level. Indonesia arranged for visits by an ASEAN delegation to fire-prone areas and, in September 1995, the ASEAN Senior Officials on the Environment agreed to set up a Haze Technical Task Force, chaired by Indonesia.[42] It was at an ASEAN meeting in

September 1997 that Suharto made his apology and the issue of transboundary haze was made a regular agenda item.

A Regional Haze Action Plan (RHAP)[43] was agreed to in December 1997 at the first of what would become bimonthly ministerial meetings on haze. With the fires having subsided temporarily, the ASEAN ministers were able to assert that the "traditional spirit of ASEAN cooperation, solidarity and understanding had continued to prevail," and that their "joint effort to combat fires and smoke haze had in fact helped bind ASEAN countries even closer together."[44] The plan did acknowledge the seriousness of the haze problem and enumerated specific actions to prevent and detect future fires, including prohibitions on open burning. However, action would be taken not on a regional level but through national plans to be developed by March 1998 and reviewed by the task force.

The return of the fires in 1998 brought a new sense of urgency to ASEAN's work, but the February meeting produced only a call to implement a joint Malaysian-Indonesian fire-fighting plan agreed to earlier. In April, the ministers took the important step of recognizing the "linkage of the haze problem to global environmental problems such as global warming, climate change, and the conservation of biodiversity." ASEAN welcomed UNEP's assistance in coordinating a response to the haze problem, and even embraced an increased role for "the private sector and Non-Governmental Organizations," at least to the extent they were involved in "worthy developments, such as public education, awareness campaigns, and fund-raising."[45] By the time of the fourth ministerial haze meeting, the rains had returned and the focus shifted to ways in which national governments could prevent future fires. One proposed legal reform was to place the burden of proof on landowners to show that they were not responsible for fires burning on their lands, since it was often difficult to prove who specifically had set individual fires.[46]

ASEAN's receptivity to UNEP involvement acknowledged the broader impact that the fires were having and the need for more resources to fight them. Initially much of the international presence was provided by NGOs led by the WWF. The WWF monitored the fires closely and used the Internet to keep the global media informed, even when regional governments might have preferred to give the fires a lower profile. During the first round of fires, UNEP remained in the background, although 16 non-ASEAN countries did offer either fire-fighting or financial assistance.[47] In October 1997, UNEP had indicated its intention to "monitor developments in the region" and had sought the assistance of the World Conservation Monitoring Centre, a body already involved with the protection of "internationally important areas" including a World Heritage site in Java and a Ramsar Convention wetland in Sumatra.[48] In February 1998, UNEP's newly appointed executive director, Klaus Töpfer, attended the second ASEAN haze meeting in Sarawak in an effort to determine how UNEP could better coordinate the international response.[49]

By the end of March, things had deteriorated. Juwono Sudarsono, Indonesia's new environment minister, had come into office earlier in the month pledging to do more to "instill a sense of crisis" to get Indonesia to respond more effectively to a problem that he recognized was of serious concern to the international community.[50] Within weeks, he was forced to admit how difficult this had been, given competing pressures on the Indonesian government.[51] Fires in East Kalimantan continued to burn out of control, and Indonesian officials were soon signaling that they had done all they could in response. A UN disaster assessment team arrived in Jakarta on 29 March. On 2 April, Töpfer met with President Suharto, emphasizing the significance of the fires even as difficult negotiations were taking place with IMF officials about Indonesia's financial situation.[52]

In mid-April, the scene shifted to Geneva, where UNEP convened a two-day conference covering three dimensions of the unfolding crisis. The first session brought together fire-fighting experts to develop what became a $10-million plan to contain the East Kalimantan fires. The second was devoted to developing strategies to prevent future fires, with officials from relevant specialized agencies and other international organizations, including ASEAN, reviewing their fire-prevention related activities. UN Secretary-General Kofi Annan designated Töpfer to coordinate the UN response. Töpfer took a tough line, encouraging improved national law enforcement and suggesting the enhanced use of satellite technology to identify those responsible for setting them. "The enforcement of law is absolutely necessary to identify those companies responsible. The behavior of the big plantation companies must be criticized and must be stopped. There is a link."[53] The final meeting of potential donors permitted Indonesia to offer thanks for the assistance already given and to assure them that Indonesia was committed to reforming its land-clearing practices.[54] In the days after the Geneva conference, Töpfer continued to press donor countries to provide the needed funds, as reports of "sporadic rainfall" in East Kalimantan led to fears of complacency. Despite the political turmoil in Indonesia in early May, Töpfer said he remained "confident that the national authorities will also take appropriate steps with regard to land use policies if we are to prevent the situation from recurring again and again."[55]

Legal Issue: State Environmental Responsibility

As ASEAN and UNEP worked to coordinate an international response, governments showed little overt interest in attempting to hold Indonesia legally responsible for what had happened. However, members of the international legal community felt a case could be made that Indonesia had legal obligations that at least ought to be acknowledged. In 1999, Alan Tan and Simon Tay, both Singaporean nationals on the law faculty at the National University of Singapore, wrote articles that offered interesting, though different assessments of the legal issues posed by the dispute.[56]

Both lawyers agreed that there was no treaty provision that states could reasonably claim Indonesia had violated. ASEAN's only environmental initiative that had the potential to be legally binding, the 1985 Agreement on the Conservation of Nature and Natural Resources, was not in force. Even if it had been, it did not provide any clear basis for enforcing the state's procedural responsibilities contained in Article 20 and merely encouraged a diplomatic resolution of any disputes that might arise. While the agreement could not be enforced directly, Indonesia's willingness to sign and ratify it would at least have made less persuasive any Indonesian claim (one it never made) that what it did on its territory regarding the fires was a matter of sovereign prerogative. The language in Article 20 suggesting that the procedural duties embraced in the treaty were already required as a matter of general international law could only reinforce the argument that Indonesia did have legal responsibilities toward neighboring states that came from customary state practice regardless of the status of the treaty. It was in the assessment of the nature of customary international law that Tan and Tay disagreed.

Alan Tan's article focused directly on issues of state responsibility and liability, and took what might be considered the more traditional approach in attempting to assess the lawfulness of Indonesia's behavior by the standards of prevailing customary international law.[57] Tan put forth three potential arguments derived from two different approaches to the question of Indonesia's state responsibility. The first approach would be to hold Indonesia responsible for the fires because it was so closely involved with the private companies that started them that the damage they caused could be attributed directly to the state. Despite the close political ties between the government and many of the timber and plantation companies, and the fact that the government was a shareholder in some, Tan made a strong case that this connection was simply insufficient to make the state directly responsible for their actions.

A second approach would be to suggest that, although the fires were started by private actors, Indonesia had a responsibility to use "due diligence" to ensure that activities on its territory did not cause transboundary harm. Within this general approach, two different though complementary arguments could be made. The first would be to adopt what Tan termed an "elevated due diligence" standard when the nature of the activity in question

is "ultrahazardous," effectively making Indonesia strictly liable for any transboundary damage that the fires might cause, regardless of what it had done
to try to prevent them. Given the common regional practice of burning
brush, Tan acknowledged that it might be difficult to apply the elevated
standard here, although one could argue that Indonesia's own nominal ban
on the use of fire to clear land suggested an awareness of the special dangers
it presented. More persuasive was a view of due diligence that examined
Indonesia's behavior before and after the fires had been set. Here, Tan felt a
compelling case could be made that Indonesia bore responsibility because
it knew of the transboundary dangers posed by the fires, given the history
of past haze events and awareness of the likely impact of the predicted El
Niño weather patterns, and because it had initially failed to enforce laws
to control and later to punish those who started the fires. Tan did not fault
Indonesia for its efforts to put out the fires once they were started, arguing that Indonesia did work with neighboring states cooperatively, if not
effectively, to attempt to extinguish them. Given the size of Indonesia and
the regulatory challenges it faced as a developing country, it might be unrea-
sonable to require the same level of due diligence expected of other states,
but this "cannot wholly exculpate a State from honouring its obligations."[58]
In the end, Tan argued that Indonesia bore state responsibility for its failure to prevent the damage caused by the fires, responsibility that would
theoretically require it to make "adequate reparation for the harm caused."
However, Tan acknowledged that this legal case seemed likely to be
trumped by "political realities."[59]

For Simon Tay, the central problem revealed by the Indonesia fires was
not political but legal. Tay argued that customary international law was
not nearly as developed in the area of state environmental responsibility
as some, including Tan, would have liked to believe. Indonesian environmental law and ASEAN regional institutions had shortcomings that needed
to be addressed. Because it emphasized cooperation over state accountability, the ASEAN way needed reform, and Tay suggested incorporating a
stronger state-to-state liability regime into regional practices. Short of this,
NGOs and other private actors could be given an enhanced enforcement
role by permitting private lawsuits in cases of transboundary damage. However, Tay also argued that there were limits to what could be accomplished
regionally, suggesting the need to bring in global institutions not simply to
provide additional resources and expertise but rather "to set neutral international standards that reflect the interests of all countries."[60]

An issue neither author addressed directly is what responsibility Indonesia might have toward the broader international community for the damage
done to shared concerns, such as protection of biodiversity. Tan did suggest

that this damage might justify expecting from Indonesia an even higher standard of due diligence,[61] and Tay, in his support of binding international standards, implicitly embraced the idea that extraregional interests deserved to have greater impact on Indonesian policies. Yet the fires also indicated the genuine challenges faced in implementing whatever rights outsiders might possess. While the views of UNEP and private organizations such as the WWF appear to have been taken seriously by the Indonesian government, their influence was political rather than legal. There was no obvious procedural mechanism by which either could attempt to force Indonesia to behave more responsibly. The fires thus again raised the question posed in Chapter 2: whether something like a doctrine of *actio popularis* deserves both formal recognition and a means to implement it.

The Resolution

Natural and political forces, not legal principles, brought a temporary end to the Indonesian fires dispute. The rains of May and June put out the most serious fires. On 21 May 1998, after weeks of street riots in which hundreds were killed, President Suharto stepped down, turning over power to a provisional government headed by B.J. Habibie. Hopes were raised that a new, more transparent Indonesian government would take more effective action to limit burning practices, particularly since Indonesia was still negotiating with the IMF over the terms of the financial support the new Indonesian government required.

Despite Executive Director Töpfer's warning to UNEP that the "environmental crisis of forest fires is far from over,"[62] international attention turned toward more pressing issues such as the implementation of the recently agreed-upon Kyoto Protocol and the negotiation of new global conventions to regulate hazardous chemicals and persistent organic pollutants. With the fires no longer burning, the haze issue simply was not on the top of anyone's agenda, and ASEAN remained the institutional focus of ongoing discussions about how to prevent future fires.

Post-Dispute Developments

The emphasis on fire prevention rather than assessing blame for past damage continued into 1999, when Abdurrahman Wahid was elected President of Indonesia by the People's Consultative Assembly. Wahid promised significant economic and political reforms and gave new voice to academics and representatives of an increasingly engaged domestic NGO community.[63] Yet Wahid's government was intended to be a government of "national unity," including members of Suharto's regime, and questions remained about Wahid's ability to deliver on the promised reforms. When fires began in Sumatra in July 2000, the Wahid government announced plans to halt operations at 12 palm oil plantations and to impose heavy fines, but officials were forced to concede that it would be difficult to enforce the new policy because of limited funds.[64] Separatist violence that picked up after Suharto's resignation also undermined the new regime's ability to enforce national policy in rural areas.[65]

When the haze returned in the summer of 1999, Indonesia's neighbors appeared more assertive. Brunei threatened to bring suit against Indonesia if it failed to control fires that might disrupt the Southeast Asian games Brunei was hosting,[66] and local environmentalists suggested that the time had come for Malaysia and Singapore to take the matter to the International Court of Justice.[67] That criticism from neighboring states was becoming more pointed seemed evident when Indonesia's forestry and plantations minister responded that Singapore and Malaysia should do more than just "make noise" about the fires. "Singapore has been receiving very expensive oxygen from us, hasn't it? . . . This concerns a common interest, so don't just make demands."[68]

Transboundary haze remained on ASEAN's agenda. In April 1999, amid widespread criticism of their ineffective response to the Indonesian fires the previous year, ASEAN's environment ministers adopted a "zero-burn" policy, specifically targeting plantation owners and timber companies and suggesting measures to identify and punish violators. The ministers also emphasized the need for additional financial support from non-ASEAN donors, given the still difficult economic situation in the region and with another El Niño predicted for the following year.[69] Haryono Suyono, the Indonesian head of a disaster and relief team in Jakarta, claimed Indonesia understood the "firm message" about the need to control the fires, but needed help to do so effectively.[70]

The zero-burn policy, like all of the initiatives taken under ASEAN's Regional Haze Action Plan, was simply a joint ministerial statement with no obvious legal significance and no enforcement provisions. Critics had argued for more fundamental institutional reform,[71] and in August 1999 ASEAN environment ministers agreed to study proposals to develop a stronger legal foundation for ASEAN anti-haze efforts. Rather than attempt to revive support for the unratified 1985 Agreement, perhaps too ambitious a leap for ASEAN states,[72] ASEAN decided to focus on transboundary haze. The result was the Agreement on Transboundary Haze Pollution,[73] signed in Kuala Lumpur in June 2002 by representatives of all ten ASEAN nations. It came into force in November 2003.

As the first binding environmental agreement among ASEAN members, the Haze Agreement represented an important break from past ASEAN initiatives. Article 3 reaffirmed the basic rule of state environmental responsibility set forth in Stockholm Principle 21. However, it added "harm to human health" as something that states must ensure did not result from "activities within their jurisdiction or control," a reflection of one of the primary concerns about transboundary haze. The agreement required the use of "precautionary measures" to prevent transboundary haze, particularly in the face of "threats of serious or irreversible damage . . . even without full scientific certainty," and called for "ecologically sound and sustainable" management of natural resources. While many of the key steps would be taken on a national level, the agreement established an ASEAN Coordinating Centre for Transboundary Haze Pollution Control to facilitate cooperation if fires did occur and required parties to designate national agencies to serve as contact points to work with the center. The agreement also provided for a conference of the parties to meet at least annually to review the implementation of the agreement and gave it the power to adopt by consensus additional protocols. Amendments to the agreement could also be made by a consensus of the conference of the parties, although they were subject to subsequent national approval.

The agreement did have limitations. The basic goal of controlling transboundary haze pollution was framed as a duty to "strengthen cooperation and co-ordination to prevent and monitor transboundary haze pollution," and even this was limited by a recognition of the parties' "respective needs, capabilities and situations."[74] Parties "should involve . . . all stakeholders" in dealing with transboundary haze, but only "as appropriate." "Appropriateness" was also a conditioning term with regard to the measures states were required to take to monitor fire-prone areas and other aspects of haze pollution, suggesting a fair degree of national discretion in the steps actually taken.[75] The Haze Agreement did not include any means for effective enforcement. Should disputes arise, Article 27 simply stated that they "shall be settled amicably by consultation or negotiation," hardly a positive response to Tay's call for the incorporation of stronger liability mechanisms into ASEAN institutional arrangements.

Until recently, the most fundamental challenge facing the transboundary haze regime was Indonesia's failure to ratify the 2002 agreement. The Indonesian government repeatedly promised to work for domestic approval from the Indonesian parliament, which rejected the agreement in 2008. Greenpeace argued that Indonesia actually wanted to protect the interests of palm oil plantations hoping to expand operations,[76] and questions were raised about whether there were sufficient financial benefits to Indonesia to justify its signing the agreement.[77] However, Helen Varkkey makes a strong case that the primary obstacle was the continuing desire to protect Indonesian sovereignty. Indonesia's historical experience of fighting against colonial control, its controversial dealings with the IMF during the 1997–98 financial crisis, and the contemporary challenges faced in governing such a diverse and geographically disparate population have made Indonesians particularly sensitive to any external initiatives that might interfere with what they consider internal matters. In 2006, Indonesia had proposed a basic change in the ASEAN approach to the transboundary haze problem, one that would build more directly on national, rather than regional, assistance plans by establishing direct connections between outside states and individual Indonesian districts and provinces. When Singapore and Malaysia offered such support to Jambi and Riau provinces, Indonesia was reluctant to accept, apparently fearing that it might erode national control over provincial policies, particularly since the forestry industry, so important to Indonesia's future development, was involved. Varkkey contends that Indonesia also needed to reassert its leadership within ASEAN, something that had been diminished during the political and economic turmoil following Suharto's resignation.[78]

What resulted were more fires and repeated Indonesian apologies, accompanied again by expressions of gratitude for the support of understanding neighbors who were actually becoming increasingly critical of Indonesia's failure to do more. Calls for Indonesia to ratify the Haze Agreement became a staple of ASEAN meetings. In June 2013, a new round of fires broke out in Sumatra. Given prevailing winds, Singapore was particularly hard hit with pollution levels exceeding those produced in 1997–98 by the fires that remain the benchmark for measuring the severity of the problem. Singapore's environment and water minister complained, "No country or corporation has the right to pollute the air at the expense of Singaporeans' health and well-being." An Indonesian minister responded that Singaporeans were behaving "like children" and reminded reporters that the companies accused of setting the fires were owned by Singaporean and Malaysian nationals, as well as Indonesians.[79] Indonesia's foreign minister suggested that calls to punish Indonesia had become "a bit redundant" and asserted (again) that the "first instinct must be one of wanting to express sympathy and . . . solidarity, rather than to apportion blame."[80] At a meeting of ASEAN energy ministers, Indonesia's representative, Jero Wacik, argued that Indonesia's neighbors should keep in the mind the economic benefits they derived from Indonesian energy supplies and tourism. Using an interesting domestic analogy in an appeal to keep the issue within the region, Jero said, "It's called sharing, you go through good times together, don't make noise to the world when things go bad. It's just like husband and wife, don't take your quarrel outside."[81]

The pattern of exchanges had become familiar, as Indonesia worked hard to maintain the ASEAN way. Noting that the real problem was the failure of the Indonesian government to take meaningful steps to prevent the burning of peat bogs, the head of one Indonesian NGO said, "If we want to stop this from happening, we will have to do something differently from what we did between 1997–98 and now."[82]

What did not seem likely in 2013 was direct UNEP involvement. Susilo Bambang Yudhoyono, a former energy minister in the Wahid regime who had been elected Indonesian president in 2004, had been chosen as one of three world leaders to chair a high-level UN panel to define future global development objectives. Issues of sustainable development were expected to be a major concern, and the fires were a sensitive issue. When asked about the Sumatran fires, a UNEP spokesperson said, "The problem is being handled by those countries in the region."[83]

By 2013, at least one new element had been added to the mix: the possibility that Singapore and/or Malaysia might consider prosecuting companies owned by their own nationals if Indonesia did not. The proposal was controversial since it ran the risk of infringing on Indonesian sovereignty. It would also be difficult to implement without Indonesian cooperation. Yet Indonesia had opened the door to this approach by blaming foreign companies for much of the burning and claiming that it lacked the capacity to enforce its own law against them. In June, Singapore sent a formal diplomatic note to Indonesia, asking for evidence about the involvement of Singapore-linked companies in setting the fires. At a 20 June press conference, Singapore's prime minister, Lee Hsien Loong, warned of potential action;[84] the next day, Lee sent a personal letter to Indonesian President Yudhoyono. Yudhoyono replied that he understood the seriousness of the problem and that those responsible for the fires would be "firmly held to account."[85] Still, at another press conference two days later, Yudhoyono stated that he did not believe that the companies involved should be named, with enforcement left up to Indonesian police. He did, however, apologize to Singapore and Malaysia, saying, "We will continue to take responsibility to deal with what's happening right now."[86] Despite the reassurances, Malaysian Prime Minister Najib Razak sent a formal note to Yudhoyono calling for more effective enforcement of Indonesian laws against offending companies, even as Malaysia's environment minister asserted that existing Malaysian laws could not be applied extraterritorially.[87]

On 30 June, ASEAN foreign ministers repeated calls for Indonesia to ratify the Haze Agreement. Indonesian officials indicated that the agreement was being resubmitted to the Indonesian parliament. This time, prospects for approval were better, since representatives in the affected Indonesian provinces, such as Riau, had come to support the treaty as a way to force Indonesia to take more effective action against the fires that were causing significant local damage.[88] Even so, the parliamentary vote to finally approve the agreement did not take place until 16 September 2014, after yet another round of fires in Riau. It also came after Singapore had moved ahead with legislation to impose fines of up to $1.6 million on companies found responsible for fires polluting Singapore. Joko Widodo, elected in July to serve as Indonesia's new president, indicated his support as long as there were "detailed protocols to guarantee the sovereignty of Indonesia."[89] What that would mean in practice was unclear, since information-sharing remained a sensitive issue within ASEAN. However, enforcement of the new law would now be aided by high-resolution maps provided by the World Resources Institute (WRI), thus reducing the amount of active Indonesian cooperation required to bring claims against companies in Singaporean courts.[90] In any case, the legislation to ratify the Haze Agreement was supported by all Indonesian parties, and the parliamentary vote was unanimous.

The Indonesian decision was greeted with relief by neighboring states,[91] although there was general recognition that key to the agreement's success would be how it was implemented.[92] The *Jakarta Post* reflected on the importance of the vote and what had been overcome in the process: "The belated move has saved Indonesia from international mockery, if not condemnation, for its failure to rein in the seasonal forest fires that have endangered the lives of its own people and those in neighboring countries. For a decade the lawmakers, without any sense of culpability, refused to endorse the government's acceptance of the pact for fear of possible infringement on Indonesia's sovereignty. . . . Such a nationalist, if not xenophobic, mindset has led to a protracted, choking haze. . . . The disaster was recurring, which simply proved that Indonesia could not address the forest fires alone."[93]

Analysis

The 1997–98 Indonesian forest fires produced a dispute that was managed, at least initially, by regional governments with a shared desire to minimize its impact on other important areas of concern. The process of non-confrontation was aided by an ASEAN regional framework that emphasized cooperation over conflict and seemed to prioritize economic development over environmental protection. The result was a dispute that was deferred, rather than resolved. It is impossible to know what earlier and more decisive criticism of Indonesian burning practices might have accomplished, but it is also true that more than 15 years later, the fires remain a source of significant environmental degradation with both regional and global implications.

UNEP, its hand strengthened by Indonesia's need for financial assistance, played a useful role in 1998 in convincing the Indonesian government that it was essential to take seriously international concerns about the fires. UNEP was also in a good position to bring to bear the resources of the larger international community to aid the response. Civil society saw its own role enhanced. Academics and NGOs, led by the WWF, were important sources of information about the origins of the fires and the extent of the dangers they posed. These groups also kept international concern alive at times when regional governments and even UNEP, distracted by other important issues, might have preferred to focus elsewhere.

Yet the unwillingness of the states most affected by the haze to confront Indonesia directly about the legal implications of what the government did and failed to do does raise serious questions about what state environmental responsibility really implies in a practical sense. Admittedly, it is difficult to know how to react to the failure of governments to assert rights they might seem to enjoy under international law. There are several different ways to explain their relative inaction without implying that it was necessarily evidence that no applicable rules existed.

As Tan argued, this could simply be a situation where political and other interests made it seem unwise to emphasize Indonesia's legal duties. First, Indonesia was a major regional power, one easily offended. Even the serious damage being done to Malaysia and Singapore might not have merited the potentially disruptive effect of bringing formal international claims. Second, not only did other states in the region, including Malaysia, use fire to burn brush, the haze was also the product of other local industries and of automobiles. Early in the crisis, the head of the Malaysian Centre for Environment, Technology and Development argued, "The (Malaysian) Government has shown it is not serious about taking steps to protect the environment. The haze is basically an internal problem. We can't just blame it on the Indonesians."[94] Third, there was good reason to try to protect the tourism industry, and the foreign exchange it provided, from the bad publicity that legal claims would likely generate. Finally, the role played by companies owned by Malaysian and Singaporean nationals provided their governments with an obvious incentive to limit their criticism.

It could also be argued that this was an unusual situation, where there were particularly compelling reasons for states not to assert otherwise applicable legal principles. Such an argument could be made to excuse the failure of downwind states to attempt to hold Russia responsible for the damage caused in 1986 by the Chernobyl nuclear accident. In that case, there was even clearer culpability on the part of the Russian government, which operated the reactor and failed to inform those potentially affected about the extent of the radiation leak. Yet Russia was going through a process of liberalization that Europeans hoped to encourage, and European governments likely viewed a legal challenge as unnecessarily confrontational, given the larger interests at stake. Moreover, they needed Russian cooperation to ensure that other Soviet-era nuclear reactors could be operated safely. Here, Indonesia's neighbors, aware of the serious financial crisis then rocking much of Southeast Asia and the major political transition taking place in Indonesia, could simply have made a calculated political decision not to confront Indonesia in legal terms at that moment. This restraint could be seen as particularly appropriate if there was reason to be concerned about the slowness and general inadequacy of the processes by which formal claims might be brought.[95]

A third approach is to suggest that how the dispute was handled reflected a genuinely alternative ASEAN way, a pattern of regional relationships that discouraged the kind of confrontational behavior represented by traditional international legal claims. In many ways, it has served the region well, limiting unwanted political conflict and helping promote impressive economic growth. Following this line of argument, the attempt to inject the IUCN-drafted Agreement on the Conservation of Nature and Natural Resources into ASEAN practices could be seen as a misguided attempt to impose views of customary international law derived from Western practice, and the failure of states to ratify it testimony to its inappropriateness in a Southeast Asian setting.

Yet these arguments dispose too easily of an important issue: the Chernobyl example is hardly exceptional, and the ASEAN way is not reflective only of how problems are handled in Southeast Asia. The history of state behavior in cases of transboundary pollution suggests a general reluctance to assert legal rights, even when serious damage is done and the rigorous Trail Smelter criteria seem to be met.[96] If this is more the norm than the exception, it is important to recognize the challenge this poses to claims that state responsibility for transboundary environmental damage has the content implied by Principle 21 and similar declarations commonly treated as evidence of customary international law.

This does not mean that there are no rules governing how states behave when serious transboundary environmental damage is done. It would seem more appropriate to acknowledge at least another strand of customary state practice offering another set of criteria for judging state behavior—criteria that might complement, not negate other customary law principles. In this instance, Indonesia never asserted that what happened on its territory was a matter of sovereign prerogative, simply a reflection of its right of permanent sovereignty over its natural resources. Indonesian presidents have repeatedly apologized for the transboundary effects of the haze and claimed to be doing all they could to put out the fires, to punish those responsible for them, and to prevent their recurrence. In context, this might be considered to be exercising "due diligence." By offering to help fight the fires rather than bringing claims for damage, Indonesia's neighbors may simply have been acknowledging Indonesia's inability to do more, thus reinforcing another dimension of the principle of "common but differentiated responsibilities." Indonesia argued, and others implicitly agreed, that they shared a responsibility to respond to a common regional threat, although their relative capacities to do so differed.

Thus, a broader implication of the Indonesian haze dispute is that it reinforces the general shift discussed in the previous chapter toward rules of state responsibility emphasizing how a state behaves before pollution occurs and the steps it subsequently takes to warn potential victims and to mitigate the damage. Within this "damage prevention" framework, the focus is on processes to promote dialogue and cooperation rather than to punish. To the extent any party should be held liable for the damage caused by the fires, the general focus on targeting the specific companies responsible for setting them indicates a preference for private claims in national courts rather than any form of international claims process.

If this does suggest a potentially complementary view of the law of state environmental responsibility, the rules are definitely permissive. Indonesia's "differentiated" responsibilities were not at all clear and a point of continuing disagreement. While Indonesia emphasized the need to avoid trying to assign blame, had affected states chosen to assert claims for damages, Indonesia would likely have argued that both the nature and extent of any Indonesian liability should be evaluated with an eye to the burden compensation would impose. Limited state funds might better be spent on prevention rather than compensation for past damage.

ASEAN's actions in the aftermath of the 1997–98 fires suggest a recognition that Tay was correct, that there was a need to strengthen the legal context in which the haze problem was being addressed. The result was the 2002 Haze Agreement, which even Indonesia, perhaps the most ardent proponent of the ASEAN way, has now ratified. The agreement represents an important acknowledgment that enhanced regional cooperation should be seen not simply as a political choice but as a legal obligation. Although the text provides room for disagreement about what states are actually required to do and lacks strong enforcement provisions, the agreement includes a mechanism for adopting amendments and protocols that can be used to strengthen it as confidence in the transboundary haze regime grows. By encouraging enhanced cooperation and information-sharing, the agreement provides a basis for more effective control over the companies and people actually setting the fires. Indonesia's apparent willingness to accept a role for Singapore, and perhaps Malaysia, to take legal action against their companies suggests that Indonesia's preoccupation with protecting its sovereign prerogative has been balanced somewhat by its recognition of the genuine need to control the fires.

Less directly addressed has been the question of what rights the international community has to intercede on behalf of broader environmental interests, such as protecting biodiversity and responding to climate change. The Haze Agreement is more narrowly focused than the 1985 Agreement on the Conservation of Nature and Natural Resources and far less clear in recognizing the parties' responsibilities to those beyond the region. Again, the agreement can be amended. It is also noteworthy that the voluntary fund established to implement its provisions permits contributions from external sources. This may provide the basis for members of the international community to influence program initiatives and priorities within a regime that might otherwise focus exclusively on the transboundary dimensions of the haze problem.

It is difficult not to be discouraged by the experience of the Indonesian fires—both the fact that they occurred and the initial responses to them. Indonesia allowed open burning to take place under dangerous conditions even after a history of damaging fires had made the risks involved apparent. The government's inability to get the fires under control resulted in serious damage. Indonesia's neighbors, as well as regional and global institutions, responded cautiously and in ways suggesting little sense that there were legal issues raised by Indonesia's behavior, that Indonesia was obligated to do more. It is unclear what the governments in the region and ASEAN as an organization gained by failing to confront Indonesia earlier and more directly about a problem that deserved to be given higher priority than it was.

However, since 1998, ASEAN nations, including Indonesia, have recognized that at least part of the response to the haze problem must be the development of more effective law and institutional procedures. The reforms undertaken thus far are incomplete and not fully implemented, but they do provide a framework offering the possibility for more effective action if the governments involved have the political will to use it.

Notes

1   This chapter draws on material previously published in Allen L. Springer, "The 1997–98 Indonesian Forest Fires: Internationalizing a National Environmental Problem," in *International Environmental Cooperation: Politics and Diplomacy in Asia-Pacific*, ed. Paul Harris (Boulder: University of Colorado Press, 2002), 291–315.
2   Asian Development Bank, *Fire, Smoke, and Haze: The ASEAN Response Strategy*, ed. S. Tahir Qadri (Manila: Asian Development Bank, 2001), 45.

3   Ibid., 55.
4   Simon Tay, "Southeast Asian Fires: The Challenge for International Environmental Law and Sustainable Development," *Georgetown International Environmental Law Review* 11 (1999): 241.
5   This was part of a global financial contagion that would spread to South America and play a role in the pulp mills dispute between Argentina and Uruguay discussed in Chapter 8.
6   International Monetary Fund, "Recovery from the Asian Crisis and the Role of the IMF," June 2000. https://www.imf.org/external/np/exr/ib/2000/062300.htm#box3.
7   Helen Varkkey, "Malaysian Investors in the Indonesian Oil Palm Plantation Sector: Home State Facilitation and Transboundary Haze," *Asia Pacific Business Review* 19, no. 3 (2013): 381–89.
8   Helen Varkkey, "Patronage Politics, Plantation Fires and Transboundary Haze," *Environmental Hazards* 12, no. 3–4 (2013): 212–13.
9   James Cotton, "The 'Haze' over Southeast Asia: Challenging the ASEAN Mode of Regional Engagement," *Pacific Affairs* 72, no. 3 (1999): 335–36.
10 H.-D.V. Boehm and F. Siegert, "Ecological Impact of the One Million Hectare Rice Project in Central Kalimantan, Indonesia, Using Remote Sensing and GIS: Land Use and Illegal Logging in Central Kalimantan, Indonesia" (paper presented at the 22nd Asian Conference on Remote Sensing, Singapore, 5–9 November 2001). http://www.crisp.nus.edu.sg/~acrs2001/pdf/126boehm.pdf.
11 See, generally, Joanne R. Bauer and Daniel A. Bell, eds., *The East Asian Challenge for Human Rights* (Cambridge: Cambridge University Press, 1999).
12 See, for example, Andrew Wolman, "National Human Rights Commission and Asian Human Rights Norms," *Asian Journal of International Law* 3 (2013): 82–83.
13 Association of Southeast Asian Nations (ASEAN), "Treaty of Amity and Cooperation in Southeast Asia, 24 February 1976," Bali, signed 24 February 1976 (in force 21 June 1976) [hereafter cited as Treaty of Amity]. http://cil.nus.edu.sg/rp/pdf/1976%20Treaty%20of%20Amity%20and%20Cooperation%20in%20Southeast%20Asia-pdf.pdf.
14 Tay, "Southeast Asian Fires," 256–58.
15 ASEAN, "Agreement on the Conservation of Nature and Natural Resources," Kuala Lumpur, signed 5 July 1985 (not in force). http://www.ecolex.org/server2.php/libcat/docs/TRE/Full/En/TRE-000820.txt.
16 Simon Tay, "Fires and Haze in Southeast Asia," in *Cross-Sectoral Partnerships in Enhancing Human Security*, ed. Pamela J. Noda (Tokyo: Japan Center for International Exchange, 2002), 58–59.
17 Cotton, "The 'Haze' over Southeast Asia," 346.
18 World Wildlife Fund (WWF), "Indonesian Fires: WWF Calls for Preventive Action," press release, 25 September 1997.
19 "1997 Forest Fires in Indonesia: New Estimates Place Damage at $4.4 Billion," *Business Wire*, 29 May 1998.
20 Asian Development Bank, *Fire, Smoke, and Haze*, 54.
21 Charles Victor Barber and James Schweithelm, *Trial by Fire: Forest Fires and Forestry Policy in Indonesia's Era of Crisis and Reform* (Washington, DC: World Resources Institute, 2000), 17–20.
22 Ibid., 17.

23 Ibid., 5–7.

24 "Indonesia Blames Timber Firms for Most Fires," *Reuters*, 3 April 1998.

25 Barber and Schweithelm, *Trial by Fire*, 8.

26 Louise Williams, "Soeharto: I'm So Sorry; Indonesia Fires Suffocating Asia," *Sydney Morning Herald*, 17 September 1997.

27 Greg Earl, "Indonesia Turns Serious at Last in Scorching Issue," *Australian Financial Review*, 6 October 1997.

28 Ibid.

29 "New Indonesian Forest Fires Raise Smog Concerns," *cnn.com*, 25 February 1998. http://www.siliconinvestor.com/readmsg.aspx?msgid=3526966.

30 Earl, "Indonesia Turns Serious."

31 Jonathan Head, "Environment Ministers Agree Concerted Action to Prevent Forest Fires," *BBC News*, 23 December 1997. http://news.bbc.co.uk/2/hi/despatches/42015.stm.

32 Indonesia, "Environmental Management Act (No. 27 of 1997)," 19 September 1997. http://faolex.fao.org/docs/html/ins13056.htm. See, generally, Laode M. Syarif, "Current Development of Indonesian Environmental Law," *IUCN Academy of Environmental Law e-Journal Issue* no. 1 (2010): 6–8.

33 Lee Siew Hua, "Indonesia Ignored Fire-Fighting Plans," *Straits Times*, 23 March 1998.

34 Economy and Environment Program for Southeast Asia (EEPSEA) and World Wide Fund for Nature, (WWF), "The Indonesian Fires and Haze of 1997: The Economic Toll" (Ottawa: International Development Research Centre, 1997), 2–3. https://idl-bnc.idrc.ca/dspace/bitstream/10625/15306/1/108153.pdf.

35 "KL to Inform Jakarta of Losses We Suffered," *New Straits Times*, 1 October 1997.

36 Seth Mydans, "Southeast Asia Chokes as Indonesian Forests Burn," *New York Times*, 25 September 1997.

37 "Indonesian Fires No Accident, Singapore Paper Says," *Reuters*, 2 October 1997.

38 Quoted in Seth Mydans, "Its Mood Dark as the Haze, Southeast Asia Aches," *New York Times*, 26 October 1997.

39 Nicholas D. Kristof, "Asian Pollution Is Widening Its Deadly Reach," *New York Times*, 29 November, 1997.

40 Quoted in Cotton, "The 'Haze' over Southeast Asia," 347–48.

41 ASEAN, "ASEAN Cooperation Plan on Transboundary Pollution," Singapore, June 1995.

42 ASEAN, "Joint Press Release. Sixth Meeting of the ASEAN Senior Officials on the Environment, Bali, 20–22 September 1995."

43 ASEAN, "Regional Haze Action Plan," Singapore, 22–23 December 1997. http://haze.asean.org/?page_id=213.

44 ASEAN, "Joint Press Statement. The ASEAN Ministerial Meeting on Haze. 22–23 December 1997, Singapore."

45 ASEAN, "Joint Press Statement. The Third ASEAN Ministerial Meeting on Haze. 4 April 1998, Brunei Darussalam."

46 ASEAN, "Joint Press Statement. The Fourth ASEAN Ministerial Meeting on Haze. 19 June 1998, Singapore."

47 Simon C. Tay, "South East Asian Fires: Haze over ASEAN and International Environmental Law," *Review of European Community & International Environmental Law* 7 (1998): 204.

48   United Nations Environment Programme (UNEP), "New Internet Resource on Indonesia Forest Fires Available," press release, 28 October 1997.

49   UNEP, "The Greatest Ecological Disaster of the Decade," press release, 19 February 2014.

50   "New Environment Minister to Make Wildfire Crisis a Priority," *Associated Press International*, 16 March 1998.

51   "Fires Low Priority for Indonesian Government," *BBC News*, 20 April 1998.

52   "Haze: Race against Time to Fight Indonesian Fires," *Straits Times*, 4 April 1998.

53   A. Bolt, "UN Urges Indonesia to Stop Forest Fires," *Courier Mail*, 23 April 1998.

54   UNEP-UN Office for the Coordination of Humanitarian Affairs (OCHA), "Meetings on the Indonesian Fires," *ReliefWeb*, 30 April 1998.

55   UNEP, "Environmental Crisis in South East Asia Is Far from Over," press release, 14 May 1998.

56   Interestingly, both had legal training in the US: Tan at Yale, and Tay at Harvard.

57   Alan Khee-Jin Tan, "Forest Fires of Indonesia: State Responsibility and International Liability," *The International and Comparative Law Quarterly* 48, no. 4 (1999): 826–55.

58   Ibid., 847.

59   Ibid., 855.

60   Tay, "Southeast Asian Fires," 299.

61   Tan, "Forest Fires of Indonesia," 848.

62   UNEP, "Environmental Crisis in South East Asia Is Far from Over."

63   Barber and Schweithelm, *Trial by Fire*, 39–40.

64   Tom McCawley, "Indonesia Gets Tough on Fires," *Financial Times*, 28 July 2000, 8.

65   Sheila NcNutty and Tom McCawley, "Autonomy Casts Haze over Indonesia's Fires," *Financial Times*, 14 August 2000, 3.

66   "Dealing with the Haze," *Jakarta Post*, 7 August 1999.

67   Stephanie Kriner, "Humans Turn Indonesian Fires into Annual Disaster," *Straits Times*, 25 August 1999.

68   "Forest Fires: Help, Don't Make Noise," *Straits Times*, 25 August 1999.

69   ASEAN, "Joint Press Statement. The Sixth ASEAN Ministerial Meeting on Haze, Brunei Darussalam, April 16, 1999."

70   Michael Richardson, "Asian Neighbors Doubt Indonesia Can Address Environmental Needs: Fear of Fires Rekindles as Jakarta Is Distracted," *New York Times*, 30 April 1999.

71   See, for example, Cotton, "The 'Haze' over Southeast Asia," 347–51.

72   Tay, "Fires and Haze in Southeast Asia," 58–59.

73   ASEAN, "ASEAN Agreement on Transboundary Haze Pollution," Kuala Lumpur, signed 10 June 2002 (in force 25 November 2003) [hereafter cited as "Haze Agreement"] http://haze.asean.org/?wpfb_dl=32.

74   Ibid., Article 2.

75   See David Seth Jones, "ASEAN and Transboundary Haze Pollution in Southeast Asia," *Asia Europe Journal* 4, no. 3 (2006): 439–40.

76   Martin Abbugao, "ASEAN Urges Indonesia to Ratify Haze Pact," *AFP News*, 30 June 2013.

77   UNEP, "Environmental Crisis in South East Asia Is Far from Over," UNEP press release, 14 May 1998, 10–12.

78   See, generally, McCawley, "Indonesia Gets Tough on Fires," 83–101.

79 Kevin Lim and John O'Callaghan, "Smog in Singapore from Indonesia Fires Could Last for Weeks," *Reuters.com*, 20 June 2013.

80 Zakir Hussain, "Haze Update: Singapore, Indonesia Officials to Discuss How to Prevent Haze," *Straits Times*, 20 June 2013.

81 "Haze Update: Malaysia, Singapore Should 'Know Themselves,' Says Indonesian Minister," *Straits Times*, 24 June 2013.

82 Ben Bland, "Indonesian Fires Highlight Weak Governance and Corruption," FT.com, 23 June 2013.

83 Thalif Deen, *Indonesia's Recurring Forest Fires Threaten Environment*, 10 July 2013.

84 Lim and O'Callaghan, "Smog in Singapore."

85 Lee U-wen, "Haze Laws May Follow Firms across Border," *Business Times Singapore*, 9 July 2013.

86 Chong Pooi Koon and Manirajan Ramasamy, "Indonesia Apologizes as Fires Cause Pollution in Region," *Bloomberg.com*, 24 June 2014.

87 Ibid.

88 Zakir Hussain, "Jakarta Moves to Ratify ASEAN Haze Pact: Law Ministry Clears Documents for Okay from Affected Ministries," *Strait Times*, 5 July 2013.

89 Brian Leonal and Fitri Wulandari, "Haze Fines Win Indonesia's Support with Caveats," *Bloomberg.com*, 30 July 2014.

90 Feng Zengkun, "Transboundary Haze Bill 'Not Shrouded in Secrecy,'" *Straits Times*, 21 May 2014.

91 See, for example, Varkkey, "Malaysian Investors."

92 Eileen Poh, "Challenges Remain Even after Indonesia's Ratification of Haze Pact: Legal Experts," *Channel NewsAsia*, 17 September 2014.

93 "Editorial: Overdue Haze Treaty," *Jakarta Post*, 18 September 2014.

94 Louise Williams and Mark Baker, "The Threatened Planet—South Asia's Year of Reckoning," *Sydney Morning Herald*, 7 October 1997.

95 This issue is explored more fully in the next chapter, in which the response to the Baia Mare cyanide spill is analyzed.

96 See, for example, Daniel Bodansky, *The Art and Craft of International Environmental Law* (Cambridge, MA: Harvard University Press, 2010), 247.

4
Baia Mare Cyanide Spill

Introduction

On 30 January 2000, water contaminated with cyanide and heavy metals breached a containment dam at the Aurul gold mine in Baia Mare, Romania, triggering what a spokesperson for the Hungarian foreign ministry called the "first global environmental pollution catastrophe of the twenty-first century."[1] Cyanide-laced water crossed into Hungary, Serbia, and Bulgaria before returning to Romania and the Black Sea. Romania and Hungary suffered extensive damage, with lesser effects in other downstream states.

The Baia Mare accident raised serious questions about the adequacy of mining standards in Romania and other parts of Eastern Europe. It also focused attention on issues of liability and compensation that were never directly addressed during the Indonesian haze dispute. Admittedly, the problem was different. The cyanide spill was a serious accident involving a deadly chemical. The Indonesian smoke was an expected by-product of land-clearing operations in a region where fires were used routinely to eliminate brush. In the case of Baia Mare, the state of Romania was also directly implicated as a part owner of the mine in a way that the Indonesian government was not. The larger political context in which the Baia Mare dispute was set made it far more difficult for the governments involved to ignore questions of private and public liability. Despite this, only minimal compensation was ever paid in a dispute in which Hungary claimed that over $100 million worth of damage had been done.

The Baia Mare dispute offers an opportunity to explore the challenges faced in making liability and compensation a significant dimension of international environmental law. This chapter describes the political and economic context in which the cyanide spill took place, the nature of the accident itself, and the responses from both within and outside the region. It then examines how liability issues were handled as the extent of the damage became clear. Almost everyone agreed that someone should pay, but there was genuine confusion about the standards of law to be applied, against whom, and how. Even the targets of potential claims, the companies involved and the state of Romania, never challenged the need to compensate victims, just their own liability. Why then were damages never paid?

Map 4.1 This map indicates the Romanian mines where the cyanide spills took place and shows the river system through which the cyanide traveled to Hungary, Serbia, and Bulgaria before entering the Black Sea.

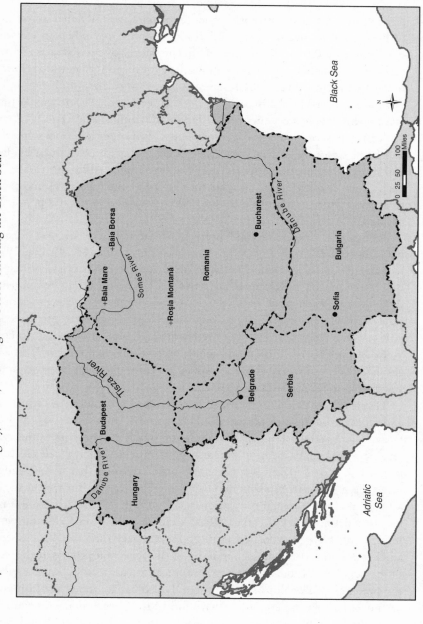

The Context

At the time of the accident, Eastern Europe had a legacy of inefficient, environmentally destructive industries requiring the capital investment and technological innovation that foreign investment could offer. An expanding European Union (EU) offered the prospects of increased trade and economic growth, but only for states capable of meeting accession requirements that included high environmental protection standards. The political disruption caused by the breakup of the former Yugoslavia and the ensuing wave of humanitarian violence had left deep wounds. The Danube River, both a key part of the region's ecology and an important regional waterway, had been seriously damaged by NATO air raids against Serbian bridges and military installations during the Kosovo conflict. Although the European Union had agreed to provide funding to help efforts to clean up the river and restore commercial traffic, Serbia remained bitter and politically isolated.

Romania was poor even by Eastern European standards. In 1998, it had a per capita GNP of only $1,600, less than half of Hungary's $4,340. Legislative measures adopted in the 1990s had written into Romanian law principles such as sustainable development and had declared a "healthy environment" to be a basic "right of all persons."[2] However, Romania lacked the administrative machinery and funds to turn these legal aspirations into effective policy. While determined to join the European Union and anxious to convince EU members of its commitment to environmental reform, Romania also had reason to worry about its reputation among foreign investors in the way it responded to the Baia Mare accident.

Hungary, the primary victim of the spill, had a broader set of bilateral and regional interests to protect. Among the most immediate was the welfare of a large ethnic Hungarian population living in Romania. Some were serving as ministers in the Romanian government, which faced elections in the fall, and Hungary was reluctant to do anything that would undermine the government's electoral prospects.[3] The two countries had signed a bilateral environmental protection agreement in 1997, but it would not be ratified until after the Baia Mare accident and a joint committee to implement it was not created until 2003. Hungary shared Romania's EU ambitions and was much farther along in the accession process at the time of the accident. Hungary's domestic political situation was complicated by the presence of a coalition government. It also had a vibrant environmental movement, strong enough to have forced the government to terminate the Gabčíkovo-Nagymaros dam project with Slovakia in 1992, and well-connected internationally.

The Dispute

The operations at the Aurul gold mine were a joint venture between Esmeralda Exploration Ltd., and REMIN, a Romanian state-owned mining company. A small West Australian company, Esmeralda held a 50 per cent ownership stake in the mine and served as the project manager for operations. The company had been brought in to help improve environmental conditions at the Baia Mare site, where toxic waste from over 200 years of mining activity had begun to leach into nearby water systems. By recycling gold and silver from waste dumps, the project offered both environmental benefits and the opportunity to produce roughly 1.2 tons of gold and 9 tons of silver per year. Created in 1992, Aurul began operations in May 1999 after receiving a series of operating permits from the Romanian government.

To extract the ore, water was pumped into a pond containing mining tailings. The resulting slurry was then pumped to a central processing plant where it was mixed with cyanide to extract the gold and silver ore. The ore-free slurry was delivered by pipeline to a lined tailings pond where the remaining tailings could be spread by hydrocyclones to create higher walls around the tailings pond itself. Water from the tailings pond was recycled through the processing plant and fed back into the water used to collect the tailings. By reusing the processing waters, what was designed as a "closed circuit" process reduced the amount of cyanide required. If everything worked as planned, no toxic waste would be emitted into nearby rivers.[4]

However, on the night of 30 January 2000, unusually heavy precipitation overwhelmed what was later determined to have been a poorly designed system.[5] The rising waters breached the walls of the tailings pond and roughly 26.4 million gallons of water containing up to 120 tons of cyanide and heavy metals spread into the nearby Sasar and Lapus rivers. The cyanide then entered the Somes River, which crosses into Hungary. Moving at 1 to 2 miles an hour, the cyanide plume traveled into the Tisza River, passing through Hungary and Serbia, where it entered the Danube and headed back into Romania, Bulgaria, and the Black Sea. Four weeks after the spill, measurable levels of cyanide were found at the mouth of the Danube, 1,200 miles from the accident site.

Though serious, the consequences of the spill could have been much worse. Quick action at the site to repair the breach in the dam and downstream to warn people about the cyanide led to no loss of life or serious health problems. The most immediate and visible effect was to fish, creating on the Tisza what a Hungarian official called a "five-kilometre-long carpet of dead fish."[6] Reportedly, 1,240 tons of fish were killed and commercial fisheries were shut down for six months. Tourism suffered and national and local governments incurred significant mitigation and remediation costs, including providing bottled water for those normally dependent on the rivers, disposing of the dead fish, and monitoring water quality in the months after the spill.[7]

Other than Romania, Hungary was the dispute's central state player. Directly downstream from Baia Mare, it suffered far more severe effects than other states in the cyanide's path. The immediate concern was to prevent further damage, which motivated Hungarian authorities to work with Romania to learn more about the spill and the potential for future accidents. The desire to appear responsible in the eyes of the European Union and the need to cooperate with Romania on other issues encouraged restraint. Hungary felt political sympathy for the Romanian government, and everyone realized that the Baia Mare accident was the last thing Romania wanted on the eve of EU accession talks. Hungary also recognized the effort being made by Romanian officials to respond. Complicating the development of any single, decisive policy were differences within Hungary's coalition government about whether to declare a state of emergency, which might have had the effect of strengthening the hand of the senior governing party.[8] At the same time, Hungary faced serious environmental damage. People were drinking bottled water, and tons of dead fish were being pulled from the Tisza. Black banners flew from homes and bridges, as many of the 15,000 members of Hungary's fishing industry were put out of work. Angry Hungarians put pressure on their government to seek compensation.

The result of these conflicting pressures was a Hungarian policy that seemed to shift almost daily from calls for cooperation to accusation. The government's initial public response was measured. Even as he announced Hungary's intention to seek restitution from Romania, Gabor Horvath, a spokesperson for the Hungarian government, avoided placing direct blame on Romania, saying only that the pollution "originated in Romania."[9] Horvath expressed confidence that Romania would be helpful, noting the link to Romania's interest in EU membership and the importance of environmental concerns to the organization.[10]

Serbia's response was far harsher. Serbian Environment Minister Branislav Blazic demanded an "estimate of the damage and that the culprits be punished" and threatened legal action against Romania.[11] However, the effects in Serbia were less significant than in Hungary and affected sites in the country were not even visited by EU representatives who later toured the region.[12] The Serb position was further undermined by its failure to have signed either the 1992 United Nations Convention on the Protection and Use of Transboundary Watercourses and International Lakes (Convention on Transboundary Waters) or the 1994 Sofia Convention on Cooperation for the

Protection and Sustainable Use of the Danube River (Danube River Convention), perhaps the two strongest legal bases for any international claim.[13]

Romania took a number of positive steps as the crisis unfolded. First, it made concrete efforts to stem the flow of pollution entering the rivers.[14] Second, as Hungary acknowledged in its own account of the accident, Romanian authorities informed their Hungarian counterparts of the problem less than 24 hours after the spill and updated them regularly.[15] This warning was critical in allowing officials to take action well before the cyanide crossed into Hungary. Third, at least initially, the Romanian government recognized publicly the seriousness of the problem, admitting that it was the worst accident in a decade, and began legal actions against the mine. The government immediately ordered the plant closed and Aurul was fined, although the minimal level of the penalty (roughly US $166) would later become a source of friction.[16] Finally, Romania offered to work directly with Hungarian officials to deal with the accident; a meeting of technical experts was held on 8 February. Two days later, Romania's Environment State Secretary met with Hungary's Environment Minister Pál Pepo at Baia Mare and agreed to set up a bilateral consultation mechanism. Among its responsibilities, at least according to Hungary, was "to establish the responsibilities of the Romanian state" for the spill.[17] Aware of the lurking issue of liability, Romania claimed that it had been playing a responsible role in overseeing the plant's operations. The Romanian Environment Protection Agency said that it had repeatedly issued written warnings to the Aurul facility to check its equipment (a claim Esmeralda disputed).[18]

Complicating scientific analyses of the impact of the Baia Mare spill were two additional pollution events occurring shortly afterwards. On 10 March, 20,000 tons of tailings sludge containing heavy metals were released from a REMIN-owned facility at Baia Borsa. Several days later, a new, though smaller spill from the same facility turned a 25-mile-long section of the Tisza visibly darker.[19] While there was no direct connection between the spills at Baia Borso and the earlier Baia Mare accident, it was hard to escape the implication that poorly designed and/or regulated Romanian mines posed a serious threat to the region's ecology, already seriously degraded by past mining and industrial activity. The sense that the Baia Mare accident was not a unique event, but part of a chronic and increasingly serious problem, helped shape the way in which Hungary and others responded to the spill.

The accident put Australia in an awkward position. It was an acute embarrassment for Australia's important mining industry and suggested that Australian companies might be going offshore in search of places to operate where they faced less restrictive regulation. Environmentalists were quick to link what happened at Baia Mare to a similar, though smaller accident at a copper/gold mine in Papua, New Guinea.[20] For the government, the accident had both domestic and international repercussions. The challenge was to demonstrate appropriate concern for the serious damage caused (indirectly) by an Australian company without taking any governmental responsibility either to provide compensation to those injured or to assume a regulatory role in controlling the actions of Australian corporations overseas.

The European Union quickly became the lead intergovernmental organization responding to the accident, assuming a far stronger directing role than that played by ASEAN in the Indonesian haze dispute. The EU goal was not simply to help two states close to Western Europe manage a serious transboundary dispute. It was also an opportunity to emphasize the political importance of environmental values in Europe and to push the governments involved to accelerate internal democratic and administrative reforms. This meant providing good information about the accident to those potentially affected and encouraging members of the public and environmental NGOs to express their concerns to authorities. The most visible sign of EU involvement was the creation of the Baia Mare Task Force (BMTF), which issued a key report in December 2000.[21]

The United Nations Environment Program (UNEP) was also actively engaged in the dispute and was actually in a position to respond even more quickly than the European Union. At the request of the Hungarian government, a joint fact-finding effort was undertaken with the Office for the Coordination of Humanitarian Affairs (OCHA). Taking advantage of the presence of scientists from a Balkans Task Force already in Serbia studying the environmental effects of the conflict in Kosovo, the UNEP/OCHA team rapidly produced a useful emergency assessment of the effect of the spill.[22]

NGOs, including the World Wide Fund for Nature, Friends of the Earth, Greenpeace, and Bankwatch, became deeply involved in the international response to the Baia Mare accident. Through public statements of concern, active protest, and critical analyses of governmental reports, they kept the accident in the public spotlight. The consistent NGO call for holding accountable those responsible for the pollution appears to have been a key factor in the continuing emphasis placed by Hungary on pursuing legal claims, even when it became clear how difficult this would actually be. NGOs also worked hard to widen the circle of potentially liable parties and to emphasize the responsibility of Australia to play a more direct role in dealing with the consequences of the spill. The Mineral Policy Institute (MPI), an Australian industry watchdog, was a particularly active participant in this effort. The importance of NGOs was underscored by the emphasis placed by both the UNEP-OCHA joint assessment mission and the BMTF on close consultation with them. The BMTF also included NGO representatives among its members.

Legal Issue: Liability and Compensation

Although liability provisions are included in many environmental agreements, formal claims of liability have never been common in international environmental law. Until recently very few international environmental disputes have led to international litigation. The problem is not simply procedural but also reflects the perceived weaknesses of the liability rules courts would apply.

Whether targeting states or private parties, liability regimes have several apparent limitations. First, they seem inherently reactive. Liability normally cannot be assigned until after environmental damage occurs. Second, there may be serious disagreement about the standard of liability to apply. Is fault on the part of an allegedly responsible party required or do rules of strict liability apply? Third, many types of environmental damage may take years to become evident or difficult to link directly to specific pollution sources, at least with the degree of certainty required to prevail in a courtroom. Fourth, because of the slowness of the claims process, there may be little immediate relief provided to those harmed. Finally, even when compensation is awarded, it may be inadequate to repair the damage done. Some injuries, for instance to endangered species or sensitive habitats, do not lend themselves easily to economic quantification, and remedial efforts may simply not be possible.

While these are reasonable concerns, there is another side. Liability rules can play two different and constructive roles in the overall design of environmental regimes, particularly in a transboundary context where the links between polluting activity and detrimental environmental effect can be established more easily than in other situations.

First, assigning liability can provide financial relief to victims and help repair environmental damage. While some effects may never be quantifiable, economists have become increasingly sophisticated in their ability to assign economic value to many forms of environmental degradation and to the cost of remedial measures. Another form of reparation comes from the psychological impact of simply holding responsible parties accountable for their actions. This was an important dimension of the public reaction to the Baia Mare accident, and represents an aspect of the "polluter pays principle" that should not be underestimated.

Second, liability regimes can actually help prevent damage from occurring.[23] Once a source of pollution is identified, changes can be made at the source to reduce the chances of a recurrence. Perhaps the most significant result of the Trail Smelter arbitration, often viewed simply as a case involving post-damage compensation, was the tribunal's order that structural changes be made in the smelter to prevent further injury to US interests.

Even before damage is done, awareness that a company or the state itself might later be held accountable can encourage more responsible behavior. For private companies, the need to secure financial backing, as well as insurance to protect against possible future claims, brings into the project development process outside parties whose self-interest is served by preventing damage. Projects that pose a predictable risk of damage should reflect that risk in increased premiums, which should provide companies with a financial incentive to take cost-effective preventive measures. Developing clear rules of state liability, if supported by the machinery to implement them, can reinforce the state's responsibility to regulate private activities taking place on its territory. This gives greater relevance to the procedural duties of states, often stated only in vague, aspirational terms.[24] It is one thing to say that a state must conduct an environmental assessment of projects that pose significant transboundary risks. It is another to suggest that its failure to do so could have practical consequences.

Less than a week after the cyanide crossed into Hungary, the Hungarian government began raising issues of liability. On 7 February, the Romanian ambassador was called to the Foreign Ministry and told that Hungary would be seeking compensation for the damage caused by the accident. There was some initial hope that Romania would simply accept responsibility and offer compensation. As it became clear that this was unlikely, a group of experts was formed to explore the legal options open to Hungary. What emerged were two different, though not mutually exclusive strategies Hungary could pursue. In neither case were the law and the odds of success clear.

The first approach was for Hungary to bring a claim against Romania on an international level. Despite early optimism that Hungary had a strong case for compensation under existing treaty law, it soon became evident that neither the Danube Convention nor a bilateral environmental agreement with Romania contained liability provisions that Hungary could easily invoke.[25] A claim directly against Romania raised questions of both substantive law and procedure. Could Romania be held responsible for transboundary environmental damage simply because it originated on Romanian soil? One Hungarian NGO argued that a doctrine of "no-fault strict liability" should apply, even if it could not be shown that the government had acted inappropriately in regulating the Aurul mine.[26] Despite Romanian state participation in the mine, this was a questionable proposition, particularly since Romania had not signed any international agreement embracing strict liability. A more promising international law strategy could be based on procedural duties Romania arguably possessed under the terms of the Transboundary Waters and Danube Conventions, to which both Hungary and Romania were party. While neither agreement contained specific liability provisions, together they still might provide a reasonable foundation for a claim against Romania, particularly when placed in the broader perspective of customary international law. An argument could be made that Romania had failed to do enough to prevent the spill by not insisting that a better method be used to construct the walls of the tailings dam, by not requiring regular monitoring of the facility, and by not having in place a better response plan. [27] Less clear under customary state practice was what it would mean to hold Romania responsible. At a minimum, Hungary would demand financial compensation (though for what damages was initially unclear) as well as a Romanian commitment to take steps to prevent further pollution.

Any international claim against Romania was unlikely to succeed without a forum in which it could be heard. The Danube Convention does provide a mechanism for binding third party settlement, either by the International Court of Justice (ICJ) or through an ad hoc arbitral process.[28] However, Romania would have to agree to the ICJ's jurisdiction for it to hear the case and the process for creating the arbitral body did not offer a quick resolution to the dispute.

The second approach, more attractive both legally and politically, was to rely on national courts in Romania, Hungary, and/or Australia to hear compensation claims brought by Hungary or by private claimants directly against the companies responsible for the accident.[29] Hungary was searching for the most favorable forum, both in terms of the liability standard likely to be applied and the court's ability to enforce any judgment. A key issue was whether to go after the Aurul mine itself, or one or both of its component companies, Esmeralda and state-owned REMIN. Even a favorable and theoretically enforceable award would be meaningless if there were no funds to cover it, and there were early indications that Esmeralda might not be able to pay, especially if the mine remained closed.[30] No obvious strategy emerged, in part because any legal action risked alienating the Romanian government, particularly if claims were brought not just by private claimants but directly by the Hungarian government. This was a virtual certainty given the collective damages Hungary had suffered in response to the spill.[31]

The debate over how to respond to the accident was also heating up in Australia, where the spill had been widely reported. There was general agreement that the image of Australian mining companies had been tarnished, but whether legislative action was needed was a source of substantial disagreement. Members of the Green Party and Democrats, supported by the Minerals Policy Institute (MPI), pushed for the adoption of rules requiring Australian companies to adhere to Australian mining standards wherever they operated.[32] Supporters of the mining industry suggested that the voluntary code adopted by the Australian minerals industry, which Esmeralda had not signed, was a better approach.[33]

Beyond possible legislative reform, could the state of Australia be expected to bear any responsibility for the accident itself? A Hungarian spokesperson announced shortly after the spill that Hungary did not intend to bring any claim against Australia because "there is no Australian state participation in the mine."[34] The Hungarian public was less forgiving. A 23 February soccer match between the Hungarian and Australian national teams was disrupted when spectators threw dead fish onto the field.[35] Two days later, protestors demonstrated outside the Australian embassy in Budapest and presented a petition calling for Australia to "recognize its *moral responsibility* for the environmental catastrophe which was caused by the irresponsible and sinful behavior of a company registered on its territory" [emphasis added].[36] This distinction between Australia's moral duty and any sense of legal responsibility would be carefully maintained by Australian officials as the dispute unfolded. Australia's Environment Minister Robert Hill met with the Hungarian ambassador in Canberra and spoke afterwards of Australia's "obligation . . . of good citizenship" in helping Hungary respond to the accident.[37] The Australian ambassador to Hungary expressed the shock of the Australian people at scenes of the accident and acknowledged its seriousness. Australia would provide technical assistance to help restore the Tisza, but could not take legal responsibility for the actions of a private company.[38]

The tenor of Hungary's public position changed at the end of the second week in February, apparently triggered by comments coming from Esmeralda's chairman, Brett Montgomery. The company had remained quiet in the first days after the accident, but Montgomery now publicly challenged both the extent of the damage and its connection to the spill at the mine. Speaking from Perth, he called the news reports "grossly exaggerated" and suggested that the fish deaths could have been caused by "a number of unrelated events."[39] The company depicted the accident as an "overflow" caused by unusually bad weather conditions and not a "structural failure or a leak,"[40] Montgomery said. "It may take some time yet but I am confident Esmeralda will be vindicated in its position on this matter."[41] He added a note of intrigue by saying he had received a phone call from someone from the MPI claiming that the group, opposed to the use of cyanide, was planning to make a major international political issue of the spill.[42] Even if claims could be brought as a result of the accident, Montgomery insisted that they would have to be directed at Aurul, not Esmeralda, which was merely a shareholder. Australian financial markets seemed unconvinced as shares in Esmeralda dropped by 40 per cent before trading in the company's stock was suspended.[43]

The Hungarian government responded angrily. Horvath expressed "sadness and incomprehension" at Montgomery's statements, claiming he was "either genuinely unaware of the facts or wants to ignore them."[44] Compensation claims would be brought. "Whoever is responsible for this will have to face claims for environmental damages caused, either by international law or civic procedure,"[45] but the government's ire was now clearly directed at Esmeralda.

Romania initially seemed happy to permit Esmeralda officials to take the brunt of the criticism, stressing that Romania was also a victim and deserved compensation.[46] However, maintaining distance from the mine and the accident became increasingly difficult. Media reports suggested that Romania was trying to downplay the incident, in one instance by only sending a deputy minister to meet with Hungary's environment minister.[47] Things worsened when Romania's environment minister seemed to echo Esmeralda's skepticism about the accident, calling the spill "serious—but not on the scale reported by the media."[48]

Romania's dilemma was clear. Given its regulatory role over the Aurul operation, not to mention its ownership stake in the company, Romania had an obvious incentive to try to undercut any sense of blame for the damage, particularly since Hungarian officials seemed to link possible international and private claims in all of their public statements about the need for compensation. On 15 February, Hungarian Prime Minister Victor Orban announced that Hungary was considering plans to sue not only Aurul and Esmeralda, but the Romanian government itself. Romania indicated that it was not prepared to pay compensation, although Hungary insisted that talks on the issue were ongoing. In an interview with an Australian newspaper, Romania's ambassador said that his government would not recognize the jurisdiction of the International Court of Justice in any claim Hungary might make.[49] On 16 February, Romania took a somewhat softer line when Foreign Minister Petre Roman, attending a news conference with an EU representative, stated that "Romania will fully respect international legal provisions." While Roman admitted "the responsibility is clear, we have never denied it," he also said that "responsibility is one thing and guilt is another," suggesting that Romania's regulatory failings need not give rise to a duty to compensate for the damage done. He also argued that to talk of legal action, when "we do not have the results of the evaluation . . . would be a purely political act . . . which serves nobody."[50]

The presence of the EU official at Roman's press conference underscored a key element that been added to the Baia Mare dispute: the increased involvement of the international community, principally the European Union. The tougher rhetoric between the parties and the growing controversy over what had actually happened provided an opportunity for a constructive outside presence. NGOs were increasingly critical of the failure of the two governments to respond more decisively to the accident.[51] On 17 February, a coalition of Hungarian NGOs issued a joint declaration stressing the need to "clarify the political and legal liabilities in the context of this catastrophe and to find fair solutions for the sake of compensation, rehabilitation and avoidance of any similar disasters." The European Union had "an essential role in this context," given the desire of both Hungary and Romania to join the organization, and should "closely assess the readiness of the candidate countries to prevent such ecological catastrophes."[52]

First on the scene, however, was the UNEP/OCHA joint assessment team, a mission particularly welcomed by Hungary considering the intensifying dispute over the accident. Esmeralda had enlisted Australian experts to study the circumstances surrounding the spill, but Hungary was understandably reluctant to rely on their evaluation. Australian papers were reporting skepticism from those familiar with cyanide about how it could have maintained so high a level of toxicity as far down the river as it allegedly had. The title of one account, "A Fishy Side to the Great Hungarian Cyanide Hysteria," suggests the level of doubt that had been generated about both the source and extent of the damage, as well as the political motives of some of those most critical of Esmeralda.[53] Some in Australia felt that Esmeralda was being unfairly targeted,[54] a concern reinforced when Peter Marinescu, director of the Romanian Water Commission, echoed earlier claims by Esmeralda that the extensive fish kill might have been caused not by cyanide, but by bleach used by authorities, including Hungarian officials, to clean up the pollution.[55]

The Resolution

The UNEP report, released in late March 2000, was not intended to assign liability or to award compensation, but to provide an objective analysis of what had happened. However, its conclusions had liability implications. According to the assessment team, the break in the dam was the result of a "combination of inherent design deficiencies in the process, unforeseen operating conditions and bad weather."[56] The facility was being operated in accordance with existing Romanian regulatory standards, which did not require special monitoring equipment. The team was unable to determine how frequently the plant had been inspected, and there was criticism of the failure to prepare adequate contingency plans in case of an accident. On the positive side, the report indicated that the company had taken reasonable steps to repair the dam once the problem was uncovered, and that "timely information exchange and measures taken by the Romanian, Hungarian and Yugoslavian authorities . . . mitigated and reduced the risk and impact of the spill."[57] The report's recommendations suggested, at least implicitly, the weakness of the international legal regime. It stressed the need to "develop a protocol on liability and compensation on accidents with transboundary impact," to be added to the UN Convention on Transboundary Waters as well as the United Nations Economic Commission for Europe (UNECE) Convention on the Transboundary Effects of Industrial Accidents.[58]

The European Union played a more direct role as mediator. In February, EU vice-president Loyola de Palacio labeled the Baia Mare accident a "true European catastrophe," and declared "there is a clear principle in the EU that . . . who contaminates will pay for the restitution."[59] EU Environment Commissioner Margot Wallström began a fact-finding tour of the Baia Mare complex on 17 February, accompanied by Romica Tomescu, Romania's environment minister. Since Romania had just begun accession talks with the European Union the previous week, Wallström's assertion that "these incidents will have no impact on Romania's negotiations with the EU"[60] was likely unconvincing to Romanians. In Wallström's presence, Tomescu recognized the need for Romania to earn the European Union's trust in the way it responded to the spill. He expressed regret for the accident, insisting that Romania "never intended to hide or downplay the seriousness of the incident."[61] When Wallström insisted that any response to the accident should "apply the 'polluter pays' principle," Tomescu affirmed that Romanian legislation did indeed embrace that principle.[62] Unstated was Romania's hope that Esmeralda, not Romania, would be seen as the relevant polluter.

On her return to Brussels, Wallström announced the formation of the Baia Mare Task Force (BMTF).[63] However diplomatically Wallström tried to package the EU visit, its presence appeared to make a difference, initially in helping to moderate Romania's official position. On 21 February, Hungary released a report, which expressed confidence that the accident would not become a "political issue" between the two states and that the bilateral consultative process established earlier would be able to resolve outstanding compensation issues.[64]

The accidents at the Baia Borsa mine in mid-March were also not as divisive as might have been expected. After the first, Romanian Justice Minister Valeriu Stoica traveled to Hungary and expressed his regret. Speaking to a Hungarian-Romanian lawyers' group, he emphasized the need to avoid accusations and to take joint action, based on principles of law, to punish those responsible and to prevent future pollution. Ibolya David, Stoica's Hungarian counterpart, agreed that this should be handled not as a political, but as a professional matter.[65] Hungary did summon the Romanian ambassador to insist that Romania adopt more stringent security measures. After the second incident at Baia Borsa, Hungarian Environment Minister Pepo organized a meeting with representatives from Romania and Ukraine to discuss a joint response.[66] The result was not a process for adjudicating international claims but a protocol among the three nations, designed to prevent future transboundary pollution.[67]

With this agreement, the interstate component of the Baia Mare dispute essentially came to an end. No formal claim for compensation was ever directed toward the Romanian government, although that option was also never renounced. The Baia Mare facility reopened in June 2000, still using cyanide, but now with higher walls around the tailings pond and using a new open circuit system designed to prevent a repeat of the January accident. After Janos Gonczy, Hungary's Government Commissioner for the Tisza and Somes Rivers, visited the mine in mid-July, Hungarian Foreign Minister Janos Martoni declared that "the international legal enforcement of the claims against the Romanian state cannot be excluded . . . and therefore it keeps the issue on the agenda. . . . [I]f trouble still occurs, the state involved should be called to account."[68] Martoni's language could be interpreted to mean that Hungary would only take action if yet another accident occurred. However, it is likely that Hungary intended to use the possibility of an international claim as leverage to help ensure Romanian cooperation in executing any award against Aurul. It would also give the Romanians an incentive to remain engaged in bilateral pollution prevention efforts.

Hungary's position was strengthened by the release of the Baia Mare Task Force report in December 2000. While targeting the company for serious criticism, the report also expressed "grave reservations over the adequacy of the permitting procedures existing when the projects were planned and constructed. . . . It was difficult for the BMTF, during its meetings with all of the authorities involved in the permitting process, to discern where exactly the responsibility for the overall safety of the facility lay."[69] That the Aurul mine was permitted to reopen, and to do so under extended "provisional" operating permits without making some of the changes it had earlier promised,[70] suggested the weakness of Romanian regulatory control.

Hungary now began what would be a lengthy and unsuccessful process to bring civil claims against the companies involved. Here the BMTF report also offered support in its criticism of the "inappropriately designed" system for managing the tailings and "inadequate monitoring of the construction and operation of the dams." It said that the accident was "triggered by severe but not exceptional weather,"[70] undercutting the argument made by Esmeralda officials that weather was to blame for the accident. The release of the report and the impending one-year anniversary of the spill brought more NGO pressure on a Hungarian government criticized for being too willing to ignore the issue.[71]

Hungary's initial target was Esmeralda. Soon after the spill, the Hungarian government employed an Australian legal firm to study the possibility of filing civil claims against the company in Australia. A complicating factor was that Esmeralda, in addition to being taken off the Australian stock exchange after the accident, was now under voluntary receivership administered by Kim Strickland, an Australian insolvency practitioner. Hungary saw this move as a trick to avoid legal responsibility for the accident.[72] In the event that Esmeralda was shielded from claims for compensation, Hungarian officials threatened to go after the banks and other investors behind Esmeralda's activities.[73] Strickland ultimately rejected the preliminary Hungarian claims against the company, arguing that the letter of complaint offered no detail as to the nature of the damages suffered. Moreover, the company simply lacked the funds to pay anything close to the roughly $100 million demanded by Hungary.[74] In the end, Esmeralda was able to escape direct liability, arguing that it was only a stockholder in the Aurul project. The company was released from receivership in October 2001 and would reemerge as Eurogold Ltd. in May 2002. Ironically, one of the factors that made the rebirth of Esmeralda/Eurogold possible was the decision by some of the financial backers of the Baia Mare plant to walk away from loans they had made to avoid the adverse publicity associated with the spill.[75]

Hungarian officials decided to focus on Aurul, the company that had actually operated the mine. In December 2001, Hungary filed a $100 million suit for damages against Aurul in a Budapest court only to discover that the defendant that appeared now identified itself as Transgold SA. The delay to determine whether Transgold was indeed the legal successor to Aurul was just the first of many. Transgold's lawyers challenged the jurisdiction of the Hungarian court, arguing that an international tribunal would provide a more appropriate forum.[76] The battle over the appropriate legal standard, Hungarian or Romanian, to apply to the accident helped drag the case out even longer.[77] A 2003 declaration by the Romanian government that the accident was attributable to bad weather led Transgold supporters to argue that this *force majeure* declaration would exonerate the company under either Hungarian or Romanian tort law, although they clearly preferred the latter.[78] In May 2005, the Hungarian court ordered Transgold to cut its production of gold by 85 per cent, citing continuing concern about potential environmental damage. While Hungarian officials argued that Romania was bound by a bilateral law enforcement agreement to implement the ruling, Romania made clear that Transgold was operating legally in Romania and would not be forced to comply.[79] On 8 May 2006, the Budapest court ruled in favor of Hungary's claims on the merits.[80] By that time, the Baia Mare mine had closed, the victim of bad weather, frozen pipes, and the declining price of gold.[81] Eurogold then shifted its operations across the border into Ukraine.[82] The case against Transgold continued into 2008, but no compensation has ever been forthcoming.

Post-Dispute Developments

Once the immediate threat posed by the spill passed, the goal was to prevent future accidents by reducing the transboundary risks posed by industrial and mining activities. Bilaterally, Hungary and Romania decided to establish more effective transboundary consultation mechanisms. Though perhaps a small step, Commissioner Gonczy's visit to make a personal inspection of the reopened mine demonstrated a shared desire to improve communication and increase the transparency of mining activities in boundary regions. The work of the Regional Environmental Center to create an emergency preparedness plan for the Tisza was intended to enhance the capacity, particularly among NGOs, to deal more effectively with pollution incidents should they occur.[83] The Danube Commission, which played an important role during the accident in helping warn people downstream of potential hazards from the spill, has also strengthened some of its response capabilities, and worked to incorporate the Tisza sub-basin into its overall water management plan.[84]

More broadly, Baia Mare indicated the need for better and more widely accepted international standards to regulate hazardous industrial activities. Both the UNEP/OCHA joint mission and the Baia Mare Task Force encouraged states, especially Romania, to ratify the 1992 Convention on the Transboundary Effects of Industrial Accidents,[85] which provides a process to identify and control hazardous activities that cause or threaten extraterritorial damage. Parties are expected to notify and consult with each other about such activities and take steps both to minimize the danger they represent and to respond to accidents.[86] While the state's role in most cases is simply to ensure that such measures are taken, the Convention does help clarify some of the state's procedural duties. The EU Commission also used the accident to build support for amendments designed to expand the range of hazardous activities covered by its earlier Seveso II directive, explicitly linking these reforms to the Baia Mare spill.[87]

The Baia Mare accident encouraged the mining industry to take more proactive measures to address concerns about the use of cyanide. UNEP convened a symposium with the International Council on Metals and the Environment after the spill. This led to the adoption of the 2002 International Cyanide Management Code, a voluntary industry program that provides detailed procedures signatories are to follow and a process of internal certification monitored by third party auditors.[88]

Baia Mare also accelerated efforts to develop rules governing the overseas activities of multinational corporations. The Organisation of Economic Co-operation and Development (OECD) had been developing *Guidelines for Multinational Enterprises* since the mid–1970s. Its 2000 Revisions were drafted shortly after the accident and reflected awareness of the issues raised by Esmeralda's role in the Aurul mine.[89] A central goal was to have firms meet the same basic environmental standards wherever they operate.[90] The *OECD Guidelines* encourage companies to consider environmental concerns when making investment decisions, to provide the public with adequate information of any environmental risks their activities pose, and to have contingency plans and emergency warning procedures to respond to environmental accidents.[91] Critics were quick to point out that the OECD standards lacked both mandatory quality and any process for enforcement.[92]

In Australia, a draft Corporate Code of Conduct Bill 2000[93] was introduced in September 2000. The measure would have created environmental, labor, and other obligatory standards covering Australian companies operating overseas. To enforce these rules, the law included a system of fines that could be imposed against the company and even company officials. A direct response to the Baia Mare experience, the draft legislation permitted those injured by a company violating the rules to bring claims in Australian federal courts for either injunctive or compensatory relief.[94] The proposal was defeated in the face of determined opposition from mining companies and other industry groups. Arguing in favor of self-regulation, lobbyists insisted that the proposed law would compromise the sovereignty of host countries.[95]

While much of the post–spill attention was focused on preventing future accidents, there were also efforts to improve what was seen as an inadequate system of civil liability for pollution.[96] Within the European Union, the spill brought new momentum to the EU Commission's attempt to develop a Community-wide approach to environmental liability. The Commission had been at work on the issue since 1989, but faced substantial industry opposition and made little initial headway. Its long-anticipated White Paper on Environmental Liability was released in February 2000, just days after the Baia Mare accident, and the discussion surrounding it was inevitably linked to what had just happened in Romania. The White Paper explored issues of private and state liability for environmental damage and the types of injury for which compensation should be available. It argued for the adoption of a new directive which would combine elements of both strict liability for damage caused by dangerous activities and fault-based liability for damage resulting from non-dangerous activities. While some environmentalists felt the Commission's proposal did not go far enough,[97] it was far more ambitious than many had anticipated and was formally approved in April 2004.[98]

As the European Union moved to expand the range of activities subject to new liability standards, members were anxious to avoid creating rules that would put EU industries at a competitive disadvantage. This provided new incentive for the UNECE to address the issue in a transboundary context. Shortly after the Baia Mare accident, Switzerland, which had learned difficult lessons from its own experience with the 1986 fire at the Sandoz chemical plant, proposed that clearer civil liability rules be added to two existing international agreements, the UN Convention on the Protection and Use of Transboundary Watercourses and International Lakes and the Industrial Accidents Convention.[99] The UNECE drafted a Protocol on Civil Liability to be added to both. It was adopted in Kiev in 2003, with Romania among the original signatories.[100] Despite fear that the commitment to environmental accountability would fade with greater distance from the Baia Mare accident, the Protocol does adopt a strict liability approach to transboundary environmental damage, subject to agreed upper liability limits. Article 12 also states that nothing in the agreement limits the obligations of state parties under general international law, thus indicating that the creation of clearer rules of private liability did not remove potential state responsibility for transboundary damage.[101]

Returning to the aftermath of the Baia Mare accident itself, the only claim for compensation brought effectively against Romania came not from Hungary, but from within Romania. Vasile and Paul Tâtar, two Romanian residents of Baia Mare, claimed to have been injured by the spill and argued successfully before the European Court of Human Rights (ECHR) that Romania had failed to provide an adequate assessment of the potential impact of the plant and had permitted the activity to continue even after the accident. Holding in 2009 that Romania had violated Article 8 of the European Convention on Human Rights, which guarantees every individual "respect for his private and family life, his home and his correspondence," the ECHR awarded the men €6,266.[102] While the compensation awarded was minimal compared to the amounts claimed by Hungary, the ruling reinforced the importance of the precautionary principle as a rule of international environmental law and put the responsibility for assessing potential damage and informing those who might be affected squarely on the Romanian government.[103]

Analysis

Perhaps the most striking aspect of the Baia Mare dispute was the central role played by outside organizations. The European Union's influence was enhanced by the membership aspirations of both Hungary and Romania, and Romania was put on the defensive by the timing of the accident just as accession talks were beginning. EU officials initially framed the problem in terms of ensuring the application of legal principles but appeared to moderate their emphasis on assigning liability as they recognized the need to defuse an increasingly acrimonious dispute. In addition to the European Union and UNEP fact-finding missions, the Danube Commission's Danube Accident Emergency Warning System, set up in 1997, made it possible for Romania to provide prompt notification of the spill.[104] The nature of the accident and the media attention it received brought a number of other actors into the process, including the victims of the spill and increasingly vocal NGOs, some working closely with local groups concerned about the continuing use of cyanide in Romanian mines. NGOs kept the liability issue before the media and tried to broaden the sense of responsible parties to include both Esmeralda and the Australian government.

Local officials have contended that this external influence has been overstated, arguing that strong bilateral relationships that had developed between middle-level government ministries was an important factor in shifting the dispute to a less politicized arena. That the European Union and UNEP seemed so involved was due, they suggest, to the nature of the dispute, which required some form of external assessment of what had happened. By entrusting that task to others, tensions were sufficiently reduced to allow more normal bilateral relations to return.[105] It is impossible to know what might have happened without the presence of the European Union, but the fact that local officials were trying to take charge of the problem and work together outside the public spotlight may help explain why Hungary never followed through with any sort of formal legal claim against Romania, despite its public pronouncements and pressure for compensation from the accident's victims.

Hungary's reluctance to bring such a claim could reinforce the sense of skepticism many have about the value of international claims proceedings, as well as the role of state liability and compensation in transboundary environmental disputes. However, four factors may help explain Hungary's restraint, without necessarily undermining the potential of liability regimes.

First, it made sense for Hungary to avoid an unnecessarily confrontational stance vis-à-vis Romania. As a landlocked, mid-riparian state, Hungary benefits from maintaining a cooperative regional regime to govern the Danube, an issue of genuine concern at the time of the spill, given the challenge of restoring transportation on the river after the Kosovo conflict. An approach based on more flexible principles such as equitable utilization seemed more attractive than one tied so directly to asserting Hungary's legal rights.

A second constraint may have been uncertainty about the legal basis for asserting Romanian liability.[106] Arguing a doctrine of strict liability might have served Hungarian interests here, but is unlikely that Hungary would want to embrace so restrictive a principle unless it was incorporated into a clearly defined international agreement. Alternatively, basing a claim on fault liability required a persuasive argument about what Romania did or failed to do that would justify demands for compensation. The reports of the UNEP/ OCHA joint mission and the Baia Mare Task Force pointed to weaknesses in Romania's regulatory process and the minimal degree of supervision government authorities exercised over the mine, but they had also recognized the impact of the unusually bad weather. Moreover, Hungary had acknowledged Romania's efforts to warn downstream states and explain the extent of the danger once the spill began, and the Task Force applauded the work of Romania for the steps taken to mitigate the effects of the accident.

Third, Romania was a poor country that was making a genuine effort to improve its environment. Paying a substantial compensation claim would be an economic hardship and could divert funds better used to develop its capacity to prevent future accidents, a concern similar to that raised in the previous chapter about possible Indonesian compensation for transboundary damage caused by the brush fires. The logic behind the principle of differential responsibilities made it difficult for a comparatively affluent country like Hungary to demand compensation when other remedies might be available. As with the Indonesian experience, it is important to recognize the positive steps Romania took, including its acknowledgment of responsibility—if not guilt—for the accident. The European Union's involvement was doubtless an important factor, but Romania never asserted a right to act as it wanted on its territory and admitted that the damage was significant. No attempt was made to treat the operation of dangerous mines within a regional watershed as just another equitable use of transboundary rivers. One possible interpretation of Hungary's decision not to bring a formal claim against Romania may be that, on balance, it felt Romania had behaved responsibly enough.

Finally, Hungary had a more attractive target, at least politically. If the spill could be attributed to Esmeralda, Hungary could try to make the polluter pay without directly attacking the Romanian government, a strategy that obviously appealed to Romania as well. Romania's strategy was to convey concern about the accident and, at the same time, separate the Romanian state from the Aurul operation by agreeing on the central place of Esmeralda in creating a problem that was affecting all the states in the region, especially Romania. Yet delinking was difficult because of Romania's ownership of REMIN and its regulatory responsibilities over the Aurul mine. To talk about reforms and improvements was to imply earlier mistakes. International investigations of the accident did not help, as they indicated that Aurul's dangerous operations had complied with Romanian rules. That Esmeralda had been brought into the Aurul project to help clean up wastes generated by previous state-run enterprises was a fact easily ignored in the vilification of Esmeralda, at least until the accidents at the Baia Borso mine (entirely REMIN-owned) suggested that dangerous mining operations were not solely attributable to Esmeralda.

Still, even with the focus on Esmeralda and later Aurul, the indecision within the Hungarian government about how to pursue civil claims suggests an awareness that legal responsibility for the spill would be difficult to assign under the law then available to it. In the beginning, Hungary may have been confident that a negotiated settlement was possible, especially with the European Union playing such a central role, and that Romania might voluntarily pay at least some compensation. Hungary also needed time to develop firm data about the damages that could actually be linked to the spill, not an easy process when pre-spill toxicity levels had already had a significant effect on the region's environment. Uncertainty about the effectiveness of existing judicial institutions likely had an impact, as well. Both the Hungarian and Romanian legal systems were in a process of development, particularly in the area of environmental protection. How either jurisdiction would treat the joint Esmeralda-REMIN venture raised complex legal questions more easily deferred than addressed.

The decision finally to go ahead with claims against Esmeralda and Aurul can be attributed to several factors. First, negotiation on compensation with Romania and Esmeralda simply was not working, and Esmeralda seemed content to wait out what officials knew would be a lengthy process. Second, the sums likely involved in any negotiated settlement acceptable to a Hungarian government that had so publicly announced a $100 million claim were more than Esmeralda or Aurul could pay. Finally, the government had little choice politically. Not only were there real people who had suffered damage and wanted compensation, there were also NGOs who saw claims by Hungary as important in vindicating the polluter pays principle and making the Hungarian state the protector of broader environmental interests. To the extent some of the government's early public statements were designed to gain political leverage against Romania in bilateral negotiations, they also created a political context in which backing away from claims was extremely difficult.

The Baia Mare cyanide spill promoted changes in international environmental law at both the bilateral and regional levels. Most were intended to prevent accidents and to improve the efficiency of institutional response mechanisms. However, both the European Union and UNECE recognized the need for clearer liability rules and better procedures to implement them. The dispute occurred in an institutional context where discussion of these issues was already underway and where treaty regimes provided frameworks in which new rules could be developed. Yet, as progressive as the 2003 Civil Liability Protocol may be, more than 10 years later it has been ratified by only one state (Hungary) and is not yet in force, a reminder that getting states to acknowledge a problem and getting them to commit to effective action can present two quite separate challenges.

The Baia Mare dispute can certainly provide ammunition for those skeptical of the value of international liability regimes. Despite the political pressure from environmental NGOs and victims of the spill, Hungary was drawn to an approach emphasizing cooperation to prevent future accidents, rather than the punishment of guilty parties. Even on a civil level, the claims that were made produced no concrete results, and Hungary made little more than a rhetorical effort to hold the state of Romania accountable. Pressing claims against a neighboring state required significant diplomatic effort, and the prospects of success were not promising.

Nonetheless, the continuing civil litigation did keep memories of the Baia Mare accident alive. There is little doubt that attitudes in Romania toward mining have changed. In June 2000, most Romanians likely saw the reopening of the Baia Mare mine as an economic necessity, and the risks posed by the use of cyanide as the unavoidable byproduct of economic development. Over the past decade, a battle has been raging over a proposal by Gabriel Resources, a Canadian mining company, to develop the nearby Roșia Montană mine again using cyanide to wash the gold and silver ore. Opponents have repeatedly invoked memories of the Baia Mare spill, and in December 2013, the Romanian parliament refused to make changes in Romanian law to allow the project, in which over $500 million has already been invested, to proceed.[107] In Baia Mare itself, the town council passed changes in local zoning ordinances in 2013 to prevent Romaltyn Mining, Aurul's successor, from reopening the mine. In an ironic twist, it is now the company that is headed to court.[108]

Notes

1   Gabor Horvath, quoted in Stephan Lunn and Tracy Sutherland, "Cyanide Spills into International Incident," *The Australian*, 10 February 2000.

2 Romania, Law on Environmental Protection, No. 137 (1995), quoted in Chris Hudson, "The Role of International Law in the Protection of the Danube River Basin," *Colorado Journal of International Law and Policy* 12 (2001): 378.

3 Nick Thorpe, "Trickery Suspected after Cyanide Spill," *The Guardian*, 17 March 2000.

4 For an overview of the Aurul design and the history of the Romanian permitting process, see United Nations Environment Program (UNEP), "Cyanide Spill at Baia Mare: UNEP/Office for the Coordination of Humanitarian Affairs (OCHA) Assessment Mission," March 2000, 6–15 [hereafter cited as "UNEP/ OCHA Assessment Mission"]. http://reliefweb.int/sites/reliefweb.int/files/res ources/43CD1D010F030359C12568CD00635880-baiamare.pdf.

5 Ibid., 44. See also European Union, "Report of the Baia Mare Task Force," December 2000 [hereafter cited as "Baia Mare Task Force Report"]. http:// viso.jrc.ec.europa.eu/pecomines_ext/docs/bmtf_report.pdf.

6 "Hungary Lashes Esmeralda Claims over Cyanide Spill," *AAP Newsfeed*, 10 February 2000.

7 "Baia Mare Task Force Report," 44–46.

8 Irena Guzelova and Robert Wright, "EU Assesses Damages as Tensions Grow over Romanian Cyanide Spill," *Financial Times*, 16 February 2000, 2.

9 "Hungary Seeks Compensation over Cyanide Pollution," *Agence France Presse*, 8 February 2000.

10 Simon Mann, "Angry Hungary Demands Compensation," *Sydney Morning Herald*, 10 February 2000.

11 "Romania Blocks Cyanide Payout," *The Australian*, 16 February 2000.

12 Guzelova and Wright, "EU Assesses Damage."

13 Aaron Schwabach, "From Schweizerhalle to Baia Mare: The Continuing Failure of International Law to Protect Europe's Rivers," *Virginia Environmental Law Journal* 19 (2000): 445–47.

14 "Cyanide Spill from Romania Polluting Hungary," *Reuters*, 8 February 2000.

15 Hungarian Ministry of Foreign Affairs, "Summary of the Environment Catastrophe Caused by the Cyanide Pollution to the River Tisza," 21 February 2000 [hereafter cited as "Environmental Catastrophe"].

16 World Wildlife Fund, "The Biggest Ever Freshwater Disaster in Central and Eastern Europe," 9 February 2000. http://wwf.panda.org/?2064/ The-biggest-ever-freshwater-disaster-in-Central-and-Eastern-Europe.

17 "Environmental Catastrophe."

18 Simon Mann, David Reardon, and Mark Metherell, "Warnings Ignored before Cyanide Spill," *Sydney Morning Herald*, 11 February 2000.

19 "Third Pollution Spill from Romania Detected in Hungary," *Agence France Presse*, 15 March 2000.

20 Tim Treadgold, "Are We Giving Our Best to the World's Mining Industry," *Courier Mail*, 12 February 2000.

21 "Baia Mare Task Force Report."

22 See "UNEP/OCHA Assessment Mission."

23 David Austin and Anna Alberini, "An Analysis of the Preventive Effect of Environmental Liability: Environmental Liability, Location and Emission Substitution: Evidence from the Toxic Release Inventory," study commissioned

by DG ENV of the European Commission, 30 October 2001. http://ec.europa. eu/environment/legal/liability/pdf/preventive_final.pdf.

24 Thomas M. Franck, *Fairness in International Law and Institutions* (Oxford: Clarendon Press, 1995), 41–46.

25 "Hungary Admits No Restitution Accord after Romania Cyanide Spill," *Agence France Presse*, 9 February 2000.

26 See opinion of the Hungarian Creators and Thinkers Independent Expert Society, in Alexander Szakats, "Cross Border Pollution: Private International Law Problems in Claiming Compensation," *Victoria University of Wellington Law Review* 32 (2000): 613.

27 Schwabach, "From Schweizerhalle to Baia Mare," 445–47.

28 "Convention on Cooperation for the Protection and Sustainable Use of the Danube," Sofia, 29 June 1994 (in force 22 October 1998) [hereafter cited as "Danube Convention"]. http://ec.europa.eu/world/agreements/downloadFile. do?fullText=yes&treatyTransId=1406.

29 Szakats, "Cross Border Pollution," 613–14.

30 Trevor Marshallsea, "Hungary Moves to Freeze Mines Assets," *AAP Newsfeed*, 24 February 2000.

31 Szakats, "Cross Border Pollution," 619.

32 "Australia Shamed by Cyanide Spill," *The Mercury (Hobart)*, 10 February 2000.

33 Adreinne Lowth, "Hungarian Cyanide Spill Prompts Calls for Tougher Laws," *Australian Broadcasting Corporation*, 9 February 2000.

34 "Romanian Cyanide Spill a European Catastrophe," 10 February 2000.

35 Trevor Marshallsea, "Soccer Fans Vent Anger at Australia over Cyanide Spill," *AAP Newsfeed*, 24 February 2000.

36 "Protest Outside Australian Embassy over Cyanide Spill," *Agence France Presse*, 25 February 2000.

37 "Australian Government Meets Hungarian Concerns over Cyanide Spill," *AAP Newsfeed*, 18 February 2000.

38 "Cyanide Pollution: Australia Promises Technical Assistance," *Hungarian News Agency*, 14 March 2000.

39 "Hungary Lashes Esmeralda."

40 Mann, Reardon, and Metherell, "Warnings Ignored."

41 "Hungary Lashes Esmeralda."

42 "Hungary to Seek Damages from Mine," *Sydney Morning Herald*, 11 February 2000.

43 "Esmeralda Expects to Escape Liability," *Australian Broadcasting Corporation*, 11 February 2000.

44 "Romanian Cyanide Spill."

45 "Hungary Lashes Esmeralda."

46 "Romania Won't Pay for Damages in Cyanide Spill," *Ottawa Citizen*, 2 February 2000.

47 Guzelova and Wright, "EU Assesses Damage."

48 "Cyanide Spill 'Exaggerated,'" *The Daily Telegraph*, 15 February 2000.

49 "Romania Blocks."

50 "Romania Admits Responsibility for Spill," *Reuters News Service*, 17 February 2000.

51 World Wildlife Fund, "WWF Demands Immediate Government Action on Toxic Spill," 14 February 2000. http://img.static.reliefweb.int/report/romania/ wwf-demands-immediate-government-action-toxic-spill.

52 World Wildlife Fund–Hungary et al., "The Ecological Catastrophe of the River Tisza: Declaration of Hungarian Non-Governmental Organizations on Occasion of the Visit of the EU Environmental Commissionaire to the Region," 17 February 2000.
53 Trevor Sykes, "A Fishy Side to the Great Hungarian Cyanide Hysteria," *Australian Financial Review*, 12 February 2000.
54 Simon Mann, "Death of a River," *Sydney Morning Herald*, 12 February 2000.
55 "Dead Fish Not Due to Cyanide: Romanian Official," *Agence France Presse*, 17 February 2000.
56 "UNEP/OCHA Assessment Mission," 44.
57 Ibid., 45.
58 Ibid., 46.
59 "Romanian Cyanide Spill."
60 "Romania Blames Bleach, Not Cyanide, for Fish Kill," *The Weekend Australian*, 19 February 2000.
61 Alison Mutler, "Romania Acknowledges Magnitude of Environmental Pollution," *Associated Press*, 17 February 2000.
62 "EU Task Force to Look into Danube Cyanide Spill," *Agence France Presse*, 17 February 2000.
63 "Pollution of the Danube: EU Commission Intervenes Following Cyanide Spill," *Europe Environment*, 22 February 2000.
64 "Environmental Catastrophe."
65 "Hungary: Romanian Minister Regrets Recent Pollution Incidents," *MTI News Agency*, 13 March 2000.
66 "Third Pollution Spill from Romania Detected in Hungary."
67 Thorpe, "Trickery Suspected."
68 "Hungary Reserves Right to Sue Romania over Cyanide Pollution," *Agence France Presse*, 18 July 2000.
69 "Baia Mare Task Force Report," 9–10.
70 Ibid., 30.
71 Friends of the Earth Hungary, "One Year after Romanian Cyanide Disaster, Not Enough Is Done," press release, 20 January 2001.
72 Thorpe, "Trickery Suspected."
73 "Danube Task Force's Mandate Extended to New Pollution Incident," *European Information Service*, 22 March 2000.
74 "Australian Company Cannot Pay 100m Dollar Cyanide Claim-Administrator," *Agence France Presse*, 15 March 2001.
75 Mark Drummond, "Rising from a Corporate Graveyard," *The West Australian*, 16 October 2004.
76 Gabriel Ronay, "Court Says Gold-Mining Firm Is Still Using Cyanide That Killed Hungarian Wildlife," *Sunday Herald*, 9 December 2001.
77 "Next Hearing in Aurul-Transgold Lawsuit Set for September 9," *MTI Econews*, 18 June 2002.
78 "Court Says."
79 "Romanian Gold Mine to Continue Production, Despite Hungarian Court Order," *Associated Press International*, 4 May 2005.
80 "Budapest Court Deems Transgold Responsible for Cyanide Poisoning," *MIT Econews*, 8 May 2006.

81   Mark Mentiplay, "Romanian Gold Mine Put to Rest," *WA Business News*, 25 February 2006.

82   John Phaceas, "Winter May Be Last Straw for Cyanide Spill Mine," *The West Australian*, 10 February 2006.

83   Peter Bodo and Robert Nemeskeri, *Emergency Preparedness Plan: Non-Governmental Organizations in Case of Pollution Accidents* (Szentendre, Hungary: Regional Environmental Center for Central and Eastern Europe, December 2001).

84   Marion Marmorat, "Local Momentum for Global Governance: The Management of Transboundary Pollution," *Health and Environment Reports*, no. 1 (2008): 42.

85   Romania did join in May 2003. United Nations Economic Commission for Europe (UNECE), "Convention on the Transboundary Effect of International Accidents," Helsinki, 17 March 1992 (in force 19 April 2000) [hereafter cited as "Industrial Accidents Convention"]. http://www.unece.org/fileadmin/DAM/env/documents/2013/TEIA/1321013_ENG_Web_New_ENG.pdf.

86   Ibid., Articles 3, 4, 6–12.

87   European Commission, "Commission Proposes to Tighten Rules on Prevention of Industrial Accidents," *Press Release*, 11 December 2001.

88   Ata Akcil, "A New Global Approach of Cyanide Management: International Cyanide Management Code for the Manufacture, Transport, and Use of Cyanide in the Production of Gold," *Mineral Processing and Extractive Metal Review* 31 (2011): 134–49.

89   Organisation for Economic Co-operation and Development, "Guidelines for Multinational Enterprises: Revision 2000," (Paris: OECD, 2000) [hereafter cited as "OECD Guidelines"]. http://www.oecd.org/investment/mne/1922428.pdf.

90   Tracy Sutherland, "Somehow Someone Must Pay," *The Australian*, 31 March 2000.

91   "OECD Guidelines," 22–24.

92   "Somehow Someone Must Pay."

93   Australian Senate, "Corporate Code of Conduct Bill 2000-C2004b01333," 6 September 2000 [hereafter cited as "Corporate Code of Conduct"].

94   Ibid., Sect. 17, 18.

95   Geoff Evans, "Where Giants May Tread, Rumblings Will Follow," *Sydney Morning Herald*, 2 November 2001, 12.

96   Stephen Stec et al., "Transboundary Environmental Governance and the Baia Mare Cyanide Spill," *Review of Central and Eastern European Law* 27 (2001): 639–91.

97   European Environmental Bureau, "EEB Analysis of the White Paper on Environmental Liability," February 2000. http://www.eeb.org/publication/2000/white_paper_on_environmental_lia.html.

98   For an overview of the history of the directive, see Geert van Calster and Leonie Reins, "The ELD's Background," in *The EU Environmental Liability Directive: A Commentary*, ed. Lucas Bergkamp and Barbara Goldsmith (Oxford: Oxford University Press), 9–30.

99   "Cyanide Spill Prompts Swiss Call for Polluters to Pay," *Environment News Service*, 17 February 2000.

100 UNECE, "The Protocol on Civil Liability and Compensation for Damage Caused by the Transboundary Effects of Industrial Accidents on Transboundary Waters," Kiev, 21 May 2003 (not yet in force), [hereafter cited as "Protocol on Civil Liability"]. http://www.unece.org/fileadmin/DAM/env/civil-liability/documents/protocol_e.pdf.

101 See, for example, comments by Laszlo Miklos, Slovakia's Minister for the Environment and chair of the UNEP's Governing Council, in "Government Meeting on Responsibility for Transboundary Pollution," *Hungarian News Agency*, 24 March 2000.

102 *Tatar v. Romania*, HUDOC case-law (2009).

103 European Court of Human Rights, "Tatar v. Romania," 27 January 2009, No. 67021/01. http://hudoc.echr.coe.int/fre?i=003-2615810-2848789.

104 Marmorat, "Local Momentum," 13.

105 Ibid., 54–55.

106 Hungary's Foreign Minister János Martoni recognized publicly that "there are factors of uncertainty" in the field of international environmental law. See "Hungary Reserves Right."

107 Cecilia Jamasmie, "Gabriel Resources Uncertain About Future of Romanian Gold Project," *Mining.com*, 14 March 2014.

108 Szabolcs Rostas, "Mining Company Sues Baia Mare in Response for the Town Banning Cyanide Mining Technology," *Budapest Telegraph*, 22 May 2013.

5
MOX at Sellafield

Introduction

In December 2001, the British government authorized British Nuclear Fuels Ltd. (BNFL) to begin commissioning a Mixed Oxide (MOX) nuclear fuel plant at Sellafield, North Cumbria. The start-up of the Sellafield MOX Plant (SMP) was an important milestone in an ongoing dispute between the United Kingdom and the Republic of Ireland, located just 112 miles across the Irish Sea, over nuclear activities at Sellafield. Opponents feared not only the potential for catastrophic accidents during shipments of nuclear materials to and from the new plant but also significant increases in the chronic radioactive pollution they believed Sellafield already generated. The risk of terrorism, enhanced by the dramatic attacks in the United States only three months earlier, heightened public concern. The United Kingdom faced opposition from not only Ireland but also other states bordering the North Sea, as well as from nations from South Africa to South America and the Caribbean whose waters would be transited by ships carrying nuclear cargoes.

No injury clearly traceable to Sellafield had been caused, certainly not by a plant that had yet to begin operating. Ireland was not in the position to bring a claim for damages similar to that which Hungary at least seemed to be after the Baia Mare accident. The issue was the risk posed by future MOX operations. How that risk should be evaluated, by whom, and what impact that calculation should have were questions at the heart of Ireland's objections. The fear that nuclear materials headed to or produced by the plant might find their way into the hands of terrorists brought another form of uncertainty. Even if the chances of diversion were small, the results could be catastrophic. To opponents this suggested that the entire MOX operation should be considered "ultrahazardous," requiring an unusually high level of UK responsibility.

The MOX dispute took place at the crossroads of a number of different international regimes. Several offered Ireland the opportunity to have its complaint heard by an international tribunal, and Ireland did initiate three separate legal proceedings against Britain. The MOX dispute thus reflects two trends in international environmental law that have recently become more pronounced: potential competition among international regimes and the increased involvement of courts in international environmental disputes.[1] In taking an adjudicative approach, Ireland was forced to frame its arguments around issues each of the courts had jurisdiction to hear. It also had to recognize the special position of the European Union. Both Ireland and the United Kingdom were EU members, and the European Union had its own legal rules and adjudicative procedures that the dispute would bring into play.

This chapter analyzes the Sellafield MOX dispute focusing on how participants dealt with the risk that Ireland claimed MOX operations posed. It explains the rationale behind the UK decision to build the plant at Sellafield and describes the intersecting regimes in which that decision was debated. It then examines how Ireland tried to invoke what it felt were the United Kingdom's procedural responsibilities to force it to respond to Irish fears about the project's potential impact. While the MOX plant opened despite these concerns, the dispute raised important questions about the British environmental assessment process and the information the United Kingdom should provide to its neighbors.

The Context

The transportation, use, and disposal of nuclear materials raise some of the most divisive questions of international environmental policy. Some consider nuclear technology so inherently dangerous that it should be banned; others see the development of nuclear power as a cost-effective way to make the transition away from carbon-emitting sources of electricity. The MOX plant dispute began during international negotiations that would lead to the Kyoto Protocol, in which states, including Ireland and the United Kingdom, would agree to targets and timetables to reduce carbon emissions.

The United Kingdom's nuclear program has been supported by a succession of British governments dating back to the 1940s. Both its purpose and form have changed over time. After World War II and the US decision to end British participation in the American nuclear program, the British government decided to focus its nuclear activities at Sellafield, a relatively less populated area in Cumbria along the northwest coast of England. Formerly the site of an explosives factory, the facility then known as Windscale was first used to develop British nuclear weapons. Nuclear reprocessing was begun there in the early 1950s, both to extract plutonium for weapons development and to conserve uranium, which was expensive and in short supply.

The first British nuclear reactors capable of producing electricity, the Magnox reactors, were relatively inefficient. The spent fuel they generated

Map 5.1 This map locates the Sellafield facility on the western coast of England, indicating its proximity to Ireland and the Isle of Man. It also shows the Irish Sea, through which ships carrying nuclear cargoes would sail to and from Sellafield.

was taken to Windscale, and the resulting plutonium was stored at the site for use in the fast breeder reactors then being developed. Although the United Kingdom ended its fast breeder program in 1992, the waste remained, becoming part of the problem the MOX plant was built to solve. The United Kingdom shifted to an advanced gas-cooled reactor (AGR), relying on uranium oxide for fuel rather than uranium metal, which thus required changes in the reprocessing process. When delays in construction of the new AGR reactors created excess reprocessing capacity at Sellafield, the British entered into contracts with foreign companies to reprocess and, normally, to repatriate their waste. The trade in nuclear materials thus became another controversial dimension of Sellafield operations. In 1971, BNFL was established as a public-owned company, still under the direct authority of the United Kingdom Atomic Energy Authority (UKAEA), but now with a more clearly commercial orientation.[2]

MOX technology was initially seen as offering a commercially viable way of recycling nuclear waste.[3] Mixed oxide fuel is produced by combining small amounts of plutonium with depleted uranium oxide to form pellets, which are sealed in fuel rods and made into assemblies to be shipped to nuclear reactors. The technology was appealing because it recycled reclaimed plutonium, limiting the amount that must be stored or disposed of, as well as reducing the demand for raw uranium. MOX fuel was also considered easier and safer to transport and a lucrative source of foreign exchange.[4]

The fuel was first intended for fast breeder reactors, but, as the British discovered, technical problems slowed their commercial development.[5] The use of MOX was thus restricted to light water reactors (LWRs) as an alternative to low-enriched uranium. Given the limited number of reactors capable of using MOX, the relatively lower cost of uranium, and the fact that four other countries (Belgium, France, Japan, and Russia) were making MOX fuel at the time the Sellafield plant was to open, a key issue was how viable the MOX industry and the Sellafield plant really were.[6]

A MOX "Demonstration Facility," with an annual output of only 8 tons of MOX fuel, was built at Sellafield in 1993. Since the fuel was usable only in LWRs, of which the United Kingdom had none, any production was destined for export, adding another international dimension to Sellafield operations. A year later, the Thermal Oxide Reprocessing Plant (THORP) was constructed, significantly increasing Sellafield's reprocessing capacity and providing the ability to recycle waste from both AGR and LWR facilities. Most foreign-generated waste was being directed to THORP, and its continued operation contributed to the controversy surrounding Sellafield. Because THORP produced the plutonium used to make MOX fuel, it became associated with the MOX plant and the dangers it was believed to represent.

In 1992, BNFL applied to build a much larger MOX production facility at Sellafield with a maximum output of 120 tons per year. While the UK government had the primary responsibility for authorizing construction of a facility being built on British territory, it did so as a member of the European Union and as a party to the Treaty Establishing the European Atomic Energy Community (EURATOM).[7] Unlike the Baia Mare and turbot cases, where the European Union was less directly involved in a regulatory capacity, here Ireland was also an EU member. EU institutions had a responsibility to protect Irish interests and a potential role in helping two members resolve their differences. The EURATOM agreement and existing EU legislation required the British to share information about the MOX project with the European Commission. However, EU nuclear policy was in a state of development, and members disagreed about the safety of nuclear energy. Environmentalists worried that EURATOM's history of promoting nuclear power might compromise the European Union's ability to provide effective oversight to the extent that EU treaties gave EURATOM regulatory power. The entire issue of nuclear power had become more important after the 1986 Chernobyl accident, especially since the organization now faced membership applications from Eastern European states with Soviet-era reactors very reminiscent of the one that had melted down in what was then the Ukrainian SSR.[8]

The dispute came at a time when general standards for assessment and information-sharing were being negotiated within the United Nations Economic Commission for Europe (UNECE), rules later implemented through EU legislation. The 1991 Espoo Convention established procedures requiring a member under whose jurisdiction "proposed activities" were "likely to cause significant adverse transboundary impact" to prepare a detailed environmental impact assessment consistent with convention standards before authorizing the activity.[9] Although Ireland had not ratified the Espoo Convention at the time when it took legal action against the United Kingdom, both the United Kingdom and the European Union had done so. Even more recent was the 1998 UNECE Convention on Access to Information, Public Participation in Decision-Making and Access to Justice in Environmental Matters (hereafter referred to as the Aarhus Convention), which Ireland had also signed but not ratified. This agreement required states to establish procedures to keep members of the public fully informed about activities that "may significantly affect the environment" and to ensure that they had an opportunity to participate in the regulatory process.[10] Although neither agreement was formally binding, both could be argued to be evidence of customary state practice that the United Kingdom was expected to follow.[11]

The semi-enclosed nature of the Irish Sea and the proximity of Ireland to Sellafield added a law of the sea dimension to what became the Irish legal claim.[12] Ships traveling to and from Sellafield were not expected to travel through Irish waters, so the right of coastal states to control the passage of hazardous ships was not the focus of the Irish complaint. Yet Irish concerns about the possible radioactive contamination of the Irish Sea, either from normal operations or from an accident at Sellafield or on a ship in transit, provided a basis to invoke the 1982 United Nations Convention on the Law of the Sea (LOSC),[13] which had come into force in 1994. Beyond the substantive treaty provisions that, Ireland could argue, the United Kingdom had violated, the convention provided compulsory dispute settlement mechanisms through which legal claims could be made.

Relevant rules and a process of arbitration were also available in the 1992 OSPAR Convention for the Protection of the Marine Environment of the North-East Atlantic.[14] This convention brought together and extended the pattern of cooperation developed in two earlier regional agreements dealing with marine dumping and land-based sources of pollution.[15] With its focus on environmental protection and explicit embrace of both the precautionary and polluter-pays principles,[16] the OSPAR Convention provided an attractive basis for Irish objections to operations at Sellafield. It also created a commission, just beginning work at the time of the MOX dispute, to which Ireland could bring its concerns.

With so many intersecting regimes, it is important to identify two that were not of immediate relevance in the MOX dispute. The Basel Convention on the Control of Transboundary Movements of Hazardous Waste specifically exempted nuclear materials from the wastes subject to its system of prior, informed consent,[17] the understanding being that those substances would be regulated on a global level by the International Atomic Energy Agency (IAEA). While the Chernobyl accident had prompted the IAEA to develop agreements covering notification and international assistance in the case of nuclear accidents, its 1994 Convention on Nuclear Safety[18] offered no substantive rules Ireland could attempt to use here and nothing more than a process of consultation in the case of disputes.[19]

The Dispute

At Ireland's request, BNFL prepared and submitted an environmental impact assessment (EIA) for the new MOX plant, even though an EIA would not have been required by British law if the discharges coming from the facility would have minimal impact.[20] The project was approved, construction began in 1994, and the plant was finished in 1996. However, commissioning of the SMP was delayed for five years as the United Kingdom took two steps required under EU law before the plant could begin operating. The first was to provide the European Commission with data on whether the plant would "result in the radioactive contamination of the water, soil, or airspace of another Member State" as required by the EUR-ATOM treaty.[21] On 11 February 1997, the Commission issued its opinion that neither normal operations nor an accident at the plant would result in discharges likely to contaminate Ireland.[22] The second required an analysis of whether the economic benefits to be derived from the SMP outweighed any risks it might pose. Since it had already been determined that any additional environmental risks were minimal, the focus was exclusively on economic aspects of the MOX operation. The UKAEA engaged in five rounds of consultations, concluding on 3 October 2001, that operating the MOX plant was economically justified. A commission opinion concurred. In late December, the United Kingdom gave its formal approval.

Ireland's objections to the SMP focused on not only the plant but also the environmental risks posed by transportation of nuclear materials to and from Sellafield.[23] Even though the fuel rods would be transported in heavy casks, if the containers were to be lost at sea they could corrode, "releasing high level radioactivity into the ocean . . . (with) devastating effects on fisheries and on human health."[24] Similar concerns were voiced about the potential loss of MOX fuel on return voyages as a result of accident or direct attack.[25] What made transporting MOX more controversial than other hazardous cargoes was the threat posed by the nuclear weapons that terrorist organizations might be able to build, using hijacked nuclear material.[26] Ireland also argued that the normal operation of the MOX plant would result in discharges of radioactive waste, exacerbating an already existing threat to the Irish Sea, which it termed "among the most radioactively polluted seas in the world."[27] While pollution emanating from Sellafield dated back to the 1950s, the SMP threatened to produce what Ireland considered an unacceptably high level of environmental damage.[28]

Irish arguments against Sellafield were generally framed in political terms until 2001. The development of nuclear energy for peaceful purposes was a lawful, if controversial, activity, one linked to important national security interests, and here taking place on territory over which the United Kingdom had acknowledged sovereign rights. As late as 1994, one frustrated legal observer (an obvious project opponent) concluded, "current domestic and international legal systems are unequal to the task of effectively regulating the nuclear industry and its insidious emissions. . . . Sellafield's fate will ultimately be decided in Whitehall, not in the ICJ, the ECJ, or the High Court."[29] However, political forces in Ireland and beyond continued to make

Sellafield and the SMP a priority for the Irish government and ultimately encouraged it to make a more direct legal challenge.

The first factor supporting a strong Irish stand was the virtual unanimity of opposition to Sellafield among Irish political groups. This was an easy issue, since Ireland derived very little benefit from Sellafield.[30] A 1957 fire at a Windscale reactor had released radioactivity later associated with increased birth defects in Ireland, and popular opposition to nuclear energy had led to a major public demonstration against a proposed Irish nuclear plant in the late 1970s. After the 1986 Chernobyl accident, the Irish Dáil unanimously passed a resolution calling for Sellafield's closure. If Sellafield posed any internal political danger for the Irish government it was the risk of appearing too soft.[31] Irish citizens fought a ten-year battle against the government in Irish courts for not taking more decisive action to prevent the THORP reprocessing plant from being built,[32] and Irish politicians of all political affiliations joined anti-Sellafield demonstrations.[33]

Second, Sellafield had become a rallying point for NGOs. Greenpeace was among the most visible, bringing together groups from Ireland, England, Scotland, and Wales, and working with Japanese anti-nuclear groups to oppose MOX trade.[34] The Norwegian-based Bellona Foundation used scientific studies exposing the effect of BNFL activities at Sellafield to put pressure on the company and UK authorities.[35] NGOs generally supported the Irish position, although they did not face the government's political constraints. When Greenpeace sent the *Rainbow Warrior* to the Irish Sea in 2002 to protest a shipment of MOX fuel, Irish leaders, including Prime Minister Bertie Ahern, were quick to visit the ship when it docked in Dublin.[36] Less welcome was a Greenpeace call to use the Irish navy to prevent UK ships from entering Irish waters, a far more provocative step that the government was not prepared to take.[37]

A third factor bolstering the Irish position was the increasing assertiveness of other states in the region. In building its legal case against the British plan, Ireland cited growing opposition from Nordic countries to increased levels of radioactivity in the Irish and North Seas, as well as from coastal states along MOX sea routes.[38]

The picture in the United Kingdom was more complicated. The government of Prime Minister Tony Blair continued to support nuclear power, a position given a stronger environmental dimension by concern about global climate change and the desire to reduce British dependence on fossil fuels.[39] Employment at Sellafield was a politically significant issue, at least in Cumbria. As the economic challenges facing expanded MOX trade became more evident, hopes for significant foreign exchange earnings dimmed. However, there was still the £473 million already invested in building the SMP, a reality any government would find difficult to ignore. Perhaps most important was the question of what to do with the plutonium and other nuclear waste accumulating at Sellafield.

On the other hand, the domestic case against the MOX plant was growing. In addition to those who shared Irish environmental concerns, there was increasing doubt that the plant could ever become profitable. A 1997 report for the Institute for Science and International Security challenged the economic viability of the entire nuclear processing program, arguing that the time had come for Britain to focus instead on long-term storage and repatriation of foreign waste.[40] Just as the SMP was authorized to begin operations, the *Economist* concluded, "Irish objections aside, the economics of MOX make no sense."[41] Despite the government's apparent unity in responding to Irish complaints, a 2004 investigation by *The Guardian* revealed that there had actually been a spirited internal debate over whether to proceed with the plant. Described was a process that put too much faith in overly optimistic estimates of future MOX orders and ignored serious concern that the MOX plant would become what the paper termed a "financial white elephant."[42] In 2011, former environment minister Michael Meacher indicated that he had consistently opposed the project as "throwing further good money after bad" and had been overruled by a prime minister "too easily bamboozled by industry lobbying."[43]

The 1999 discovery that data about a shipment of MOX fuel to Japan from BNFL's MOX Demonstration Facility (MDF) had been falsified created a political environment in which it was easier for the Irish government to proceed with its legal case against the United Kingdom. Ireland's subsequent claims made specific reference to the incident as evidence of BNFL's failure to follow safe operating practices. The MDF was closed and BNFL ordered to make changes before it could reopen. Although there was no evidence that the MOX fuel was actually faulty, the Japanese demanded that BNFL take back the MOX shipment. With Japanese customers threatening to stop further purchases of MOX[44] and German and Swiss companies suspending orders, BNFL announced a major management reorganization.[45] This came at a particularly sensitive time for the British government, which was still engaged in consultations to demonstrate the economic viability of the much larger SMP. In July 2000, BNFL agreed to take back the MOX and to pay £40 million in compensation to the Kansai Electric Power Company.[46]

The agreement rekindled the argument over the safety of maritime nuclear cargoes. The Third United Nations Conference on the Law of the Sea had worked for over ten years to negotiate an appropriate balance between the principles of free navigation and the right of coastal states to protect their maritime interests in what became a series of different zones of ocean space. Unfortunately for those advocating enhanced coastal state authority over ships with "ultrahazardous" cargoes, the LOSC effectively limits their control except in the band of internal waters closest to the coast. Even in a coastal state's territorial sea, foreign ships enjoy a right of "innocent passage," which the coastal state cannot normally suspend unless there is an "act of willful and serious pollution."[47] Simply transiting the zone, even with dangerous nuclear materials, would not violate this standard. Moving seaward into the exclusive economic zone and the high seas, the extent of coastal state jurisdiction becomes even more limited.[48] The International Maritime Organization (IMO) and IAEA had been working to strengthen rules governing shipments of nuclear cargoes, but many coastal states, especially those situated on key international shipping channels, did not believe they went far enough.[49] Among the most contentious issues was that of "prior notification," since coastal states had an understandable desire to know when dangerous cargoes were heading their way. However, shipping companies, backed by flag states, could also reasonably claim the need for tight security to protect against potential terrorist attacks.

The ships chosen to make the voyage had been involved in several earlier disputes. Long before leaving Japan, they became the target of criticism from nations whose leaders feared that the ships' undisclosed sea route would take them close to their shores. The ships left Japan in June 2002, arriving in England two months later amid demonstrations led by the *Rainbow Warrior*. Assured by BNFL that the ships would not enter Irish waters, Ireland used ships and aircraft to simply monitor their voyage.[50] Despite the furor, by the time the MOX shipment had been returned to Sellafield, the British government had approved the SMP.

Ireland's decision to add a legal dimension to its opposition to Sellafield was likely the result of growing frustration with British regulatory procedures, domestic political pressures, and new opportunities provided by the entry into force of the LOSC and OSPAR Conventions. However, Irish leaders recognized this to be an important step. Ireland was not simply making legal claims against the United Kingdom; it was going to court against a neighboring state with which it had a complex and critical relationship. As Prime Minister Ahern later told the Dáil, "These cases have been the most significant legal actions taken by Ireland. . . . They represent the government's absolute commitment to ensuring that our rights under these conventions in relation to Sellafield and its operations are vindicated."[51] Legal action also carried risks, not the least of which was the possibility that negative decisions could undercut Ireland's political position opposing Sellafield.

Ireland's preferred legal strategy would have been to challenge all aspects of Sellafield's operations from the THORP reprocessing plant to the construction of the SMP, if its ultimate goal was to shut down Sellafield as the government insisted.[52] However, Ireland needed a court that could hear such a broad claim. In theory, the matter could be referred to the International Court of Justice (ICJ) with Ireland's case based on alleged violations of both treaty obligations and customary international law. Unfortunately, Ireland had no basis for invoking the Court's compulsory jurisdiction, and the British government had made clear that it had no intention of litigating the dispute there.[53] More promising might have been to work within the framework of EU law with the possibility of taking the matter before the European Court of Justice (ECJ).[54] The Irish cabinet considered this strategy but did not pursue it,[55] apparently concerned that the European Union would require evidence of a level of damage coming from Sellafield that Ireland could not provide.[56] In addition, the European Commission had supported the United Kingdom's assessment that SMP operations would not harm Ireland, as well as the economic justification for the plant, and seemed unlikely to be sympathetic to the Irish position.[57]

Instead, Ireland decided to bring almost simultaneous claims within the narrower frameworks provided by the OSPAR and LOSC Conventions. Ireland tailored its complaints specifically to the issues each tribunal could address. While the history of Irish concerns about Sellafield was part of the broader legal context, Irish arguments focused specifically on British plans to open the MOX plant and the failure of British authorities to take Irish interests into account. Ireland argued that the United Kingdom had violated accepted rules of international procedure in its evaluation of the plant's likely impact, the information it shared with Ireland, and its process of consultation with those potentially affected. That serious material consequences could result was part of the overall claim, but Ireland's argument was focused on preventing future pollution rather than seeking compensation for past injury.

Ireland filed its first action against the United Kingdom in June 2001 under the terms of the OSPAR Convention, which allows parties to bring a claim involving the "interpretation or application of the Convention" to an ad hoc arbitral tribunal created under the Permanent Court of Arbitration (PCA).[58] Ireland argued that the British had failed to provide information Ireland had requested concerning the economic viability of the MOX plant in violation of the "access to information" obligation found in Article 9 of the convention. On 16 October 2001, Ireland brought a second claim, this to be heard by an Annex VII arbitral tribunal formed under LOSC's compulsory dispute-settlement provisions. Ireland raised a series of objections to the United Kingdom's decision to commission the MOX plant, arguing that it had breached procedural obligations imposed by the convention and had approved a facility whose operations represented a significant threat to the Irish Sea. Since it would take time for the tribunal to begin hearing the case, Ireland asked the International Tribunal on the Law of the Sea (ITLOS) to order the United Kingdom to suspend the authorization of the MOX plant, a request the ITLOS denied in December. While the cases went forward before both the OSPAR and Annex VII tribunals, the EU Commission began "infringement proceedings" against Ireland for failing to resolve its differences with the United Kingdom within the European Union, a case that would ultimately reach the European Court of Justice. A battle within and between competing courts was underway.

Legal Issue: Regulating Risk

Although it would take different forms before different tribunals, Ireland's argument against the MOX plant was ultimately based on questions of risk. How much of a threat did the facility and maritime traffic to and from Sellafield pose to Ireland? Had the United Kingdom done all that was required to assess and weigh this risk in its regulatory decisions? Procedurally, what Ireland was challenging was the adequacy of the United Kingdom's environmental impact assessment process and its level of cooperation in sharing information and consulting with Irish authorities. The problem was compounded by the fact that the risk was exposure to ionizing radiation. Questions persisted about whether there was any safe level of exposure, particularly since the effects of radiation might not be evident for years. Moreover, the most serious potential effects would likely result from accident or deliberate attack, and the likelihood of either was extremely difficult to predict. The problem was how to develop these concerns in ways that each of the tribunals could consider.

Ireland faced a particular challenge before the OSPAR tribunal. OSPAR had an environmental mandate, and with Ireland's support had been working to control radioactivity levels in the waters covered by the convention. However, because the United Kingdom had exercised its right to opt out of OSPAR restrictions on dumping low- and intermediate-level nuclear waste, Ireland was unable to use the OSPAR arbitral process to directly attack the British reprocessing operations at Sellafield.[59] In introducing its claim, Ireland took the opportunity to provide extensive background on the problems at Sellafield—assertions the United Kingdom dismissed as "irrelevant to the dispute"[60]—and, in the four-volume memorial it submitted as part of its legal case against the UK, acknowledged the need to focus on the MOX plant. Its goal was to show that the British had violated the OSPAR Convention by failing to include information redacted from the public versions of two reports prepared by independent experts hired to assess the MOX plant's economic feasibility.[61] The SMP's profitability was clearly not Ireland's primary concern. However, the European Union's "economic justification" rules required that, when ionizing radiation was involved, even low levels of potential risk needed to be balanced against the benefits the activity would produce.[62] The justification process had become particularly controversial, since the analysis had not included the £473 million spent in constructing the plant in its cost-benefit analysis, treating the finished plant as a "sunk cost."[63] Given the substantial doubt even in Britain about the economic viability of the MOX industry, it was an issue that resonated politically.

The United Kingdom argued that the tribunal lacked jurisdiction, because Article 9 was never intended to give any person a "direct right to receive information," but simply required parties to set up an internal process to disclose it.[64] Moreover, much of the information Ireland requested was irrelevant to OSPAR because it focused on economic factors relating to MOX production, not on any threat to the marine environment. For the British, their earlier environmental impact assessment, accepted by the EU Commission and not challenged at the time by Ireland, made clear that the SMP posed no meaningful environmental risk.[65]

In its July 2003 decision, the OSPAR tribunal took a middle path, recognizing Ireland's right to information under the convention but not the specific information Ireland had requested. The tribunal rejected the British argument that Article 9 simply required the parties to set up a process for releasing information; instead, an "outcome of result" was required.[66] However, the tribunal did not accept Ireland's argument supporting a broad reading of the types of information that must be disclosed, or that the tribunal should interpret the meaning of Article 9 in light of goals and obligations developed in other agreements like the Aarhus Convention. For the tribunal to take this approach "would transform it into an unqualified and comprehensive jurisdictional regime" that there was no reason to believe the parties to the OSPAR Convention ever intended to create.[67] The tribunal held that the information must relate to an activity that "affects adversely" the "state of the maritime area," which the requested information did not.[68]

The LOSC dispute settlement process offered Ireland an opportunity to discuss more directly the risk posed by MOX operations, although the challenges posed in the various phases of the case differed somewhat. In approaching the ITLOS for an order to suspend authorization of the MOX plant, Ireland had to convince the court that there was a *prima facie* basis for presuming that the Annex VII tribunal would have jurisdiction. Moreover, it had to show that provisional measures were needed to "to prevent serious harm to the marine environment" until the case could be decided[69]—in short, that there was risk of damage that was both real and immediate. In order to demonstrate the LOSC violations that were the basis of its case, Ireland argued that by failing to notify Irish authorities and provide them with appropriate information about the operation of the MOX plant[70] and by preparing an inadequate environmental impact assessment,[71] the United Kingdom had not cooperated to protect the Irish Sea. Ireland also invoked the precautionary principle, a "recognized rule of customary international law," arguing that the British "must apply caution, and take preventive measures even where there is no conclusive evidence of a causal relationship between the inputs and the effects."[72] Ireland claimed that the principle was relevant to its case not only on the merits—thus giving the court *prima facie* jurisdiction—but also to explain why the court should see this as an urgent matter justifying provisional measures.[73] To indicate the risks posed by MOX operations, Ireland outlined the general impact of operations at Sellafield, the particular threats posed by the proposed MOX plant, the dangers of transporting nuclear materials to and from the plant, and concerns about potential acts of terrorism. The need to impose provisional measures now was based on the imminence of the United Kingdom's decision to "release plutonium within the MOX plant . . . [which] will become contaminated and releases into the environment, including the marine environment of the Irish Sea, will occur. Such releases are irreversible."[74]

The United Kingdom challenged the court's jurisdiction on several grounds. Most important was the claim that the issues raised by Ireland were more appropriately handled through OSPAR or by the European Union, which had "exclusive jurisdiction" over key matters in dispute.[75] The British also asserted that there was no "urgency" to justify imposing provisional measures. "The only event that Ireland can identify . . . is the commissioning of the MOX Plant . . . [which] will not, even arguably, cause serious harm to the marine environment or irreparable prejudice to Ireland's rights."[76] The United Kingdom attacked Ireland's substantive arguments about the dangers posed by Sellafield and the MOX plant and defended the thoroughness of its eight-year review of the SMP proposal, using the Commission's 1997 Opinion to support its position.[77]

While denying Ireland's request for provisional measures, the ITLOS agreed that there was a *prima facie* basis for the Annex VII tribunal to assert jurisdiction. The existence of several different venues for dispute resolution should not be seen as an obstacle, since each agreement provided rights with a "separate existence," which could be enforced within that regime.[78] Given Ireland's allegations about the United Kingdom's violation of the LOSC, there was a valid basis for the Annex VII tribunal to proceed. However, the ITLOS concluded that the measures sought by Ireland were not necessary, quoting assurances given by the British that, "there will be no additional marine transports of radioactive material either to or from Sellafield as a result of the commissioning of the MOX plant . . . there will be no export of MOX fuel from the plant until summer 2002 . . . [and] there is to be no import to the THORP plant of spent nuclear fuel pursuant to contracts for conversion to the MOX plant within that period either."[79] Nonetheless, the tribunal ordered its own provisional measures, requiring the parties to "cooperate . . . and enter into consultations" to exchange information, monitor risks posed by the plant, and develop measures to prevent any pollution that might result.[80]

Ireland made its first written submission to the Annex VII tribunal in July 2002. Ireland asked the tribunal to order the British not to allow the MOX plant to operate or to permit transportation of radioactive materials to or from the plant until a "proper assessment of the environmental consequences" of these activities had taken place. Ireland also wanted assurance that the plant's operations would result in "deliberate discharge of no radioactive materials" into the Irish Sea and the development of a joint strategy to deal with possible terrorist attacks.[81]

The British argued again that they had followed all required procedures and that nothing associated with the MOX plant presented the threat Ireland suggested. The United Kingdom took its "regulatory responsibilities . . . seriously," and its actions were fully compatible with the LOSC.[82] Procedurally, the British continued to challenge the tribunal's jurisdiction to hear a case the United Kingdom believed belonged elsewhere.

With the European Commission moving ahead with infringement proceedings against Ireland, the tribunal decided in November 2003 to suspend proceedings until the European Court of Justice had time to consider the case.[83] In its Order No. 3, the tribunal held that the risk of further delay was offset by the need to have issues of EU law that were outside its purview "definitively resolved." Referring to the "considerations of mutual respect and comity which should prevail between judicial institutions," the tribunal worried that conflicting decisions would only hinder the dispute settlement process.[84] Given the new delay, Ireland asked the Annex VII tribunal for provisional measures similar to those requested of the ITLOS, but was once again turned down because it could not demonstrate that there was an "urgent and serious risk of irreparable harm."[85] The tribunal extended the ITLOS's earlier order and recommended that the parties set up an intergovernmental consultation mechanism to coordinate the work of key agencies.[86]

In 2006, the ECJ agreed with the Commission that Ireland had acted improperly in taking the dispute to the LOSC dispute settlement procedures, given the European Union's preeminent role in dealing with maritime matters between member states. In February 2007, Ireland announced that it was dropping its claim against the United Kingdom.[87]

The Resolution

None of legal proceedings brought by Ireland succeeded in achieving its stated goal of blocking the opening of the MOX plant. At least in the short run, the process of litigation may have complicated the process of reaching a diplomatic solution. The months immediately following the ITLOS proceedings were tense, since the decision permitted Ireland's case to go forward but also allowed the SMP to begin operations. The return shipment of MOX fuel from Japan created a particularly divisive political atmosphere. As late as May 2003, when proceedings at The Hague were still underway, British Energy Minister Brian Wilson blasted those in Ireland who were engaged in a "dishonest debate" about Sellafield. Wilson acknowledged that the Irish Government had "its own political pressures ... but I hope we could reach a stage where it acts as a critical friend rather than a participant in an auction of indignation." On a more positive note, Wilson suggested that the conclusion of the litigation would provide a clearer context in which to move forward. "When a line is drawn under these proceedings we will have a good basis to develop a more balanced view and more rational dialogue."[88]

After the OSPAR tribunal ruled against Ireland, Irish Environment Minister Martin Cullen still spoke of the case as setting "an important international precedent—the UK is now accountable to an international tribunal for information it must disclose to another State under OSPAR. We are closer to achieving our objectives today than we were yesterday."[89] In fact, Ireland was having more success in the OSPAR Commission, where environmentalists hoped to publicize concerns about Sellafield and put pressure on Britain. When the Commission met in 1998, British Deputy Prime Minister John Prescott had declared, "I was ashamed of Britain's record in the past but now we have shed the tag of the 'Dirty Man of Europe' and have joined the family of nations."[90] Britain pledged to reduce radioactive discharges from Sellafield.

In the days leading up to the OSPAR Commission's 2003 session in Bremen, the first ministerial meeting since 1998, leaders of Greenpeace were quick to remind the United Kingdom of Prescott's pledge. Jean McSorley claimed that Britain had "misled the public and the OSPAR countries with its hollow promises. . . . Far from shedding the 'Dirty Man of Europe' tag, Britain looks to become the deceitful man of Europe too."[91] Another Greenpeace campaigner called upon OSPAR "to act immediately and decisively to stop reprocessing. . . . Ireland and other OSPAR contracting states must . . . hold the UK to account."[92] This reflected an unrealistic assessment of OSPAR's institutional power, but the political pressure was clear. Just before the Bremen meeting, Greenpeace had released a study that found traces of Technetium-99 (TC-99) in farmed salmon from Scotland. Britain's environment secretary, Margaret Beckett, promptly asked BNFL to place a nine-month moratorium on emissions of radioactive materials from Sellafield while work continued to develop technology that would prevent future pollution.[93] Two days later, Britain agreed to phase out all radioactive discharges into the North Sea from Sellafield by 2020.[94]

With the end of the OSPAR arbitration and the suspension of the LOSC proceedings, the prospects for cooperation brightened. The new British energy minister, Stephen Timms, asserted, "We want to work constructively with Ireland on Sellafield. If there have been failures or misunderstandings in the past, let us correct them."[95] Irish representatives also sounded optimistic, arguing that even the failed OSPAR litigation had been part of a process of building the "case, piece by piece, in every available forum." The Irish goal was "at the very minimum . . . to bring an end to all discharges into the Irish Sea,"[96] a more negotiable objective than the complete closure of Sellafield that had been the stated aim of Irish policy. Environment Minister Cullen argued that the Annex VII tribunal had criticized the United Kingdom's limited cooperation and claimed, somewhat optimistically, that the tribunal's extension of the ITLOS provisional measures meant that "we now have a UN referee overseeing the implementation of Britain's obligations."[97]

What undoubtedly had changed was the role of the European Commission, which had become more assertive on issues related to Sellafield, creating discomfort for both Ireland and the United Kingdom. The Irish were unhappy with the Commission's 1997 opinion about the limited risk posed by the MOX plant and what they saw as the general inaction of the Commission in responding to the problems at Sellafield. Cullen indicated that Ireland had not supported an EU directive on environmental liability because it did not include liability for radioactive discharges into the ocean.[98] Irish Greens were even more critical of the way the European Union appeared to be promoting the nuclear industry.[99] However, British storage practices at Sellafield also became a target of Commission concern. In March 2004, the Commission threatened to take the United Kingdom to the European Court of Justice for failing to provide adequate information to EURATOM inspectors about plutonium wastes deposited in a 50-year-old storage pond. Concerns about the message its actions would send to EU applicants were not far from the surface. In the words of one EU official,

"We cannot ask the Slovaks, Czechs and Lithuanians to change things and improve their nuclear sites if then nothing is done in countries like the UK."[100] However, some British officials saw the action as punishment for the United Kingdom's lack of support for enhancing the European Union's role in regulating nuclear power,[101] while one British EU opponent termed it "an ol' fashioned power grab."[102] Whatever the true motivation, the waste storage issue provided the Commission the opportunity to appear more even-handed in its approach to Sellafield. In September 2004, the Commission rejected British waste-monitoring plans and threatened legal action, a decision welcomed by Irish politicians who hoped that this new Commission toughness might even lead to the closure of what one termed the "unsafe nuclear cesspit at Sellafield."[103]

The Commission was not prepared to go that far, but EU pressure helped create an environment that encouraged the United Kingdom to reduce tensions with Ireland. On 10 December 2004, an agreement was signed calling for regular visits to Sellafield by Irish police and representatives of the Radiological Protection Institute of Ireland (RPII). The two nations agreed to cooperate in the event of nuclear accidents or terrorist attacks, and Britain gave Ireland access to data from its nuclear monitoring system set up after the Chernobyl accident. While the Irish environment minister insisted that Sellafield's closure remained Ireland's goal,[104] both the tone and substance of relations over the Sellafield issue had improved significantly.

Post-Dispute Developments

The new spirit of cooperation would not resolve all differences. Early in 2005, an audit by the UKAEA indicated discrepancies in the amount of plutonium stored at Sellafield, with roughly 30 kilograms unaccounted for. While there was no evidence the material had been removed from the site, the report angered Irish officials. A Fine Gael spokesperson called on Prime Minister Ahern to meet with Tony Blair, saying Ireland could "not kick up enough stink" over the issue.[105] A new dispute arose in May with the revelation of a major leak of radioactive fuel that had forced the THORP reprocessing plant to be shut down. Although he had been notified of the problem in April, Ireland's new environment minister, Dick Roche, was still very concerned after he received information suggesting that the leak might have begun the previous August. "The pattern with Sellafield is well established and consistent. . . . This is something that you'd expect from Homer Simpson."[106] The incident prompted calls by the EU energy commissioner for an EU-wide mechanism to ensure nuclear safety rather than leaving the issue up to member states.[107]

In the end, economic factors determined the fate of the MOX plant. In 2002, BNFL was forced to buy MOX from a competitor, France's COGEMA, to fulfill contractual obligations to foreign utilities.[108] When the plant finally began producing MOX in 2004, industry representatives insisted that the commercial situation was improving. A spokesperson for the department of trade and industry claimed, "The economic and environmental case for the (MOX plant) remains as strong as ever,"[109] ironically a point on which both supporters and critics would likely have agreed. While production of MOX fuel never lived up to the expectations of the early 1990s, proposals to make significant changes in British nuclear policy were consistently stymied by the enormous costs of decommissioning and the question of what to do with the plutonium stored at Sellafield.

The Japanese tsunami and subsequent Fukushima nuclear accident in March 2011 finally sounded the death knell for the SMP. The Japanese government undertook a thorough review of Japanese nuclear policy and decided to suspend operation of the Hamaoka nuclear plant, depriving the SMP of its sole contracted MOX customer.[110] On 3 August 2011, officials announced the closure of the MOX plant. At a cost to British taxpayers of roughly £1.4 billion,[111] the SMP had produced only 13 tons of MOX fuel, a "monumental scandal" in the eyes of critics.[112]

Irish officials and anti-nuclear activists applauded the decision. However, Sellafield remained an active nuclear site, and major differences between Ireland and the United Kingdom on nuclear policy quickly resurfaced.[113] With demand for electricity growing as old coal-fired plants were retired, the United Kingdom began planning to build two new nuclear reactors at Hinkley Point in Somerset, the first of what Prime Minister David Cameron hoped would be many new British nuclear power projects.[114] To deal with the continuing problem of the waste plutonium stored at Sellafield, the Nuclear Decommissioning Authority (NDA) was considering reviving efforts to construct an American-designed fast breeder reactor or, even more controversially, to build a new MOX fuel plant at Sellafield.[115]

Irish objections to these proposals have echoed those against the SMP, but clearer avenues now exist for bringing them to the attention of the British government. The bilateral consultation mechanism put in place during the SMP dispute has provided an opportunity for direct and ongoing government-government contact.[116] With the Espoo and Aarhus Conventions now in effect, there would seem to be greater clarity about Britain's procedural obligations toward potentially affected parties. Several revised directives have been passed to implement these agreements within the European Union.[117] Directive 2003/4/EC clarified the types of "environmental information" public authorities are required to provide and limited some of the exceptions permitted in an earlier formulation. In 2003, the Public Participation Direc-tive was amended, in part to clarify the consultation procedures required in cases of potential transboundary impact. The Environmental Impact Assess-ment Directive, first passed in 1985, was revised in 1997 and again in 2003 and 2011, to expand the number of projects requiring impact assessment and define more explicitly what an assessment should entail. The European Union has also taken steps to implement the Espoo Convention's Protocol on Strategic Environmental Assessment (SEA),[118] which attempts to inte-grate environmental impact assessment procedures into the planning process before the point at which individual projects are approved. With clearer legal standards have come more opportunities for legal challenges in both UK courts and the European Court of Justice in the event of alleged violations. The Espoo Convention has also established an implementation committee, which can receive communications not only from member states, but also from concerned NGOs.[119]

This has not meant the end of disputes, as was made evident by continu-ing differences over the Hinkley project. In December 2013, an Irish NGO challenged in UK courts what it felt was inadequate consultation with the Irish public by the British government, now invoking the Espoo and Aarhus Conventions as well as the EU's Environmental Impact Assessment Direc-tive.[120] The claim was heard, but ultimately rejected. Greater progress of a sort was made within Espoo's implementation committee. In September 2013, the committee began considering a complaint about Hinkley brought by the Irish NGO Friends of the Environment. The committee spoke of the need for states to notify others of projects even when the chances of trans-boundary impact were minimal. "Even a low likelihood of such an impact should trigger the obligation to notify affected Parties." Embracing the pre-cautionary principle, the committee added, "Notification is necessary unless a significant adverse transboundary impact can be excluded." Yet, even as the committee expressed its "profound suspicion of non-compliance," it simply invited the United Kingdom to meet with it in December 2014 in a closed-door session to discuss committee concerns.[121]

From an Irish perspective, these procedural improvements have not produced stricter international controls over British nuclear activities. In October 2014, the EU Commission approved plans for the Hinkley pro-ject, angering Irish officials and anti-nuclear groups.[122] As in the case of the MOX plant, the Commission's concern was not the reactor's safety and possible transboundary impact, but how it would be paid for and whether the £24.5 billion in financial support Hinkley required was justified or rep-resented an unwarranted subsidy by British taxpayers. Greenpeace's legal adviser blasted the EU decision to back the project. "There is absolutely no legal, moral or environmental justification for turning taxes into guaranteed profits for a nuclear power company whose only legacy will be a pile of radioactive waste."[123]

The Commission's decision seemed to confirm environmentalists' fears that the European Union has a pro-nuclear bias, which could prompt other EU members to expand their own reliance on nuclear power. In reality, deep divisions exist among European states about the role that nuclear power should play, making it difficult for the European Union to move ahead with any common policy. Substantive nuclear safety regulations remain very much in the hands of national authorities.[124] European states remain divided even on the seemingly less controversial issue of civil liability for damage caused by nuclear accidents.[125] Nuclear damage was explicitly excluded from the EU's 2004 Directive on Environmental Liability,[126] in favor of two potentially competing international conventions negotiated within the IAEA and the OECD.[127] Efforts to bridge the differences between these two liability regimes, even within a European context, have thus far been unsuccessful.[128]

Analysis

The most interesting procedural question posed by the MOX dispute is whether it was wise for Ireland to frame its differences with the United Kingdom in such explicitly legal terms and to pursue a strategy in which litigation featured so prominently. In one sense, the answer would appear to be no, since Ireland's legal claims both failed and the issues at the core of dispute were not resolved through adjudication. The source of the dispute remained unresolved until the MOX plant was closed, a decision prompted by economic and political rather than legal pressures. Taking the United Kingdom to court was a confrontational approach, one that governments often consider unnecessarily hostile and divisive. From a cynical perspective, a legal strategy could be viewed simply as a way for Ireland to offer tough rhetoric but delay confronting a difficult transboundary problem, a strategy designed more to satisfy domestic constituents than to achieve a constructive diplomatic outcome.

Evident here was also the reality that bringing legal claims forced the Irish to focus on issues that could be litigated, rather than addressing directly the concerns that were at the center of the dispute. The terms of the OSPAR Convention required Ireland to treat the issue as one of information-sharing. The larger problem of how that information was used to make regulatory decisions was one the tribunal could not address. As a result, even if a definitive answer were given to the question posed, it may do little to resolve the dispute.

The limited nature of treaty commitments may also have the perverse effect of lowering the bar in terms of what domestic policy or even customary international law might otherwise require. After the ruling by the Annex VII tribunal, Prime Minister Tony Blair told Parliament, "All of these [nuclear energy] issues are governed by international rules that we are obliged to abide by. . . . On each occasion this issue has been looked at, the allegations made in respect of Sellafield have turned out to be wrong."[129] Defeating Ireland's claim may actually have reinforced within the United Kingdom a sense that environmentally risky behavior was justified and had been given international backing, especially among members of the general public who may not understand clearly the tribunal's limited purview.

Finally, given the recent proliferation of international tribunals, there is the risk of competition between them and the potential for inconsistent rulings that only cloud the meaning of the rules themselves. The possible conflict between the Annex VII tribunal and the ECJ could be seen as symptomatic of a larger structural problem facing international environmental law. The special hierarchical position and the wide-ranging economic and political concerns of EU institutions only added to an already complex institutional landscape.

Despite these concerns, one can also see the role of adjudication in the MOX dispute in a more positive light. Much depends on one's expectations. Ireland's broadest stated goal—to force the United Kingdom to shut down Sellafield—was essentially unachievable, and the chasm between the two states over the role of nuclear power was unbridgeable. Ireland was not going to bring about a complete resolution of its grievances over Sellafield through adjudication, and the Irish government made a point throughout the dispute that litigation was only part of a broader strategy. Defending the litigation in 2007, even as Ireland was accepting the ECJ verdict that it should terminate the Annex VII proceedings, Irish Environment Minister Roche insisted that it had served Irish interests in promoting better nuclear cooperation with the British and putting Sellafield "center stage" before the European Commission and the ECJ.[130]

Choosing adjudication was indeed a confrontational approach and deliberately so. It came after years of genuine frustration that the British were not taking Irish concerns seriously. Bringing a legal claim raised the stakes, but it also placed the issues in a form the British could not ignore. Framing the dispute in legal terms also helped shape the language of the dispute, as it was argued by not only government representatives but NGO leaders as well. A debate over environmental impact assessment procedures or the form Anglo-Irish consultation should take could never capture fully the anger Ireland felt over the threat posed by Sellafield, or the British sense that their

Irish counterparts were caught up in an emotional opposition to nuclear power that too often ignored the facts. However, it did channel some of the disputants' energy into more negotiable arenas.

While the tribunals that became involved did not find satisfactory solutions to all of the problems before them, they did contribute to modest improvements in the way the two governments worked with each other behind the scenes. Both Ireland and the United Kingdom came out of the litigation anxious to show they had not only prevailed but were also reasonably conciliatory afterwards. The December 2004 agreement did not solve the Sellafield problem, but it appears to have created a better system of communication.

Some observers regretted that the OSPAR tribunal did not take the opportunity provided by the MOX case to help develop the rules governing transboundary information-sharing by expanding upon the information the United Kingdom was required to provide to Ireland. However, the tribunal offered a convincing interpretation of what the OSPAR Convention was actually intended to mean by the states that had created it. The tribunal's conservatism may encourage states to see adjudication as a predictable process they will be more willing to entrust with complex environmental issues.[131] Empowering adjudicative bodies with a legislative function, however appealing, creates the risk of backlash and may do little in practical terms to develop the law.

The MOX dispute also reflects tensions that continue in three areas of international environmental law involving the procedural responsibilities of states in transboundary situations where the issue is not compensation for damage but rather the risk that damage will occur.

First, there are the questions posed by environmental impact assessment. Ireland's objection to the way the United Kingdom evaluated the potential effects of the MOX plant was more than a technical concern; it went to the heart of the Irish belief that the British cared too little about the risks they were imposing on others. The Irish critique and the United Kingdom's defense of its 1993 Environmental Impact Assessment and other review procedures suggest significant differences in perspective about what an appropriate review should entail, an issue central to the pulp mills dispute analyzed in Chapter 8. Given the importance of cost-benefit analysis in the way many governments make and defend decisions with environmental impact, the debate over how the United Kingdom determined that the SMP plant was economically justified is worth closer scrutiny. The government's decision not to consider the "sunk costs" involved in constructing the plant had obvious implications for the outcome of its cost-benefit calculations. As a matter of process, to conduct the calculation after the plant had already been built, with the promise of jobs and other economic benefits, created a reality that was simply too difficult to write off, at least in 2001. This is a particular problem in the field of nuclear energy, where the costs of decommissioning can be so staggering.

Second, the dispute reveals continuing differences about what consultation and information-sharing, two widely accepted components of the duty to cooperate, really do require. It is important to stress that the United Kingdom never suggested that these duties did not exist or were not a priority. The ITLOS tribunal reinforced the importance of principles of transboundary cooperation in articulating its own provisional measures. The dispute was over what kinds of information to share, with whom, and at what stage, and whether the ongoing contact between the United Kingdom and Ireland satisfied the requirements of international law. As matters of transboundary pollution have become the concern of not only national governments but also local governments and private actors, these practical questions of process take on added significance.

Third, the dispute raised questions about how the precautionary principle should be applied. Ireland gave it a prominent place in its argument before the ITLOS for provisional measures to block the opening of the MOX plant, even though the principle was not explicitly included in the LOSC being cited by Ireland as the basis for its claim. While they did not agree that precautions were needed in this situation, the British again never challenged the existence of the principle and the tribunal defended its decision not to accede to the Irish request, referring directly to the precautionary principle.[132] Still, as would be true in the case brought by Uruguay against Argentina, how to make this principle operational remains a source of substantial disagreement.

It is dangerous to try to attribute specific changes in international environmental law to the MOX dispute, since the procedural rules being developed within the Espoo and Aarhus Conventions during this period were influenced by many factors. The SEA Protocol's emphasis on early and strategic environmental assessment resonated well with the concern Ireland was raising with the British about when and how it evaluated the transboundary impact of the MOX plant. The bilateral United Kingdom–Ireland nuclear consultation mechanism was a specific product of the MOX dispute, and its effectiveness may well encourage more widespread use of similar procedures, particularly as European states look for ways to manage their differences over nuclear power.

Perhaps the most tangible result was the United Kingdom's decision to follow through on its 1998 commitment to the OSPAR Commission, reaffirmed in the course of the MOX dispute, to phase out emissions of radioactive waste into the Irish Sea. While technically the British were not bound by earlier OSPAR regulations, by signing the OSPAR Convention the United Kingdom had accepted an obligation to "take . . . all possible steps to prevent and eliminate pollution from land-based sources."[133] The United Kingdom's "Strategy for Radioactive Discharges" reaffirms the country's legal commitment to meet OSPAR radioactive waste objectives, even though the document also admits that the 2002 pledge was made at a very different time, when nuclear power was seen as a declining industry rather than as an important source of future energy, as it is viewed today in the United Kingdom. The document also recognizes the United Kingdom's obligation to develop its nuclear policy within a legal framework that includes the precautionary principle.[134] Translating this commitment into practice remains a challenge, as does the larger problem of the future of Sellafield operations and the safe storage and disposal of the site's plutonium waste.

Ireland and the United Kingdom have long disagreed about the benefits and risks posed by nuclear power and view operations at Sellafield from opposite sides of the Irish Sea. However, the United Kingdom now clearly recognizes that the transboundary risk those operations may pose is a matter of legitimate concern to Ireland and other neighbors and that the assessment and management of that risk are governed by rules of international law.

Notes

1   Each of these two developments is explored more directly in Chapters 7 and 8 respectively.

2   For a useful summary of the development of nuclear operations at Sellafield, see Terry Hall, "'Carried by the Wind out to Sea'—*Ireland and the Isle of Man v. Sellafield*: Anatomy of a Transboundary Pollution Dispute," *Georgetown International Environmental Law Review* 6 (1994): 641–45.

3   For an overview of the process see International Tribunal for the Law of the Sea (ITLOS), "MOX Plant Case: Ireland v. United Kingdom (Request for Provisional Measures and Statement of Case of Ireland)," Case No. 10, 9 November 2001, 15–17 [hereafter cited as "ITLOS—Ireland's Memorial"]. http://www.itlos.org/fileadmin/itlos/documents/cases/case_no_10/request_ireland_e.pdf.

4   A good summary of the case for MOX can be found at UK, Queen's Bench Division, "R (On the Application of Friends of Affairs and another," 15 November 2001, EWHC Admin 914, CO/402/20 [hereafter cited as "R v. Secretary of State"]. http://www.lexisnexis.com/hottopics/lnacademic.

5   Some consideration has recently been given to reviving the fast breeder program by importing a US-designed reactor and building it at Sellafield. See Steve Connor, "Revealed: New Nuclear Plant to Tackle UK's Plutonium Mountain: Radical Plan to Deal with Record Deposits of Nuclear Waste Represents a Dramatic Policy U-Turn," *The Independent*, 3 April 2012.

6 Peter Bunyard, "Making a Mess of MOX," *Ecologist* 32, no. 1 (2002): 65–68.

7 "Treaty Establishing the European Atomic Energy Community (EURATOM)," Rome, signed 27 March 1957 (in force 1 January 1958). http://eur-lex.europa.eu/legal-content/EN/TXT/?uri=CELEX:12012A/TXT.

8 See, generally, Regina S. Axelrod, "The European Commission and Member States: Conflict over Nuclear Safety," *Perspectives* 26 (2006): 5–22.

9 United Nations Economic Commission for Europe (UNECE), "Convention on Environmental Impact Assessment in a Transboundary Context," Espoo (Finland), signed 25 February 1991 (in force 10 September 1997), Art. 2 2(2) [hereafter cited as "Espoo Convention"]. www.unece.org/env/eia/about/eia_text.html.

10 UNECE, "Convention on Access to Information, Public Participation in Decision-Making and Access to Justice in Environmental Matters," Aarhus (Denmark), signed 25 June 1998 (in force 30 October 2001), Art. 5(1)(b) [hereafter cited as "Aarhus Convention"]. www.unece.org/fileadmin/DAM/env/pp/documents/cep43e.pdf.

11 Simon Marsden, "MOX Plant and the Espoo Convention: Can Member State Disputes Concerning Mixed Environmental Agreements Be Resolved Outside EC Law?" *Review of European Community & International Environmental Law* 18, no. 3 (2009): 316–17.

12 Daud Hassan, "International Conventions Relating to Land-Based Sources of Marine Pollution Control: Applications and Shortcomings," *Georgetown International Environmental Law Review* 16 (2004): 658.

13 "United Nations Convention on the Law of the Sea," Montego Bay (Jamaica), signed 10 December 1982 (in force 16 November 1994), *International Legal Materials* 21 (1982): 1283 [hereafter cited as "LOSC"]. www.un.org/depts/los/convention_agreements/texts/unclos/unclos_e.pdf.

14 "Convention for the Protection of the Marine Environment of the North-East Atlantic," Paris, 22 September 1992 (in force 25 March 1998) [hereafter cited as "OSPAR Convention"]. http://sedac.ciesin.org/entri/texts/acrc/MEofNE.txt.html.

15 For more on the regime created by the OSPAR Convention, see Ellen Hey, Ton Ijlstra, and André Nollkaemper, "The 1992 Paris Convention for the Protection of the Marine Environment of the North-East Atlantic: A Critical Analysis," *International Journal of Marine and Coastal Law* 8, no. 1 (1993): 1–49.

16 "OSPAR Convention," Art. 2(2).

17 United Nations Environment Program (UNEP), "Convention on the Control of Transboundary Movements of Hazardous Waste and Their Disposal," Basel, signed 22 March 1989 (in force 5 May 1992), Art. 1(3). www.basel.int/Portals/4/Basel%20Convention/docs/text/BaselConventionText-e.pdf.

18 International Atomic Energy Agency (IAEA), "Convention on Nuclear Safety," Vienna, signed 17 June 1994 (in force 24 October 1996). https://www.iaea.org/sites/default/files/infcirc449a1.pdf.

19 IAEA, "Convention on Nuclear Safety: Background," IAEA website. https://www.iaea.org/publications/documents/treaties/convention-nuclear-safety.

20 Marsden, "MOX Plant and the Espoo Convention," 314.

21 Though neither were original signatories, both the UK and Ireland became parties at the time of their admission into the European Community in 1973.

"Treaty Establishing the European Atomic Energy Community (EURATOM)," Rome, signed 27 March 1957 (in force 1 January 1958) [hereafter cited as "EURATOM Treaty"]. www.ab.gov.tr/files/ardb/evt/1_avrupa_birligi/1_3_antlasmalar/1_3_1_kurucu_antlasmalar/1957_treaty_establishing_euratom.pdf.

22 ITLOS, "Ireland v. United Kingdom: MOX Plant Case (Request for Provisional Measures: Written Response of the United Kingdom)," 15 November 2001, para. 36, p. 15 [hereafter cited as "ITLOS: UK's Written Response"]. http://www.itlos.org/fileadmin/itlos/documents/cases/case_no_10/response_uk_e.pdf.

23 "ITLOS: Ireland's Memorial," para. 13, p. 8.

24 Ibid., para. 27, p. 15.

25 How serious the actual risk was had been the subject of much disagreement, with at least some observers arguing that the clean record of the nuclear transport industry offered evidence that nuclear materials could be carried safely. See, for example, Raul A.F. Pedrozo, "Transport of Nuclear Cargoes by Sea," Journal of Maritime Law and Commerce 28 (1997): 207–36.

26 "ITLOS: Ireland's Memorial," para. 33–43, pp. 17–23.

27 Ibid., para. 16, p. 6.

28 Ibid., para. 142, p. 60.

29 Hall, "'Carried by the Wind,'" 641–81.

30 Ireland did keep some low-level nuclear waste at a site near Sellafield, thus undercutting the purity of its anti-nuclear position. Ibid., 657.

31 Ibid., 655–57.

32 Mary Carolan, "Court Finds for BNFL over Sellafield," The Irish Times, 3 April 2004, 4.

33 Paul Brown, "Threat Across the Water Unites the Irish," The Guardian, 16 September 2002 .

34 Shawn Pogatchnik, "Irish Antinuclear Activists Set Sail to Intercept British Ships," Sydney Morning Herald, 13 September 2002; Greenpeace International, "UK Nuclear Installations Inspectorate Confirms BNFL Falsification Scandal to Plutonium Fuel Now in Japan," press release, 15 December 1999.

35 See Erik Martiniussen, "Final Decision Today: Radioactive Technetium-99 to be Cleansed from Sellafield Discharges," Bellona Report, 21 April 2004. http://bellona.ru/bellona.org/english_import_area/energy/nuclear/sellafield/33433.

36 Alison Healy, "'Warrior' Hoping to Turn the Tide against Sellafield," The Irish Times, 13 September 2002, 5.

37 Valerie Robinson, "Fears Grow over Nuclear Shipment," Irish News, 5 September 2002, 24.

38 Permanent Court of Arbitration (PCA), UNCLOS Annex VII Arbitral Tribunal, "Ireland v. United Kingdom: Mox Plant Case (Memorial of Ireland)," 26 July 2002, Vol. 1, para 1.68, p. 24, and paras. 2.43–2.49, pp. 35–39 [hereafter cited as "Annex VII Tribunal-Ireland's Memorial"]. http://www.pca-cpa.org/Ireland%20Memorial%20Part%20I8c9a.pdf?fil_id=222.

39 Tom Dalyell, "Westminister Diary," New Scientist, 19 April 2003, 47.

40 William Walker, "Britain's Policies on Fissile Materials: The Next Steps," Special ISIS Report on the Future of UK Nuclear Weapons, Fissile Materials, Arms Control and Disarmament Policy no. 2 (1997).

41 "With One Bound," Economist, Vol. 361, no. 8250, 29 November 2001, 52.

42 Paul Brown and Rob Evans, "Nuclear Plant Backed by Blair is £600m 'White Elephant,'" *The Guardian*, 26 July 2004, 1.

43 Michael Meacher, "Mox Plant Was a Total Waste from Start to Finish," *Morning Star*, 4 August 2011.

44 "Horrid Stuff," *Economist*, Vol. 354, no. 8160, 4 March 2000, 64.

45 Sinead McIntyre, "Sellafield Shake-up at Top Level," *Independent.ie*, 18 April 2000.

46 Matthew Jones, Bayan Rahman, and Cathy Newman, "Pacific Nations Concerned by Deal to Take Back Nuclear Fuel from Japan," *Financial Times*, 12 July 2000, 12.

47 "LOSC," Art. 19.

48 For more analysis of these issues see Robert Nadelson, "After MOX: The Contemporary Shipment of Radioactive Substances in the Law of the Sea," *International Journal of Marine and Coastal Law* 15, no. 2 (2000): 193–244; and Maki Tanaka, "Lessons from the Protracted MOX Plant Dispute: A Proposed Protocol on Marine Environmental Impact Assessment to the United Nations Convention on the Law of the Sea," *Michigan Journal of International Law* 25, no. 2 (2004): 337–428.

49 See Nadelson, "After MOX," 222–33.

50 Pogatchnik, "Irish Antinuclear Activitists."

51 "Irish PM Says Sellafield Nuclear Case 'Most Significant' Ever," *Agence France Presse*, 11 June 2003.

52 Ibid.

53 Hall, "'Carried by the Wind,'" 678.

54 See, for example, Marsden, "MOX Plant and the Espoo Convention," 316–17.

55 Markus G. Puder, "The Rise of Regional Integration Law (RIL): Good News for International Environmental Law (IEL)?" *Georgetown International Environmental Law Review* 23 (2001): 199.

56 Hall, "'Carried by the Wind,'" 674.

57 For other limitations of an EU approach, see Robin Churchill and Joanne Scott, "The MOX Plant Litigation: The First Half-Life," *International and Comparative Law Quarterly* 53 (2004): 666–69.

58 "OSPAR Convention," Art. 32(1), 17.

59 Hall, "'Carried by the Wind,'" 678.

60 PCA, OSPAR Arbitration, "Ireland v. United Kingdom: MOX Plant Case (Counter-Memorial of the United Kingdom)," 2 June 2002, para. 1.21, p. 7 [hereafter cited as, "OSPAR: UK's Counter-Memorial"]. http://www.pca-cpa.org/UK%20-%20Counter%20Memorial7e9d.pdf?fil_id=437.

61 PCA, OSPAR Arbitration, "Ireland v. United Kingdom: MOX Plant Case (Memorial of Ireland)," 7 March 2002, paras. 55–60, pp. 18–20 [hereafter cited as "OSPAR: Ireland's Memorial"]. http://www.pca-cpa.org/Ireland%20-%20Memorial904c.pdf?fil_id=435.

62 Malgosia Fitzmaurice, "Dispute Concerning Access to Information under Article 9 of the Ospar Convention," *International Journal of Marine and Coastal Law* 18, no. 4 (2003): 544.

63 This issue was raised in suit filed in the UK by Greenpeace and other opponents of the project. See "R v. Secretary of State," 13–14.

64 "OSPAR: UK's Counter-Memorial," para. 4, p. 1.

65 Ibid., paras 2.6–2.7, pp. 10–11.

66   PCA, OSPAR Arbitration, "Ireland v. United Kingdom: MOX Plant Case (Final Award)," 2 July 2003, para. 140, p. 46 [hereafter cited as "OSPAR: Final Award"]. http://www.pca-cpa.org/OSPAR%20Awarde17f.pdf?fil_id=447.
67   Ibid., para. 85, pp. 29–30.
68   Ibid., para. 179, p. 57.
69   "LOSC," Art. 290.
70   "ITLOS: Ireland's Memorial," paras. 55–80, pp. 27–37.
71   Ibid., para. 84, p. 38.
72   Ibid., paras. 97–101, pp. 44–45.
73   Ibid, para. 101, p. 45.
74   Ibid., para. 142, p. 60.
75   "ITLOS—UK's Written Response," paras. 162–67, pp. 59–62.
76   Ibid., paras. 199–200, p. 70.
77   Ibid., para. 36, pp. 15–16.
78   ITLOS, "Ireland v. United Kingdom: MOX Plant Case (Order of 3 December 2001)," 3 December 2001, paras. 49–50, p. 9 [hereafter cited as "ITLOS: December 3 Order"]. https://www.itlos.org/fileadmin/itlos/documents/cases/case_no_10/Order.03.12.01.E.pdf.
79   Ibid., paras. 78–79, p. 12.
80   Ibid., para. 89, p. 18
81   "Annex VII Tribunal: Ireland's Memorial," Vol. 4, para. 10.1, p. 251.
82   PCA, UNCLOS Annex VII Arbitral Tribunal, "Ireland v. United Kingdom: Mox Plant Case (Counter-Memorial of the United Kingdom)," 9 January 2003, para. 7.156, p. 238 [hereafter cited as "Annex VII Tribunal: UK's Counter-Memorial"]. http://www.pca-cpa.org/UK%20Counter%20-Memorial1504.pdf?fil_id=227.
83   For a discussion of the Annex VII Tribunal's ruling, see Tanaka, "Lessons from the Protracted MOX Plant Dispute," 389–94.
84   PCA, UNCLOS Annex VII Arbitral Tribunal, "Ireland v. United Kingdom: Mox Plant Case (Order No. 3)," 9 January 2003, paras. 24–27, pp. 8–9 [hereafter cited as "Annex VII Tribunal: Order No. 3"]. http://www.pca-cpa.org/MOX%20Order%20no3a614.pdf?fil_id=81.
85   Ibid., para. 62, p. 18.
86   Ibid., para. 66, p. 19.
87   Helen Bruce, "The Sellafield War That Ireland Could Never Win," Daily Mail, 11 April 2007.
88   Paul Cullen, "Irish Debate on Sellafield 'Dishonest,'" Irish Times, 29 May 2003, 3.
89   "State Loses UN Legal Battle to Get Key Data on Sellafield Risk," Irish Independent, 2 July 2003.
90   "Row Brews over UK's Failure to Cut Pollution," The Herald (Scotland), 23 June 2003.
91   Ibid.
92   Peter Roches, "UK Reneges on Sellafield Discharge Pledge," Irish Times, 19 May 2003.
93   Graham Hiscott and Keith Sinclair, "Beckett Acts after Sellafield Salmon Findings," The Herald, 24 June 2003, 8.
94   "Britain Agrees to Phase out Sellafield Radioactive Discharges," Deutsche Presse-Agentur, 26 June 2003.

95 "UNCLOS Tribunal Rejects Ireland's Bid to Stop Operation of Sellafield Plants," *M2 PressWIRE*, 25 June 2003. The litigation may also have played a role in encouraging the British to strike a deal with Norway on the disposal of TC-99 waste rather than face the prospect of another set of legal claims. See "Ireland Threatened over Sellafield Row," *Independent*, 29 June 2003.

96 "State Loses."

97 Sorcha Crowley, "UN Issues Ruling on Sellafield Nuclear Safety," *Irish Times*, 25 June 2003, 4.

98 "Cullen Fury over Suspension of Sellafield Court Fight," *Irish Independent*, 16 June 2003.

99 Paul Cullen, "Ireland and UK Both Claim Win on Sellafield Irish Times," *Irish Times*, 26 June 2003.

100 Ralph Minder and Andrew Taylor, "Brussels in Court Move on Sellafield Nuclear Waste Storage," *Financial Times*, 25 March 2004, 5.

101 Stephen Castle, "UK Told to Clean up Nuclear Waste," *The Independent*, 30 March 2004, 3.

102 Richard North, "An Ol' Fashioned Power Grab?" *EUReferendum.com*, 4 September 2004.

103 Geoff Meade, "Brussels Launches Legal Action over Sellafield," *Press Association Limited*, 3 September 2004.

104 David Hencke, "Deal Allows Irish to Check on Sellafield," *The Guardian*, 11 December 2004, 12. That a deal was possible now may also have been influenced by increased cooperation between the two governments on the issue of Northern Ireland. Ibid.

105 "Political Storm Brewing over Nuclear Plant's 'Lost' Plutonium," *Irish Independent*, 18 February 2005.

106 "Ireland Slams Sellafield Leak as Further Damning Indictment," *Agence France Presse*, 27 May 2005.

107 Andrew Rettman, "Nuclear Disaster Test Staged in Romania," *EUObserver.com*, 11 May 2005.

108 Jason Nisse, "BNFL Forced to Go to France for MOX Fuel," *The Independent*, 3 August 2003.

109 Brown and Evans, "Nuclear Plant Backed by Blair Is £600m 'White Elephant.'" *The Guardian*, 26 July 2004, 1.

110 World Nuclear Association, "Nuclear Power in Japan," 14 November 2014. http://www.world-nuclear.org/info/Country-Profiles/Countries-G-N/Japan/.

111 Fiona Harvey, "Sellafield Mox Nuclear Fuel Plant to Close," *The Guardian*, 3 August 2011.

112 Meacher, "Mox Plant Was a Total Waste."

113 Peter Geoghegan, "Sellafield Will Remain a Threat to Ireland," *The Guardian*, 4 August 2011.

114 "Britain's Nuclear Move," *The Irish Times*, 23 October 2013.

115 Connor, "Revealed: New Nuclear Plant."

116 As an example, see Ireland, Department of the Environment, Community and Local Government, "Minister Hogan Discusses Sellafield with Secretary of State Huhne," 28 March 2011. http://www.environ.ie/en/Environment/EnvironmentalRadiation/News/MainBody,25751,en.htm.

117 See, generally, Marsden, "MOX Plant and the Espoo Convention." See also Nikolaos Lavranos, "The Ospar Convention, the Aarhus Convention and EC Law: Normative and Institutional Fragmentation on the Right of Access to Environmental Information," in *Multi-Sourced Equivalent Norms in International Law*, ed. Tomer Broude and Yuval Shany (Oxford: Bloomsbury, 2011), 143–69.

118 UNECE, "Protocol on Strategic Environmental Assessment to the Convention on Environmental Impact Assessment in a Transboundary Context," Kyiv, 21 May 2003 (in force 11 July 2010) [hereafter cited as "SEA Protocol]. http://www.unece.org/fileadmin/DAM/env/eia/documents/legaltexts/ protocolenglish.pdf.

119 UNECE, Espoo Convention, "Implementation Committee," created February 2001. http://www.unece.org/env/eia/implementation/implementation_ committee_meetings.html.

120 "Irish Challenge against 'Unlawful' British Nuclear Plant Starts Tomorrow," *thejournal.ie*, 4 December 2013.

121 UNECE, "Report of the Implementation Committee at Its Thirtieth Session: Meeting of the Parties to the Convention on Environmental Impact Assessment in a Transboundary Context," 25–27 February 2014 [Doc. ECE/ MP.EIA/IC/2014/2], paras. 35–36, p. 9. http://www.unece.org/fileadmin/ DAM/env/documents/2014/EIA/IC/ece.mp.eia.ic.2014.2.as_resubmitted.pdf.

122 Valerie Robinson, "Irish Anger at Europe over Consent for UK Nuke Plant," *Irish News*, 9 October 2014, 3.

123 "Europe Backs Hinkley Nuclear Plant," *bbc.com*, 9 October 2014.

124 See "Nuclear Power in the European Union," *World Nuclear Association*, December 2014. http://www.world-nuclear.org/info/Country-Profiles/ Others/European-Union/.

125 While this issue was not raised directly in the MOX dispute, the failure to establish a strong liability regime can be evidence of continuing disagreement about the seriousness of the threat posed by specific activities.

126 EU, European Parliament and the Council. "Directive 2004/35/CE on Environmental Liability with Regard to the Prevention and Remedying of Environmental Damage," 21 April 2004, *Official Journal of the European Union* (30 April 2004) [L143/56], Art. 4(4). http://eur-lex.europa.eu/legal-content/ EN/TXT/PDF/?uri=CELEX:32004L0035&from=EN.

127 On some of the issue posed by the Vienna and Paris Conventions, see Duncan E.J. Currie, "The Problems and Gaps in the Nuclear Liability Conventions and an Analysis of How an Actual Claim Would Be Brought under the Current Existing Treaty Regime in the Event of a Nuclear Accident," *Denver Journal of International Law and Policy* 35, no. 1 (2006): 85–127. http://www.law.du.edu/ documents/djilp/The-Problems-Gaps-Nuclear-Liability-Conventions- Analysis-How-Actual-Claim.pdf.

128 For an overview of the pattern of ratifications and recent Commission efforts to try to bridge the differences within the EU, see EU, "Public Consultation: Insurance and Compensation of Damages Caused by Accidents of Nuclear Power Plants (Nuclear Liability)," Consultation Period, 30 June–22 October 2013.

129 "Blair Opposed to Closure of Sellafield Nuclear Plant," http://www.publications. parliament.uk/pa/cm200203/cmhansrd/vo030625/debtext/30625-03.htm.

130 Republic of Ireland, Dáil Éireann, "Written Answers—Nuclear Debate," Vol. 635 (5 April 2007). http://debates.oireachtas.ie/dail/2007/04/05/00056.asp.

131 On this point see Ted L. McDorman, "Access to Information under Article 9 of the Ospar Convention (Ireland v. United Kingdom)," *American Journal of International Law* 98 (2004): 337–38.

132 Barbara Kwiatkowska, "The Ireland v. United Kingdom (Mox Plant) Case: Applying the Law of Treaty Parallelism," *International Journal of Marine and Coastal Law* 18, no. 1 (2003): 38–46.

133 "OSPAR Convention," Art. 3.

134 United Kingdom, Department of Energy and Climate Change, "UK Strategy for Radioactive Discharges," (July 2009). https://www.gov.uk/government/uploads/system/uploads/attachment_data/file/249884/uk_strategy_for_radioactive_discharges.pdf.

6

Turbot War[1]

Introduction

On 9 March 1995, Canadian authorities boarded and seized the Spanish trawler *Estai*, about 220 miles east of Newfoundland, for violating Canadian fisheries regulations. Shots were fired during the lengthy chase, and Spanish ships were dispatched to protect other Spanish fishing ships. The European Union denounced the arrest of a vessel flying the flag of an EU member as a "flagrant violation of the laws of the high seas" and EU Fisheries Commissioner Emma Bonino called it an "act of organized piracy."[2] Fortunately, the dispute between Canada and Spain was a war fought more with words than guns and ended without serious injury or damage.

The ensuing diplomatic confrontation centered on the rules governing marine fisheries, the role of regional fisheries organizations, and the rights of coastal states. On another level, the arrest of the *Estai* was a dramatic example of unilateral state action to protect environmental interests, something normally viewed as a sign of failure rather than a force for positive change. Yet over five decades of international environmental diplomacy have shown how difficult it can be to reach broad-based agreement on policies that deal decisively even with widely recognized environmental problems. When existing regimes are slow or unresponsive, internal pressures can build to push governments to act on their own, even in the face of substantial international criticism. The virtue of the ends sought may be seen to overcome the normal objections to the unilateralist means being used.

The focus of the next three cases shifts to issues of process, how international environmental law is developed through individual state action, intersecting environmental regimes, and international adjudication. This chapter, "Turbot War," explores some of the legal issues associated with the use of unilateral measures in the environmental arena through an analysis of the verbal debate surrounding the Canadian action, most notably within Canada itself. For all the overblown rhetoric, the exchanges between government representatives and the reactions in the popular media reflected competing views about the circumstances under which states can legitimately take independent steps to protect what they consider vital environmental interests, especially when this might violate existing international law. Examined here are not just the formal legal arguments put forward by government

Map 6.1 This map indicates the seaward limits of Canada's Exclusive Fishing Zone. It also shows where the Spanish fishing ship *Estai* was seized and St. John's, the Newfoundland port into which the arrested ship was taken.

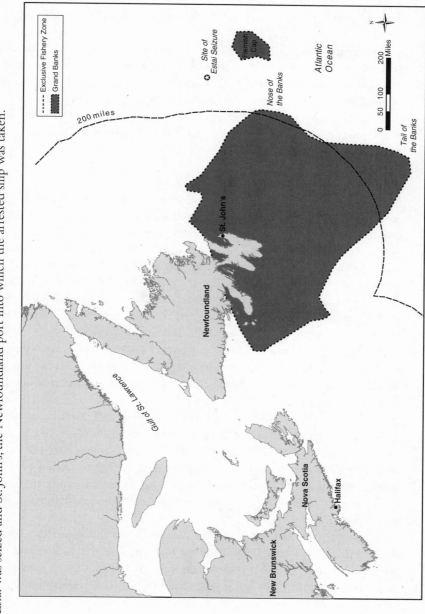

officials but also the comments and opinions of members of the fishing industry, journalists, editorial writers, and private citizens confronting the question of whether Canada had the right to take this action, to use armed force in an area of the ocean generally understood to be beyond its lawful jurisdiction.

The chapter begins by examining the problems faced in the Northwest Atlantic as states attempted to manage fisheries crossing between national and high seas fishing zones. It then explains the steps taken by Canadian authorities and the public reactions to Canadian unilateralism coming from both international and domestic audiences, as well as the broader impact of the dispute on the development of regional and global fisheries law.

The Context

No area of international law has been more affected by unilateral state action than the law of the sea. A series of individual national claims helped transform a body of law built around the concept of freedom of the seas and narrow limits of coastal state jurisdiction into one where states now enjoy sovereign control over ocean resources out to 200 nautical miles and beyond. It has been a confrontational process. In 1945, the United States issued the Truman Proclamations, under which it claimed sovereign rights to the resources of the continental shelf and the right to establish conservation zones to protect high seas fisheries. Several Latin American nations, with little to gain from extending control over their own narrow continental shelves, soon followed with far more extensive claims over marine fisheries. While the US challenged these actions as violations of international law, they became the basis for the exclusive fishing zones now enjoyed by most coastal states, as international conferences in 1958 and 1960 failed to halt the seaward expansion of coastal state jurisdiction. Hopes raised in 1967 by Avi Pardo, Malta's Ambassador to the United Nations, that the oceans would become the "common heritage of mankind" were dashed as coastal states, skeptical about the ability of the international community to manage maritime resources to their benefit, opted for extended coastal state control rather than global sharing.

The result was the 1982 United Nations Convention on the Law of the Sea (LOSC), a complex agreement that established jurisdictional rules governing a wide range of marine activities, including fishing. The LOSC codified what was by then emerging state practice by recognizing the right of each coastal state to establish an Exclusive Economic Zone (EEZ) in which it enjoys sovereign rights over living resources out to 200 nautical miles from the baseline from which its 12-mile territorial sea is measured.

This includes most fisheries, although the Convention makes provision for special regimes to govern highly migratory species, such as tuna, and anadromous species like salmon. The hope was to provide more effective single-state regulation of the large percentage of the world's fisheries found close to shore, as nations would presumably have a strong incentive to protect what would now be national rather than common resources. That national management has not been as effective as many had anticipated is a significant problem and was one of the pressures at work in the dispute between Canada and Spain.

Extending the limits of national jurisdiction still meant that boundary lines would be drawn at sea, and some fish stocks would inevitably pass either between different EEZs (transboundary stocks) or between the EEZ and the high seas (straddling stocks). In the high seas, all states continue to enjoy the freedom to fish. The framers of the 1982 Convention recognized the problems this could cause, and Canada was among the nations arguing for some form of joint management.[3] However, Article 63 of the Convention simply calls upon coastal and distant water fishing states to "seek, either directly or through appropriate subregional or regional organizations, to agree upon the measures necessary for the conservation" of straddling stocks.[4] The record of the multilateral fisheries organizations formed during the 1950s and 1960s to regulate what were then high seas fisheries was hardly encouraging. Yet the need to provide fishing opportunities for the heavily capitalized distant water fleets of key conference participants militated against any more extensive roles for the coastal states.

The fisheries of the Northwest Atlantic have traditionally been among the world's richest. Given their proximity to both Europe and North America, they have also been among the most heavily fished. After expanded fisheries zones were created in the mid-1970s, Canada and the United States focused on extending their effective control out to 200 nautical miles, moving foreign fishing ships out of their national zones and drawing up a boundary between them in the Gulf of Maine. The Grand Banks became a prime target for distant water fishing interests as two key sections, the Nose and the Tail, lie beyond the 200-mile limit of Canada's Exclusive Fishing Zone (EFZ). Economic and political factors combined to encourage the overcapitalization of the world's fishing fleets, putting tremendous pressure on marine fisheries. The situation facing Grand Banks fisheries was made even more difficult after the 1986 entry of Spain and Portugal into the European Community. Under the terms of their accession agreements, these two major fishing nations agreed that only part of their fleets would initially be permitted to fish in the Community's already depleted waters, thus forcing their ships to look outside the region for fishing opportunities.[5]

The Northwest Atlantic Fisheries Organization (NAFO)[6] has provided the institutional framework for much of the management of the Grand Banks fisheries. Formed in 1979, NAFO succeeded the International Commission for the Northwest Atlantic Fisheries (ICNAF), which had been responsible for regulating fish stocks over a far broader geographical range in the days before Canada and the United States created their exclusive fishing zones. NAFO's principal regulatory body is the Fisheries Commission. While its formal regulatory powers are limited to high seas areas, the so-called Regulatory Area, the Fisheries Commission is expected to coordinate its work with conservation measures being undertaken by coastal states. Regulatory measures, normally in the form of individual quotas or percentages of the Total Allowable Catches (TACs) established for each stock, are currently approved by majority vote of the members of the Commission with each member having a single vote. However, under Article XII of the NAFO Convention, parties retain the right to object to adopted proposals within a set period and thus opt out of their assigned limits. The Convention calls for a system of joint international enforcement, which permits all parties the right to board and inspect ships of other parties fishing in the area. The prosecution of violators is a flag state responsibility.

The other regional organization that played a central role in the turbot dispute was the European Union, represented by the fiery Emma Bonino, here serving as the EU Fisheries Commissioner.[7] By 1994, the European Union was a NAFO member, representing the interests of all EU nations, here principally Spain and Portugal, whose individual NAFO memberships ended when they joined the European Union. However, developing a single EU policy would become more complicated when the United Kingdom, also an important EU member, came to sympathize with the Canadian position, and other key EU countries hoped to end the dispute quickly. Throughout the dispute, Spanish officials would remain uncertain about the degree of support, beyond tough rhetoric, the EU would actually provide.

The Dispute

While the immediate trigger of the conflict between Canada and Spain was the arrest of the *Estai*, the dispute had begun much earlier. Since the late 1980s, Canada had consistently protested the European Union's failure to accept quotas on NAFO straddling stocks, whose yields declined precipitously in the early 1990s. The situation became so severe that, in 1992, the Canadian government declared a two-year moratorium on all commercial fishing for northern cod within the Canadian zone, putting thousands of Canadians out of work. Later that year, NAFO accepted a Canadian proposal to extend the ban to all fishing for northern cod on the Nose of the Grand Banks. However, the European Union took advantage of the opting out process to establish its own quotas. Similar findings of severe depletion on the Tail involving not only cod, but also flatfish stocks of yellowtail and witch flounder, led the Commission to adopt moratoria or major cutbacks in fishing for all significant groundfish stocks in the Regulatory Area. Again, Canada was initially frustrated by the European Union's adoption of higher independent quotas for many closely regulated species.[8] In early 1994, the European Union finally went along with the NAFO moratorium.

The focus shifted to ships flying the flags of non-NAFO members. This included ships genuinely linked to countries like South Korea, where the fish would be targeted for home consumption, and others flying flags of convenience, often owned by western Europeans, whose catches were headed to European markets. In April 1994, Canada took its first new enforcement measures when it arrested the *Kristina Logos*, a ship flying the Panamanian flag, for cod fishing just outside the 200-mile zone. This first seizure of a "foreign" ship in international waters had been carefully chosen. The *Kristina Logos* was owned by a Canadian who had failed to cancel his Canadian registry when the ship was reflagged, thus giving Canadian authorities an unusually strong basis on which to seize it. In May, the Canadian parliament passed amendments to the Coastal Fisheries Protection Act (CFPA)[9] whose stated purpose was to give Canada the power to enforce NAFO regulations. The government claimed that the targets of the new law were stateless "pirate" and flag of convenience ships, not those from Europe or the United States.[10] However, the European Union and the United States recognized that the law could easily be amended to change the classification of ships subject to the new rules.[11]

The passage of the CFPA should hardly have surprised the international community; it was also not an isolated act. Following the demarcation of a boundary line in the Gulf of Maine, Canada had conducted controversial hot pursuits into US waters of American fishing ships accused of violating Canadian law. The Liberal Party government of Jean Chrétien had promised in its 1993 campaign to take tough measures to protect Canadian fisheries and Chrétien selected Newfoundland's charismatic Brian Tobin as his fisheries minister. Tobin became a key actor in what a *New York Times* reporter later termed the "great television theater" of the Canada-EU fisheries dispute.[12] In June 1994, Canada imposed a $1,500 per-trip fee on American salmon fishermen transiting Canadian waters in an effort to push the United States toward a more effective system of joint management under the 1985 Pacific Salmon Treaty.[13] The next month, Canada arrested two US ships dragging for scallops on the Grand Banks beyond the 200-mile limit, justifying the action on the grounds that Canada had special rights to regulate scallops as "sedentary species" on its continental shelf even beyond 200 miles.[14] The legislation had its intended effect and non-NAFO ships quickly left the Regulatory Area.

Precipitating the arrest of the *Estai* and the dispute with the European Union was Canada's decision to go after Spanish and Portuguese ships fishing for turbot, otherwise known as Greenland halibut. For years, most turbot had been located in Canada's EFZ. However, the stock's movement to just beyond the 200-mile limit and a tremendous EU-subsidized increase in the Spanish and Portuguese fishing effort combined to make NAFO regulation of turbot catches a high Canadian priority. By the time NAFO did impose management quotas in 1995, EU ships were responsible for over 75 per cent of the turbot catch. In January of that year, the Fisheries Commission agreed to set a 27,000 ton TAC for turbot, but allocated to Canada, as the coastal state, 50 per cent of the TAC plus a reserve, giving it a total of 16,300 tons. Other quotas were determined on the basis of historic catch, with the result that the entire European Union received only 12.6 per cent or 3,400 tons. The European Union had been outvoted in the Fisheries Commission six to five with two abstentions and took immediate exception. While purporting to object not to the TAC, but to the apportionment of individual quotas, the European Union determined for itself a quota of 18,000 tons, which it felt represented a more equitable division of the catch. Thirty-nine Spanish fishing boats moved into the NAFO zone.

On 3 March, Canada amended the CFPA regulations to permit Canadian authorities to board and seize Spanish and Portuguese ships fishing in excess of the EU's NAFO-determined quota. Canada believed that limit to have been reached by the beginning of March. On 6 March, Fisheries Minister Brian Tobin announced Canada's intent to act if the dispute was not resolved diplomatically.[15] Within the Canadian cabinet, a heated debate had been taking place between advocates of tough action, led by Tobin and the members of the Department of Fisheries and Oceans (DFO), and foreign relations professionals in the Department of Foreign Affairs and International Trade (DFAIT), very much concerned about the effect this would have on Canada's international reputation.[16] Chrétien backed Tobin, and three days later the *Estai* was seized in a dramatic four-hour chase. After warning shots were fired over the ship's bow, the *Estai* was boarded and towed back to a jeering crowd in St. John's, Newfoundland. The *Estai*'s captain was arrested and Canadian authorities claimed to have found large numbers of undersized turbot and other illegal fish on board. The ship's net, which had been cut during the chase, was seized. In Spain, huge street demonstrations took place in Vigo, and the Canadian embassy in Madrid was pelted with fish.[17]

Legal Issue: Unilateral State Action

In the highly publicized dispute that followed, the European Union defended the right of Spanish ships to fish in international waters. The central issue was the alleged illegality of Canada's unilateral action, particularly since it involved the use of force and because Canada was a member of a multilateral fisheries organization responsible for managing the fishery.

International law has traditionally provided states with substantial jurisdictional freedom. However, when a state takes action beyond its territory and in potential violation of treaty obligations, there is a presumption that it must provide a legitimate basis for doing so. There are at least two distinguishable ways in which states might defend a decision to act unilaterally that might otherwise violate international law. Both are relevant to Canada's turbot war with Spain.

One form of justification is implied by what is variously termed self-help, self-protection, and self-preservation. The goal here is modest: not to change the law but to make a temporary exception to it in response to a threat to the state's vital interests. Unlike the related doctrine of self-defense, self-help is less a right to be asserted in the face of an actual or imminent attack than an excuse to be given when the state is forced to take action that would seem to violate international law. In order to invoke self-help, two elements borrowed from self-defense are traditionally required. The first is a *necessity* to act, a serious and immediate problem threatening significant damage to the legitimate interests of the state. The second is that the state's response is *proportional*, one tailored carefully to the nature of the threat. The generality of the self-help concept and the ambiguity of the circumstances under which it can be invoked have given rise to understandable fears of abuse. However, those who once proclaimed its demise predicated their arguments on what seem unduly optimistic assumptions about the ability of the UN system of collective security to provide adequate protection for state's rights. A strong argument can be made that self-help continues to exist in international law and is particularly relevant in the environmental arena.

One of the best examples of environmental self-help occurred after the *Torrey Canyon* oil spill. In March 1967, a Liberian oil tanker carrying almost 120,000 tons of Kuwaiti oil ran aground off the coast of southern England beyond the limits of the United Kingdom's territorial sea. Heavy oil spewed from the ship; ultimately 35 million gallons were released causing extensive damage to property and sea life along British and French beaches. The British waited for several days before taking action against the ship, instead permitting salvagers to try to regain control of the vessel. Finally the Royal Air Force was ordered to sink the tanker to prevent further damage. Given the clear and imminent threat posed by the ship and the fact that other measures had failed, the British were not criticized for their action. Indeed, there was some suggestion that Great Britain owed a duty to France and other states potentially affected by the spill to take such measures, perhaps even sooner and more decisively.[18] The *Torrey Canyon* disaster became the catalyst for the development of the 1969 Intervention Convention, which now provides for all coastal states a right to take such preventive measures even on the high seas.[19] However, the United Kingdom's goal at the time was not to develop international law, but to protect British coastlines.

Second, a state may attempt to change the law by asserting a right in an otherwise unregulated area or in one where it believes the law is outdated. Canada made such a claim in 1970 when it enacted the Arctic Waters Pollution Prevention Act (AWPPA). Designed to prevent the marine pollution that it feared would result were the United States to ship crude oil from Alaska's North Slope through Arctic waters adjacent to Canada's coast, the legislation extended Canadian jurisdiction over Arctic waters out to a limit of 100 miles for the purpose of controlling potential polluting activities. While some chose to defend this action in terms more closely associated with the right of self-help,[20] the legislation amounted to an attempt to change international law to extend a form of control, albeit limited and far short of sovereignty, over waters considered vital to Canada.[21] In the words of the former legal adviser to the Canadian Department of External Affairs, Canada though "well aware of the controversial nature of these measures . . . was aware also that international law is developed by state practice, that is, by unilateral measures gradually acquiesced in and followed by other states."[22]

In the turbot dispute, Spain felt that international law was clear, authoritative, and completely supportive of Spain. Spanish ships, like those of all other nations, enjoyed the time-honored rights to navigate and to fish on the high seas. Spain was operating lawfully within NAFO, which recognized the right of members to opt out of rules they opposed, as the European Union had done. Spain also had the "exclusive responsibility over any ship sailing its flag,"[23] and the right to respond to Canadian "piracy" by sending ships to protect its nationals. Should "any accident" occur as a result, "it would not be the fault of the Spanish government."[24] Contrasting itself with Canada, Spain pledged not to "respond to a violation of international laws with yet another violation of international laws."[25] Spain had sufficient confidence in its argument to file a formal complaint before the International Court of Justice, contending that Canada had violated provisions of the NAFO Convention as well as rules of general international law in amending the CFPA and seizing the *Estai*.[26]

The ICJ claim brought a new level of institutional complexity to the dispute. The European Union, asserting its competence to represent the interests of EU members in all maritime fisheries matters, claimed the sole right to challenge Canadian actions within NAFO. However, since the European Union is not a state, it could not bring a case before the ICJ. Spain could do so, but only if it could provide a jurisdictional foundation for its claim against Canada.[27]

The European Union initially seemed even more adamant than Spain in condemning Canadian behavior. When the CFPA amendments were passed, an EU spokesperson compared the new law to the actions of Saddam Hussein. While admitting that this matter was "of a different magnitude," it was nonetheless "outside international law."[28] Fisheries Commissioner Bonino entered the fray, concurring that the Canadian actions were even more than unlawful, accusing Canada of turning the Grand Banks into "some sort of a Far West, with one state acting as the only self-appointed lawmaker, sheriff, and judge."[29]

The seizure of the *Estai* attracted broad support in Canada. Yet, while most Canadians thought it both appropriate and justified, whether it was legal posed a more difficult question. Four lines of argument emerged.

The first was that the *Estai*'s arrest was morally right and acceptable under international law. Former Canadian ambassador J. Alan Beesley, who led the Canadian delegation at the Third UN Conference on the Law of the Sea, suggested two different legal rationales. The first was based on the doctrine of self-help, given the seriousness of the threat to turbot stocks and the measured nature of the Canadian response.[30] The second focused on the coastal state's right to impose conservation measures over fish stocks adjacent to its coast when other states fail to cooperate in taking measures to protect those stocks. This approach drew support from past state practice dating back to the Truman Proclamations and from the decisions of the ICJ in the Anglo-Norwegian Fisheries and Anglo-Icelandic Fisheries cases.[31]

A second line of argument was that the rules governing straddling stocks were unclear or nonexistent. The result was a legal vacuum in which Spain could not prove that Canada had behaved unlawfully. One writer, using one of the myriad nautical metaphors that dominated media coverage of the dispute, suggested that Canada had "stepped into uncharted legal water," while also quoting Dalhousie's David VanderZwaag that the "case seems to fall between the cracks of international law."[32] The *Times* of London offered its editorial support to Canada in part because it recognized Canada's need to "fill the legal breach" in managing straddling fish stocks.[33] In an interview with *Maclean's* at the height of dispute, Tobin reflected a similar attitude. "No nation has authority to set the rules, and more importantly, no nation has the authority to enforce the rules. Therefore there are no rules, and it's a free for all. . . . It is the tragedy of the commons."[34]

A third approach was to admit that the actions were probably unlawful, but just, according to some other set of normative criteria. Few were prepared to celebrate the seizure of the *Estai* as a simple act of Canadian power; even the most jingoistic Canadian seemed compelled to offer some justification. Writing in the *Vancouver Sun*, Barbara Yaffee proclaimed that Canadians were "Pirates! and proud of it" and admitted forthrightly that, under international law, Canada had committed an "act of aggression . . . beyond the limits of Canada's jurisdiction." Still she was certain that the act was "morally defensible," in part because it served broader global interests, in part because it punished those violating NAFO rules.[35] However, the sense of a gap between what was right and what was legal was, for others, not so easily overcome. More attractive was to argue that international law provided few protections for fisheries. One observer complained, "there are few areas of international law so inadequate."[36] Another declared the law "as leaky as a fishnet," lacking both restrictive rules and effective enforcement.[37] Others tended to see the legal challenge as somewhat less daunting. The NAFO quotas served as the "rules of law" to be followed, whatever the significance of NAFO's opting-out procedure. Canada's unilateral enforcement, though in one sense a "lawless act of Canadian self-interest," thus was also "overdue, and justified" since "only enforcement can give international law any practical effect."[38] An editorial in the *Buffalo News* concurred. While the Canadians "in strictly legal terms . . . are overstepping their bounds," their action was "perfectly reasonable" given the failure of other states to "tightly observe international rules on conservation."[39] Canada had become, in the words of the *New York Times*, a "high-minded conservation vigilante."[40] Somewhat ironically given the organization's own history of direct action, a Greenpeace spokesperson opposed Canada's "clear violation of international law," even as he agreed that the law of the sea "has done very little to prevent continued and relentless overfishing."[41]

A final argument was that Canada's action would promote needed reforms in international fisheries law, just as Canada's earlier AWPPA had helped bring about extended coastal state enforcement jurisdiction over marine pollution.[42] A *Globe and Mail* reporter saw Canada as "extending the bounds of international law through action rather than talk."[43] Newfoundland's Premier Clyde Wells compared the Canadian action to the British decision to send the Royal Navy to the African coast to stop the slave trade.[44] A representative of the fishing union in Newfoundland argued that, if states had simply waited for changes to happen through negotiation, "we'd still have a three-mile limit. . . . International law . . . evolves by countries taking action and backing it up."[45] Such a catalytic effect was clearly the intent of the Canadian action. Several observers noted that the timing of the seizure of the *Estai* was hardly coincidental, coming on the eve of a key session of the United Nations Conference on Straddling Fish Stocks and Highly Migratory Fish Stocks.[46]

Not everyone found the logic in favor of unilateralism convincing. After the seizure of the *Estai*, even the sympathetic British emphasized the need to move quickly to the conference table to resolve the immediate dispute and produce an effective long-term management regime.[47] Prime Minister John Major suggested that prolonged enforcement actions against Spanish ships could "undermine [Canada's] own good case."[48]

That states targeted by the Canadian action would claim it undermined prospects for cooperation is hardly surprising. More interesting were concerns expressed in Canada that the precedent established by unilateralism might come back to haunt Canadians. Even as it celebrated Canada's "victory" in the fish dispute, the *Ottawa Citizen* expressed editorial concern about the effect of the "un-Canadian methods by which it was achieved" on other Canadian diplomatic initiatives. "In the future, will combatants accuse us of a double standard when we urge them to settle their differences without violence? If Canada is ready to act unilaterally over a bunch of fish, how can we disparage Bosnian Muslims for using guns to save their cities?"[49] The *Globe and Mail* envisioned a future in which Canadians would awake one morning to find that an "outlaw nation—one with less capital than Canada, acting on intentions less honourable than conservation" has seized a ship on the high seas and "to justify its piracy . . . cites Canada as precedent."[50] Europeans angry at British support for Canada also suggested that the United Kingdom might view the Canadian actions differently were it to think in terms of their potential precedent value in areas closer to British interests. A source within the EU Commission remarked, "What would happen if the next vessel seized in international waters was a Cornish or Scottish vessel operating . . . off the coast of Norway? Would they be happy if Spanish fishermen started waving Norwegian flags?"[51] At least in this respect, both supporters and opponents of the Canadian action seemed to agree on one thing: Canada's unilateralism could be catching, even if they disagreed on whether the contagion would be a positive or negative thing.

A related issue was Canada's attitude toward the International Court of Justice. When the CFPA was amended in 1994, Canada made a reservation to its earlier declaration accepting the Court's jurisdiction to remove from the Court's purview cases involving the application of the new law. This was defended as a "temporary step in response to an emergency situation,"[52] necessary to avoid delays in protecting endangered fish stocks during a potentially lengthy adjudicative process.[53] While critics viewed this as tacit admission of Canada's weak legal position, Canada did invoke the amendment in its response to the Spanish claim, arguing that the Court lacked jurisdiction to hear the case. In a statement reminiscent of the attitude adopted by the US in response to the claim brought against it by Nicaragua in 1984, Canada suggested that it would reject any decision by the Court in the matter, since it was better left to "negotiated settlement."[54] The parallel was not lost on observers. One French diplomat reportedly commented that "Canada is becoming more like America every year . . . taking international law into their own hands."[55] However the *Times* of London wrote that Canada's "modification" of its acceptance of the Court's jurisdiction "should carry no stigma," since 11 members of the European Union, including Spain, had their own reservations in place.[56] It was left to a Canadian lawyer to remark with regret, that the "precedent-setting withdrawal of the jurisdiction of the World Court . . . for a country committed to the rule of international law and its progressive development, should at the very least have merited some public questioning and debate."[57]

The Resolution

Despite threats to retaliate against Canada, the European Union did not impose economic sanctions, partly due to British sympathy with the Canadian position.[58] Progress was made on 15 March 1995, when the *Estai*'s owners agreed to post a $500,000 bond for the ship's release; Spanish fishing vessels left the zone, and Canadian and European officials agreed to reopen talks. However, Spanish fishing ships returned on 21 March, now accompanied by a Spanish patrol boat. Talks ended on the 25th without agreement; the next day Canadian ships using new equipment cut the nets of the trawler *Pescamero Uno*, and Spain announced plans to send a second naval vessel to the area. On 28 March, as Spain was taking its legal claim to The Hague, Tobin used a visit to New York to the meeting of the UN Straddling Stocks Conference to offer a graphic exhibit supporting the Canadian position. On a barge in the East River, he produced an "illegal" small-meshed net, which Canadian authorities had recovered from the *Estai*, cut off during the ship's attempted escape.

Renewed talks led to a settlement announced on 15 April just hours before Canadian authorities were preparing to arrest several Spanish ships fishing on the Nose section of the Grand Banks. The agreement[59] represented a significant victory for the Canadian position although Canada did agree to repeal the provisions of the CFPA used to arrest the Spanish ships and to reimburse the *Estai*'s owners for the $500,000 bond. To bring the European Community under the TAC set by NAFO for turbot, Canada agreed to reduce its own quota, thus giving Canada and the European Union approximately 10,000 tons apiece. For 1996, they agreed to propose to NAFO that each receive roughly 41 per cent of whatever TAC was established. More important to Canada, the agreement called for a significant improvement in NAFO enforcement procedures with independent inspectors placed aboard all vessels fishing in the NAFO area and the introduction of satellite tracking equipment to monitor at least 35 per cent of the boats.[60] In September, NAFO adopted most of the agreement's key provisions.

Spain and the European Union publicly welcomed the outcome as a return to more normal, acceptable behavior. Commissioner Bonino declared that the "rule of law has been restored on the high seas" and listed as the first point of the agreement Canada's repeal of the offending provisions of the CFPA. The deal reaffirmed that "European vessels, operating in full respect of International Law and NAFO regulations, may not be prevented from fishing. Reestablishing security and International Law was our primary aim during all these negotiations."[61]

Post-Dispute Developments

The dispute's most immediate effect was within the UN Straddling Stocks Conference, whose first session had been held in April 1993. By 1992, the declining state of the world's high seas fisheries and increased conflict between distant water fishing fleets and a growing number of assertive coastal states had brought recognition of the need for a more comprehensive approach to managing straddling stocks. Of the many issues negotiators faced, none was more critical or divisive than enforcement, and the Canadians had led the charge for an enhanced coastal state role. However, a 1994 draft agreement left much of the effective enforcement up to flag states; the right of coastal states to board and inspect stateless vessels was recognized, but they had no other formal role.[62]

Fresh off the turbot victory, Brian Tobin addressed the conference in July 1995 sounding a tough, defiant note. Canada would not accept any agreement that lacked strong enforcement provisions. "For Canada, no agreement is better than a bad agreement." It was important to "fill the gaps in international law." Tobin suggested that conference participants look to the 15 April agreement between Canada and the European Union as a model. Flag states and coastal states have a "parallel set of legitimate concerns . . . there must be some means to deal with the situation where the flag state is unable or unwilling to control its vessels fishing on the high seas."[63]

The United Nations Fish Stocks Agreement (UNFA) included tougher enforcement provisions. Article 21 provides all parties with the right to board and inspect ships of all other parties fishing in high seas areas covered by regional and subregional agreements in order to enforce agreed conservation measures. Where there are "clear grounds for believing that a vessel has committed a serious violation," and the flag state, once notified, has failed to take action against it, the inspecting state may take the ship into port. Actual punishment is left to the flag state but the hand of the coastal state is noticeably strengthened by the agreement.[64]

It was up to individual regional organizations to implement the new measures. Work began within NAFO even before the UNFA went into force to negotiate more conservation-minded limits for a range of threatened fish species and to improve NAFO's enforcement capacity. In the first months after the dispute, the enhanced enforcement system appeared to be working,[65] and NAFO experienced a period of relative harmony.[66]

By 2002, tensions had resurfaced. Members of the Canadian fishing community and their political representatives from the maritime provinces complained that EU nations were not taking the promised action against ships violating NAFO rules and that excessive use of the Convention's opting out provisions continued. Critics from industry and the environmental community, led by World Wildlife Fund Canada, claimed NAFO "lacked teeth." Three possible strategies emerged. The first would be for Canada to extend its jurisdiction seaward to bring fisheries straddling the Canadian EFZ and the NAFO Regulatory Area completely within Canadian jurisdiction. The second was to adopt a "custodial management" approach. Canadian marine conservation jurisdiction would be extended over fisheries beyond 200 nautical miles, but not over the water column itself. Recognizing some historic rights for foreign ships to fish the stocks being regulated might make this more acceptable than an outright extension of Canada's EFZ. In either case, Canada would have to withdraw from NAFO and would almost certainly face legal challenges that it had violated the 1982 Law of the Sea Convention.[67] The third option would be to try to reform NAFO far more significantly than had thus far been possible.

NAFO's future was hotly debated in the lead-up to the 2006 Canadian national election. Campaigning in Newfoundland and Labrador, Conservative challenger Stephen Harper promised to extend Canadian jurisdiction over the Flemish Cap and the Nose and Tail of the Grand Banks if fundamental NAFO reforms were not enacted within five years. Canadian waters were being "raped. . . . When the country's national interests are at stake, when our stewardship of the country's resources are at stake, we will not hesitate to have diplomatic battles."[68] It was unclear how far Harper was prepared to go militarily to enforce these new claims, but the message rekindled memories of the turbot war. The Liberal government of Paul Martin had also called for improved NAFO enforcement. In December 2004, it closed Canadian ports to Danish-flagged shrimp boats from Greenland and the Faroe Islands accused of overfishing just beyond Canada's EFZ.

Harper's election in January 2006 brought new Canadian pressures for NAFO reform, although what was ultimately negotiated did not go as far as many had hoped, given Harper's campaign rhetoric. In 2007, NAFO adopted changes designed to emphasize that "sustainability," rather than "optimal utilization," would be the guiding NAFO objective.[69] The parties agreed to streamline NAFO's institutional structure to create a single decision-making Commission. The Commission will try to reach consensus on key management decisions; where that is not possible, votes require a two-thirds majority, rather than a simple majority, thus presumably increasing the likelihood that more states would support and actively enforce the new regulations. Crucially for Canada, the opting-out procedure was also changed. While it is still available, dissenting states are now required to explain their objections and outline alternative steps they plan to take to achieve the Convention's objectives. This explanation is then submitted to an ad hoc panel of experts, subject to review by the Commission, and the Convention's dispute settlement procedures could later be invoked. The agreement also clarifies flag state responsibilities regarding treatment of ships allegedly violating NAFO rules.[70]

Although critics feared that the new agreement could actually undermine Canada's control over its fisheries,[71] the progress made was likely possible only because of Canadian threats to leave the negotiations, threats made all the more credible by Canadian actions during the turbot war.[72] While the amendments have yet to receive the nine ratifications needed for the agreement to come into effect, both Canada and the European Union have ratified the changes and appear to be working together more effectively to enforce existing NAFO rules than was true in the past.

Analysis

Canada was the driving force behind the turbot dispute. Well aware of the larger political environment in which it was acting, the Canadian government, essentially led by Brian Tobin, took deliberate action and, by most criteria, emerged the winner. Canada almost certainly triggered the dispute to affect negotiations at the Straddling Stocks Conference, as well as to promote changes within NAFO. Though aggressive, it was an easy policy for the Canadian government to adopt, given the strong and virtually united support it enjoyed among domestic fishing interests and environmental organizations. Only concern for Canada's image abroad, largely a worry of foreign policy officials, provided reason for governmental restraint.

The dispute was resolved through bilateral diplomacy with the European Union, with Spanish officials relegated to a secondary role. While the European Union attempted to support the Spanish position, and did win changes in turbot quotas benefiting Spanish ships, it was unable to take any decisive economic action against Canada given Britain's position. NAFO's institutional weakness in 1995 prevented it from playing a more decisive intermediary role, and the International Court of Justice was effectively removed from the process by its jurisdictional limitations. The Spanish ICJ claim served a limited political purpose, but little more.

The substantive area of international environmental law most directly affected by the turbot dispute was the acceptance of an enhanced enforcement role for coastal states in regulating marine fisheries. Canada had a clear set of goals and put a high priority on achieving them. By combining direct action and negotiation, Canada made significant progress both in the North Atlantic and beyond. International negotiations underway at the Straddling Stocks Conference offered Canada an opportunity to graft stronger rules onto the development of a global treaty regime at the moment of formation. In NAFO it had an existing institutional framework in which enhanced fisheries enforcement could be implemented while still providing protection for wary distant water fishing states. Moreover, the rules it hoped to develop reflected a reasonable extension of a trend already underway for over 40 years in a dynamic area of international law.

Of more general significance to the development of international environmental law was the grudging international recognition that states, under certain circumstances, do have a right to take unilateral action to protect legitimate environmental interests. Three factors help explain the degree of support that Canada received from states and observers without a direct stake in the outcome of the dispute, although they also reveal areas of disagreement among the disputants. Two are derived from the rules governing self-help, the necessity to act and the proportionality of the action taken, while a third can be traced to the effect of the actions on the development of new legal standards governing fisheries.

First, with regard to necessity, Canada's seizure of the *Estai* was defended as a response to a "grave and imminent threat . . . [to] an essential interest," a "peril not caused by Canada."[73] That North Atlantic fisheries, and turbot in particular, were in trouble could hardly be denied given declining yields. Yet did this constitute a problem sufficient to cross something like the "grave and imminent" threshold? No one seemed prepared to say otherwise, and even Spain found it difficult to challenge the sense that North Atlantic fisheries were in bad shape. The European Union acknowledged the seriousness of the problem by approving the overall TAC for turbot; the difference with Canada was on the distribution of the quotas.

There was more room for disagreement on the question of who was responsible for the "peril." Canada never denied its past history of overfishing, but felt that its self-imposed moratorium within its own EFZ indicated its commitment to fisheries reform.[74] Spain and the European Union saw things quite differently, viewing the overfishing problem as the result of bad management within the Canadian zone. Spanish Fisheries Minister Luis Atienza argued that it was "absurd" that Canada, "a country which has exhausted its resources should set itself up as guardian of the 10 per cent outside its control."[75]

Also contentious was the question of whose "essential interest" was threatened. Here the focus was less on the importance of the fisheries, something both sides conceded, than in whose interest they were. While self-help traditionally focuses on the state's ability to take extraordinary measures to defend its own rights, Canada stressed throughout the dispute that it was acting to protect the interests of the international community rather than any special interest of Canada's. "If we do not protect these fragile stocks now, we—not we as a nation, but we as a planet—may lose them forever," declared Tobin.[76] Canada was assuming the role of protector not just of a shared resource important to humans but of the larger planetary ecology and even its small, otherwise defenseless components. At perhaps the zenith of his rhetorical assault on Spain and using the *Estai*'s captured net, all 16 storeys' worth, as a backdrop, Tobin told the assembled press in New York, "We're down now finally to one last, lonely, unattractive little turbot clinging on by its fingertips to the Grand Banks, saying 'reach out and save me in this eleventh hour.'"[77]

Not everyone defending Canada approached the issue in such selfless terms. The fall 1993 cod survey had indicated that even a complete ban on fishing in the Canadian EFZ, imposing tremendous costs on Canada's fishing industry, was achieving little as long as exploitation of straddling stocks continued on the high seas.[78] As the *Ottawa Citizen* put it at the time of the CFPA amendments, "The self-interest of Canada is transparent and unembarrassing. Straddling stocks must be protected if Atlantic Canada's cod fishery is ever to revive."[79]

Spain challenged Canadian claims that it was protecting a global resource, suggesting instead that this was simply a case of Canadian greed.[80] Atienza also saw the action as politically motivated, an attempt to deflect attention from its own failed policies and blame a "foreign enemy . . . for all its problems."[81]

The Spanish government was less inclined to argue that it had any special interest in the fisheries, other than as a nation exercising its right to fish on the high seas. However, one Spanish editorial argued that, "For centuries before Canada existed, ships sailed by people of the [Spanish] coast have fished for cod. History supports our right to continue fishing."[82] The closest the Spanish came to making a historic rights argument was in their frequent criticism of the NAFO quotas, which they felt did not adequately recognize past Spanish catches of turbot.

A second factor was the nature of the Canadian response. Even if legitimate interests were endangered, should Canada not have tried to protect them through multilateral channels? This naturally questioned NAFO's ability to manage the fisheries. The Canadian government had reason to mute its criticism of NAFO as an institution, since part of the Canadian justification for its action was the need to implement NAFO rules. Canada stressed repeatedly that it had no desire either to extend its national jurisdiction over the fisheries or to replace NAFO with another institution. The issue was enforcement, and Canada was able to claim after the settlement that it had helped create a "total enforcement regime" for NAFO.[83]

The European Union argued that NAFO was working reasonably well. The problem was Canada's unwillingness to permit the organization to function as intended. After the seizure of the *Estai*, Spain criticized Canada for delaying efforts to discuss the dispute within NAFO and used past NAFO inspections of the *Estai* to argue that the ship had not been engaged in illegal fishing.[84] It also argued that NAFO had procedures that would have permitted Canada a reasonable right of inspection, which Canada refused to exercise.[85] EU officials went to great length to insist that their disagreement was over how NAFO apportioned the turbot quotas, not the 27,000-ton TAC it had imposed. The European Union had exercised its right under the Convention to opt out of the allotment formula, and the reapportionment of the quotas now answered their primary objection.[86]

Canadians were far more direct and colorful in suggesting that whatever system existed had failed to curtail abusive Spanish fishing practices. The Spanish "sat like grim reapers" just beyond Canada's EFZ, "harvesting stocks to the point of extinction."[87] "The European devils" had been "raping the seas."[88] Spain had a "reputation for ignoring conservation practices"; having "destroy[ed] their own waters . . . they're over here trying ours."[89] The arrest of the *Estai* brought further evidence of the problem. The discovery of immature turbot, a "hidden compartment" containing other illegal fish, and a "secret logbook," not to mention the much-celebrated small-meshed net, all indicated an ongoing Spanish defiance that could not be tolerated.[90] Another line of argument, which reinforced the Canadian position at the UN Straddling Stocks Conference, was that it was simply too difficult for flag states to police their own fleets far from home.[91] Tobin did try to suggest that the problem lay not with hard-working people on board the boats, for whom many Canadians actually had sympathy, but with the "pirates . . . in the blue suits who sit in the corporate boardrooms and own these vessels."[92]

Canada also saw this action as a last resort after years of diplomatic efforts had failed and after Spain had been warned of the consequences of non-agreement. "We have conducted diplomacy down to the last few pounds of fish," declared Tobin.[93] The European Union's Bonino disagreed, arguing that Canada's "aggressive" behavior suggested little interest in a negotiated settlement.[94] In a series of Internet messages entitled "Latest Fridays" and "Friday's Specials," Spain contended that the entire pattern of Canadian diplomacy during the dispute was calculated not to reach a resolution but to keep the Spanish government off balance by forcing it to respond to a series of carefully timed weekend ultimatums.[95]

Spain also claimed that the Canadian naval actions posed an unnecessary threat to Spanish civilians and ships, what Bonino termed a "wave of terror" unleashed by Canadian authorities.[96] High speed chases through dangerous seas and under difficult weather conditions, warning shots, the cutting of nets, and the failure to control bellicose crowds in St. John's created an aggressive pattern of behavior that could not be justified. In the civil claim brought later in Canada by the *Estai*'s owners, much was made of the actions of Canadian authorities during the seizure of the ship.[97] The Canadian judge rejected that argument, holding that the actions of the crew attempting to escape triggered the chase, and that the force used in boarding the ship was not excessive.[98]

A third factor that supports the Canadian action is that it seemed designed to change, and ultimately did change, a fisheries regime that needed reform. To be sure, it was difficult to know at the time the *Estai* was seized that this would result, but it is important that institutional reform was a genuine Canadian goal and not simply political rhetoric to mask a Canadian grab for more fish. The reforms agreed to by NAFO and the success of the Straddling Stocks Conference provided for many the ultimate vindication of the Canadian position in the turbot war. "The appropriate but illegal tactics that Brian Tobin . . . used last spring to intimidate some unscrupulous Spanish fishermen may now, in the eyes of international law, become imminently acceptable."[99] What had been morally right was now being given legal sanction, though admittedly after the fact.

Canada could make a reasonable case that it had acted within the bounds of necessity and proportionality. There was a generally recognized threat to a resource in which Canada and the international community had a genuine interest. It took action only after years of unsuccessful negotiation within the framework of a weak multilateral regime and only after Canada had imposed significant and costly restrictions on its own fishing industry. Appropriate warning was given, and the seizure was conducted so as to minimize risk. Canada ultimately accepted a negotiated settlement in which its nationals would be able to take fewer turbot than NAFO had authorized. Moreover, its actions helped change the rules in NAFO and UNFA in ways that would strengthen multilateral institutions responsible for managing marine fisheries.

Spain and the European Union never accepted the legality of the Canadian actions, and Canada never offered a full legal justification, since Spain's ICJ case was dismissed on jurisdictional grounds.[100] Canada agreed to rescind the amendments to the CFPA, and its more restrained actions in the later shrimp dispute with Denmark may suggest Canadian recognition of the diplomatic costs associated with aggressive unilateralism. While the turbot dispute made clear that there are circumstances under which unilateral action to protect the environment can be both effective and justifiable, it may also have helped develop guidelines about when it is appropriate.

Notes

1   This chapter draws on material previously published in Allen L. Springer, "The Canadian Turbot War with Spain: Unilateral State Action in Defense of Environmental Interests," *Journal of Environment and Development* 6 (1997): 26–60.
2   "EU Halts Meetings with Canadians," *Moscow Times*, 14 March 1995.
3   Peter J. Stoett, "Fishing for Norms: Foreign Policy and the Turbot War of 1995," in *Ethics and Security in Canadian Foreign Policy*, ed. Rosalind Irwin (Vancouver: University of British Columbia Press, 2001), 255.
4   "United Nations Convention on the Law of the Sea," Montego Bay, 10 December 1982 (entered into force 16 November 1994), *International Legal Materials* 21 (1982): 1283 [hereafter cited as "LOSC"].
5   Douglas Day, "Tending the Achilles Heel of NAFO: Canada Acts to Protect the Nose and Tail of the Grand Banks," *Marine Policy* 19 (1995): 268.
6   NAFO's governing agreement is the "Convention on Future Multilateral Cooperation in the Northwest Atlantic Fisheries," Ottawa, 24 October 1978 (entered into force 1 January 1979) [hereafter cited as "NAFO Convention"]. http://www.nafo.int/about/frames/convention.html. Described here is how the convention currently operates. As will be discussed, significant changes would be made in NAFO if reforms adopted in 2007 are ratified.
7   As seen in the previous chapter, Emma Bonino would go on to play a more conciliatory role as EU Environment Commissioner in the Baia Mare dispute.
8   "NAFO Convention."
9   Canada, "Coastal Fisheries Protection Act as Amended in 1994," *International Legal Materials* 33 (1994): 1383.
10   Clyde H. Farnsworth, "Canadian Law Pushes Past 200-Mile Limit," *Portland Press Herald*, 16 May 1994, 1: 5.
11   Day, "Tending the Achilles Heel," 264–65. See also, "New Canadian Law on Inspection of Vessels Runs Counter to International Law, Says Council," *Reuter Textline, Agence Europe*, 14 June 1994.

12 Clyde Farnsworth, "Mellow Canadians Bellow over Their Fishing Rights," *Brunswick Times Record*, 31 March 1995, 11.

13 "License Fee Announced for U.S. Vessels," *Reuter Textline*, 9 June 1994.

14 Colin Nickerson, "Canada Seizes Massachusetts Scallopers; 2 New Bedford Boats Boarded in International Area," *Boston Globe*, 27 July 1994, 1.

15 Andrew Flynn, "Tobin Vows Tough Action to Stop EU Fishing Fleet," *Ottawa Citizen*, 6 March 1995.

16 Brendan Howe and Matthew Kerby, "The Canada-EU Turbot War and the Cybernetic Model of Decision-Making," *The Round Table* 98, no. 401 (2009): 173–74.

17 Marvin S. Soroos, "The Turbot War: Resolution of an International Fishery Dispute," in *Conflict and the Environment*, ed. Nils Petter Gleditsch, *NATO ASI Series* (Dordrecht, Netherlands: Springer, 1997), 240.

18 Jan Schneider, *World Public Order of the Environment: Towards an International Ecological Law and Organization* (Toronto: University of Toronto Press), 151.

19 "International Convention Relating to Intervention on the High Seas in Cases of Oil Pollution Casualties," Brussels, 29 November 1969 (entered into force 6 May 1975), *International Legal Materials* 9 (1970): Art. 1(1), 25 [hereafter "Intervention Convention"].

20 Albert E. Utton, "The Arctic Waters Pollution Prevention Act, and the Right of Self-Protection" in *International Environmental Law*, ed. Ludwik A. Teclaff and Albert E. Utton (New York: Praeger, 1974), 140–53.

21 For more on the rationale behind the AWPPA, see comments of the Canadian Secretary of State for External Affairs, Mitchell Sharp, 4 June 1969, *Canadian Yearbook of International Law* 8 (1970): 344–45; and 16 April 1970 *Canadian Yearbook of International Law* 9 (1971): 284–85.

22 J. Alan Beesley, "The Canadian Approach to International Environmental Law," *Canadian Yearbook of International Law* 11 (1973): 5.

23 Spanish Foreign Ministry spokesperson, quoted in Andrew Kelly, "Spain Takes Canada to World Court in Fishing Dispute," *Reuters*, 28 March 1995.

24 Garcia Vargas, Spanish Defense Minister, in Robert Hart, "Spanish Ships Resume Fishing in Disputed Atlantic Area," *Reuter Textline*, 28 March 1995.

25 Spanish Foreign Minister, Javier Solana, "Statement to the Media," *Si Spain*, 27 March 1995.

26 International Court of Justice (ICJ), "Fisheries Jurisdiction Case (Spain v. Canada) (Spain, Application Instituting Proceedings)" 28 March 1995. http://www.icj-cij.org/docket/files/96/7197.pdf.

27 Adela Rey Aneiros, "Spain, the European Union, and Canada: A New Phase in the Unstable Balance in the Northwest Atlantic Fisheries," *Ocean Development and International Law* 42, no. 1–2 (2011): 157.

28 Farnsworth, "Canadian Law."

29 Emma Bonino, European Commissioner for Fisheries, comments on "Fish Story," *The MacNeil/Lehrer NewsHour*, 29 March 1995, 10.

30 J. Alan Beesley and Malcolm Rowe, "Why Canada Was Right in the Turbot Fight," *Vancouver Sun*, 24 May 1995, A15.

31 William T. Burke, "The Law of the Sea Convention Provisions on Conditions of Access to Fisheries Subject to National Jurisdiction," *Oregon Law Review* 63 (1984): 113.

32   John DeMont, "Gunboat Diplomacy," *Maclean's*, 20 March 1995, 10.

33   The Times Editorial, "Canadian Practices," *Reuter Textline*, 31 March 1995.

34   Brian Tobin, quoted in Chris Wood, "Who Owns the Sea?," *Maclean's*, 27 March 1995.

35   Barbara Yaffe, "Pirates and Politics," *Vancouver Sun*, 14 March 1995, A14.

36   Runku Varadarajan, "Hook, Line and Sink'em," *Reuter Textline*, 14 April 1995.

37   Wood, "Who Owns the Sea?."

38   "No More Codswallop," *Ottawa Citizen*, 5 April 1994, A8.

39   "May the Canadians Defeat the Spanish Fish Armada: In Overfished World, Our Neighbors Take a Stand," *Buffalo News*, 14 April 1995, 2.

40   John Darnton, "2 Feuding Nations with Fish Stories," *New York Times*, 2 April 1995, E4.

41   Matthew Gianni, "Fish Story," 13.

42   See, generally, Ted L. McDorman, "Canada's Aggressive Fisheries Actions: Will They Improve the Climate for International Agreements?," *Canadian Foreign Policy* 2, no. 3 (1994): 5–28.

43   Edward Greenspon, "Canada Vows to Stop Pirates," *Globe and Mail*, 4 April 1994, A1.

44   Clyde Wells, Premier of Newfoundland, in "Fish Story," 12–13.

45   Earle McCurdy, President of the Fishermen, Food and Allied Workers Union, quoted in Gavin Will, "Fishing War of Words May Become Violent," *Financial Post*, 5 March 1994, (1)8.

46   See, for example, "Turmoil over Turbot Points to Need for High Seas Fishing Deal," *Vancouver Sun*, 16 March 1995, A20.

47   See comments by Michael Jack, junior UK fisheries minister, in Juliet O'Neill, "British MPs Throw Support Behind Canada," *Ottawa Citizen*, 14 March 1995, A4.

48   See comments of UK Prime Minister John Major in John Carvel, Stephen Bates, and Clare Dyer, "Talks to Raise EU Fish Quota," *Reuter Textline*, 31 March 1995.

49   "Victory at Sea," *Ottawa Citizen*, 18 April 1995, A14.

50   "A Dubious Victory in the Fish War," *Globe and Mail*, 18 April 1995.

51   Unidentified diplomat, quoted in "Talks to Raise EU Fish Quota."

52   Statement of the Canadian government, quoted in Charles Trueheart, "Canada Vows to Police High Seas," *Washington Post*, 11 May 1994, A30.

53   Canada, Fisheries and Oceans Canada, "Tobin and Wells Respond to Misinformation on the Canada-EU Turbot Dispute," 24 March 1995 (Document NR-HG-95–34E).

54   "Canada Will Reject World Court Ruling," *Agence France Presse*, 29 March 1995.

55   Unidentified French diplomat, quoted in Eric S. Block and Jonathan D. Tepperman, "Overfishing in Troubled Waters," *Washington Times*, 10 April 1995, A19.

56   "Canadian Practices."

57   Lawrence Herman, "Law of the Sea Is Seen as a Bit of Museum Piece," *Financial Post*, 7 December 1994, 1(17).

58   See, for example, the comments by Prime Minister John Major before the House of Commons, in Carvel, Bates, and Dyer, "Talks to Raise EU Fish Quota."

59   Canada-European Community, "Agreed Minute on the Conservation and Management of Fish Stocks," 20 April 1995, *International Legal Materials* 30 (1995): 1260.

60 On the terms and importance of the settlement, see Tim Buerkle, "Fishing Pact Ends Dispute between EU and Canada," *International Herald Tribune*, 17 April 1995; and Clyde H. Farnsworth, "North Atlantic Fishing Pact Could Become World Model," *New York Times*, 17 April 1995, A2.

61 Emma Bonino, "Statement on the Occasion of the Initialing of the Agreement between the European Union and Canada on Fisheries (16 April 1995)," *Reuter Textline*, 10 April 1995.

62 United Nations General Assembly, "Draft Agreement for the Implementation of the Provisions of the United Nations Convention on the Law of the Sea 10 December 1982 Relating to the Conservation and Management of Straddling Fish Stocks and Highly Migratory Fish Stocks Prepared by the Chairman of the Conference," 1994 (Doc. A/Conf.164/22), Art. 20.

63 Brian Tobin, "Notes for an Address to the United Nations Conference on Straddling Fish Stocks and Highly Migratory Fish Stocks," 24 July 1995. See also Stephen Handelman, "Tobin Warns U.N. on Fish Law for Canada," *Toronto Star*, 25 July 1995.

64 United Nations General Assembly, "Agreement for the Implementation of the Provisions of the United Nations Convention on the Law of the Sea 10 December 1982 Relating to the Conservation and Management of Straddling Fish Stocks and Highly Migratory Fish Stocks," 4 August 1995 (entered into force 11 December 2001), *International Legal Materials* 34 (1995): 1542–91, Art. 21, 1563–65.

65 Canada, Department of Foreign Affairs and International Trade, "Fisheries Statistics Show 100 Per Cent Observer Coverage Effective," 1995 (Document NR-HQ-95-86E).

66 Aneiros, "Spain, the European Union, and Canada," 158.

67 Ibid., 158–59.

68 Allan Woods, "Harper Would Use Force to Protect Fish Stocks," *Calgary Herald*, 7 December 2005, A6.

69 North Atlantic Fisheries Organization (NAFO), "Amendment to the Convention on Future Multilateral Cooperation in the Northwest Atlantic Fisheries," 28 September 2007 (not yet in force) (GC Doc 07/4). http://www.nafo.int/about/frames/convention.html.

70 Aneiros, "Spain, the European Union, and Canada," 162–64.

71 "Canada Ratifies NAFO Changes, Despite Sovereignty Concerns from N.L.," *Maclean's*, 11 December 2009.

72 "Canada Won Fisheries Reforms after Threatening to Leave Talks," *CBC News*, 26 September 2006.

73 Beesley and Rowe, "Why Canada Was Right in the Turbot Fight," A15.

74 "Victory at Sea."

75 Luis Atienza, "Personal View: Estai's Boarding Tantamount to Piracy," *Financial Times*, 28 March 1995, 3.

76 Tobin, quoted in Trueheart, "Canada Vows to Police High Seas," A14.

77 Tobin, quoted in John DeMont, "Tobin's War," *Maclean's*, 10 April 1995, 14.

78 Will, "Fishing War of Words May Become Violent."

79 "No More Codswallop."

80 Atienza, "Personal View: Estai's Boarding Tantamount to Piracy."

81 Ibid.

82   Unnamed source, quoted in Wood, "Who Owns the Sea?"
83   Buerkle, "Fishing Pact Ends Dispute between EU and Canada."
84   Juan Antonio Yanez-Barneuvo, Representative of Spain to the United Nations, "Letter to the Editor," *New York Times*, 3 April 1995.
85   Atienza, "Personal View: Estai's Boarding Tantamount to Piracy."
86   Bonino, "Statement."
87   Tom Regan, "Canada Follows Talk with Action," *Portland Press Herald*, 12 March 1995, B2.
88   Harris Bartholomew, Canadian fisherman, quoted in Colin Nickerson, "Thousands Jeer Captured Spanish Trawler," *Brunswick Times Record*, 13 March 1995, 9.
89   William McCloskey, "Some Countries Continually Ignore International Fishing Treaties," *Portland Press Herald*, 3 May 1995, 9A.
90   "Turmoil over Turbot."
91   "Coastal States Need Power to Conserve Fish Stocks," *Reuter Textline*, 28 March 1995.
92   Tobin, quoted in Greenspon, "Canada Vows to Stop Pirates."
93   Farnsworth, "Canadian Law," 5A.
94   Bonino, in "Canada Will Reject."
95   See, for example, "Friday's Specials," *Si Spain*, 1995.
96   Bonino, quoted in Wood, "Who Owns the Sea?"
97   Bonnie Belec, "Estai Lawsuit Begins," *St. John's Telegram*, 11 January 2005.
98   "Estai Boarding Upheld," *Halifax Daily News*, 31 July 2005, 26.
99   "High Hopes for High Seas: Canada Scores for Fish Stocks," *Montreal Gazette*, 6 August 1995, B2.
100 International Court of Justice (ICJ), "Fisheries Jurisdiction Case (Spain v. Canada) (Jurisdiction of the Court)," 28 March 1998. http://www.icj-cij.org/docket/files/96/7533.pdf.

7
Voyage of the *Clemenceau*

Introduction

On 8 February 2009, the decommissioned French aircraft carrier *Clemenceau* was towed into port in Hartlepool, England, for dismantling. This brought to an end a nearly decade-long dispute surrounding the disposal of a once proud ship labeled "toxic" by environmentalists because of the tons of asbestos and other dangerous chemicals it contained. Plans to process the *Clemenceau* at India's Alang shipbreaking yards had become the focus of an intense global debate over the regulation of an industry that in recent years had shifted to developing countries like India and Bangladesh, where environmental and safety regulations were either nonexistent or poorly enforced. While the battle over the *Clemenceau* had ended, the question of how to dismantle aging ships was still very much alive.

There is serious disagreement about what body of law should apply to shipbreaking, a practice that cuts across several different international regimes. Shipbreaking has attracted the attention of the parties to the Basel Convention,[1] the International Maritime Organization (IMO), the International Labour Organization (ILO), and the European Union (EU). Despite the adoption of the Hong Kong International Convention for the Safe and Environmentally Sound Recycling of Ships (hereafter referred to as the Hong Kong Convention)[2] soon after the *Clemenceau* arrived in Hartlepool, reconciling their different perspectives on how to manage the shipbreaking industry represents a serious challenge.

This chapter analyzes the *Clemenceau* dispute and the broader questions it raises about how a decentralized system of environmental governance and a fragmented body of international environmental law respond to a problem that does not fall easily into pre-existing categories. It begins by describing the shipbreaking industry and the problems it presents, and then shows how the controversy over what to do with the *Clemenceau* both reflected and helped shape the international debate over the rules to govern what soon became known, at least within the IMO, as ship "recycling."

The Context

The *Clemenceau* dispute took place at a time of serious international disagreement over what had become a lucrative, but controversial industry.

Map 7.1 This map depicts the route taken by the *Clemenceau* after France decided to have it broken in India. Sailing from Toulon, France, the ship transited the Suez Canal and headed into the Indian Ocean toward Alang, before the French government ordered it to return. The *Clemenceau* traveled to Brest where it was moored until its final trip to Hartlepool, England.

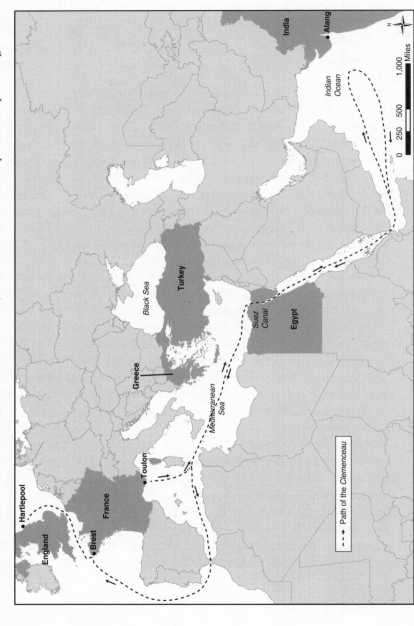

Once primarily conducted in the reasonably well-regulated shipyards of the Organisation for Economic Co-operation and Development (OECD), by the mid-1990s much of the shipbreaking activity had moved to the beaches of South Asia, in particular Pakistan, India, and Bangladesh. Low wages in what is a labor-intensive industry, few local regulatory constraints, and an increasing demand for the steel that could be recycled from existing ships created strong economic incentives for shipowners to have their ships broken in South Asia, where they would realize the highest financial return. For countries like India, shipbreaking provided substantial employment opportunities, both directly and for those involved in industries that depend on the products that can be recovered from recycled ships. At the height of its operations, India's Alang shipyard employed over 40,000 people.[3] As business has shifted to South Asia, once profitable yards in OECD countries have been forced to scale back operations or closely entirely. Even Turkey, which has had among the most competitive shipbreaking industries, found it difficult to compete with Indian yards that could pay nearly twice per ship what their Turkish counterparts could offer.[4]

The migration of the shipbreaking industry to South Asia coincided with a significant increase in demand for shipbreaking capacity. With a global fleet of ocean-going ships estimated at just under 100,000 vessels over 100 GWT in 2009,[5] the year the Hong Kong Convention was signed, even under normal conditions approximately 600 to 700 ships needed to be retired each year. A building boom in the 1970s had produced a particularly large number of ships reaching the end of their productive lives.[6] In 2009, the average age of the world merchant fleet was 22 years.[7] Compounding the challenge was the 2003 decision of the IMO, in the wake of the *Exxon Valdez* and *Erika* oil spills, to begin phasing out single-hulled oil tankers.[8] It was estimated that over 2,200 tankers flying flags of the European Union states alone would need to be decommissioned by 2015.[9]

There are alternatives to direct recycling. Some ships have been transformed into offshore casinos, others scuttled to create artificial reefs, but such reuse still requires expensive cleaning.[10] It is also possible to delay scrapping by holding ships in reserve fleets, as the United States had done since the early 1990s, when concern about shipbreaking practices led the Clinton Administration to order a moratorium on the export of government-owned vessels. However, the cost of maintaining these ships and the environmental risks they present make this at best a stopgap solution.[11]

Shipbreaking in Asian shipyards is a simple but fast-moving process, one of the many reasons it can be difficult to control.[12] Ships destined for breaking are moored offshore until a full moon and high tide make beaching conditions optimal. Each vessel is driven into the beach at full speed, and holes are cut in the ship's hull to allow the waters of the next high tide to wash out to sea pollutants still left in the ship. The ship is stripped of anything of value, and workers armed with acetylene torches then scramble aboard to cut the ships into sections, which can then be sent to steel re-rolling mills. Among the chief concerns about the shipbreaking process are the conditions under which the shipbreakers live and work. Wages are low, training minimal, and protective safety equipment virtually non-existent. Since the ships to be broken are old and seldom precleaned before their arrival, workers are exposed to high levels of asbestos, PCBs, tributyltin (TBT), lead, and other toxic substances. The environmental impact on coastal areas is also significant, particularly along the beaches where the ships are broken and in the coastal estuaries into which the pollutants from the ships flow.[13]

In the late 1990s, the media and environmental NGOs began to alert the public to what was happening in Asian shipbreaking yards. In 1997, Will Englund and Gary Sund published a series of articles in the *Baltimore Sun* linked to the possibility that the United States was reconsidering its ban on exporting retired government-owned vessels. Their reporting won the 1998 Pulitzer Prize for investigative journalism and brought public attention to the dangers of shipbreaking practices, both in the United States and abroad, and drew vivid images of the Alang shipyard to which the ships were rumored to be headed.[14] NGOs led by Greenpeace and the Basel Action Network (BAN) combined with a number of other organizations under the umbrella of the NGO Shipbreaking Platform[15] to publicize the realities of shipbreaking practices and to lobby both nationally and internationally to uncover and oppose what they viewed as illegal activities. In 1998, Greenpeace launched a global campaign against shipbreaking and in 2002 began identifying and tracking what became a list of 50 Toxic Ships it believed were headed to Asian shipbreaking yards. NGOs have remained very active players both in disputes over the disposition of individual ships and in the broader international debate over the best regulatory response.

While there have been highly publicized disputes over governmental efforts to dispose of aging warships like the *Clemenceau* and state-owned merchant vessels, even greater regulatory challenges are posed by privately owned vessels. Often sailing under flags of convenience, their ownership and nationality may change many times. This problem can become particularly acute as a ship reaches the end of its working life, when the shipowner commonly engages a cash buyer to serve as an intermediary in the hope of maximizing the financial return from the ship's dismantling. The new owner, with limited connection to the vessel, becomes a key player in the process by which the ship makes its way to the recycling yards. A buyer may decide to reregister the ship in the process, thus providing even greater distance between those who were responsible for the ship over its active lifetime and those who will recycle it.[16]

The Dispute

What became the *Clemenceau* dispute began in July 2004 when the French government announced plans to the send the aging ship for recycling at Alang. The 870-foot carrier had been launched in 1957 and saw extensive action off the coast of Lebanon during US-led peacekeeping operations in the early 1980s and again in the Persian Gulf during the UN response to Iraq's invasion of Kuwait. The *Clemenceau* was decommissioned in 1997, and the decision was made to send the ship abroad for disposal, given the value of the 26,000 tons of steel it contained (estimated at €8 million) and the cost of dismantling it in France. The original plan called for the ship to be transferred to Spain, then later to Turkey, which maintained perhaps Europe's most competitive ship-recycling facilities, but authorities in both countries refused permission, citing concern about the chemical hazards alleged to be on board. The ship returned to France after Greece declined to participate in its decontamination.[17] As part of an agreement by which Shree Ram Scrap Vessels Pvt. Ltd., an Indian shipbreaking company, would recycle the *Clemenceau* at Alang, France agreed to have 90 per cent of the asbestos the ship still contained removed in Toulon, France, before allowing the hull to be towed to India. Significantly, the French government would maintain ownership of the *Clemenceau* until the ship had been recycled, at which point title would pass to the Panamanian company to which the ship had earlier been sold. French authorities argued that in order to ensure the ship's structural integrity, the rest of the asbestos could not be removed for the trip to Alang—but how much asbestos the ship actually contained both before and after the work was done in Toulon would remain a matter of controversy.[18]

What followed was a well-publicized dispute over the appropriateness of the *Clemenceau*'s transfer to Alang, a dispute in which the national governments of India, France, and Egypt were all directly involved. India was the state in whose territory the ship would be broken and through whose territorial waters it would pass. France was the owner and flag state of the vessel. Since the ship was to be towed to Alang through the Suez Canal, Egypt also had the power to influence events. However, the context in which these governments acted was shaped by forces over which they had only limited control. Environmental NGOs had a significant impact on the outcome, both through legal challenges against the transfer and by using intense media coverage to create a political climate that pressured the French government to reconsider its decision. Judicial bodies in France and India provided arenas in which the legal dimensions of the issues posed by the *Clemenceau* were aired, and their actions ultimately limited the options open to French officials.

The legal dispute began in French courts as environmentalists challenged the transfer as a violation of the Basel Convention and an EU directive designed to prevent shipments of hazardous waste from the European Union to non–OECD countries. The focus was on the dangers posed by the asbestos still on board the ship. A spokesperson for the French ministry of defense claimed that the 115 tons of asbestos removed from the *Clemenceau* "was the maximum we could do without damaging the ship's structure and flotation capacity."[19] In both French and Indian courts, the French government also argued that the rules of the Basel Convention did not apply to warships, and that ships generally could not be classified as "hazardous waste," regardless of the materials they contained.[20] Environmentalists took strong exception to all three assertions,[21] but on 30 December 2005, French courts ruled in favor of the government.[22] The *Clemenceau* was towed from Toulon the next day.

While Indian courts studied the issues posed by the impending arrival of the *Clemenceau*, the immediate focus was on Egypt as the ship made its way toward the Suez Canal. Egyptian authorities ordered the convoy to stop before entering Egyptian waters while the government determined whether the ship's passage would breach the Basel Convention. While the ship was still about 50 miles from Egypt, two Greenpeace activists boarded the vessel and called upon the Egyptian government to refuse passage to a ship that presented "an immediate danger to the Indian environment and to the workers at the Alang ship-breaking yard."[23] Egypt accepted written French reassurances about the lack of environmental hazard posed to Egypt by the *Clemenceau*, agreed that the rules of the Basel Convention did not apply, and permitted the ship to transit the Canal.[24]

Attention shifted to Indian courts, where a debate was raging over whether the *Clemenceau* should be allowed to enter Indian waters. By 2006, the Indian judiciary had begun taking an active role in dealing with environmental matters, fueled most notably by the disastrous 1984 fire at a chemical factory in Bhopal, which had killed thousands and injured many more, revealing serious limitations in India's environmental protection laws.[25] Article 21 of the Indian Constitution, which states that "no person shall be deprived of his life or personal liberty except according to the procedure established by law," was now being viewed by the Indian Supreme Court as providing the legal basis for the right to a clean and healthful environment.

When linked to procedural rights guaranteed by other constitutional provisions, the result, according to one observer, was that "citizens can now approach High Courts or the Supreme Court on any problem that affects the environment."[26]

Shipbreaking practices had become the focus of particular Indian judicial attention. As early as 1995, the Supreme Court had taken on questions involving the dumping of hazardous waste on Indian territory. Two years later, it created a High Power Committee (HPC) to investigate hazardous waste issues, including the failure to decontaminate ships before they arrived in Indian waters. The HPC's "Report on the Management of Hazardous Wastes" established the foundation for a set of guidelines on shipbreaking issued in conjunction with the Supreme Court's 2003 decision in the case of Research Foundation v. Union of India, and Others.[27] The guidelines put responsibility on shipowners to ensure that a ship be "properly decontaminated by the ship owner prior to the breaking" and that "a complete inventory of hazardous waste on board of ship" also be provided. Moreover, the guidelines required the "proper consent from the concerned authority stating that it does not contain any hazardous waste or radioactive substances" before a ship destined for breaking could be permitted into port.[28] A Supreme Court Monitoring Committee (SCMC) was created to help oversee the implementation of the new standards.[29]

The 2003 guidelines were in put in place well before the *Clemenceau* dispute began. However, by 2006 they were already under attack by those claiming that they went too far and were undercutting an important Indian industry facing increased international competition, particularly from neighboring Bangladesh.[30] The SCMC had been aware of the possible arrival of the *Clemenceau* for over a year before the ship actually passed through the Suez Canal and had prepared recommendations to the Alang shipyard about how the ship should be handled. As the carrier approached India, the SCMC grappled with the question of how much asbestos remained on board. The French government claimed that all but 45 tons had been removed, but the French company that had decontaminated the ship, when contacted by the SCMC, indicated that almost 500 tons remained. On 6 January 2006, the Indian Supreme Court issued a temporary order preventing the *Clemenceau* from entering Indian waters until it could determine the amount of asbestos on board and whether its transfer violated the Basel Convention.[31] A split SCMC recommended that the order not be lifted until it could issue a final report; the Supreme Court decided on 13 February to create another expert body to look into the special problems caused by demolishing warships.[32] Meanwhile, French officials offered to return any removed asbestos to France.[33]

Legal Issue: Regime Complexity

At the center of the *Clemenceau* dispute was the question of what body of international law should govern the movement and dismantling of the ship. There were two general approaches that could be taken, although the extent to which they were incompatible was a source of disagreement. The first, favored by environmentalists, was to focus on the hazardous nature of the materials that remained on board the *Clemenceau* and would cross international borders along with the ship. This suggested that the rules of the Basel Convention should apply, supplemented and reinforced by the Stockholm Convention on Persistent Organic Pollutants (hereafter referred to as the Stockholm Convention)[34] and the Rotterdam Convention on the Prior Informed Consent Procedure for Certain Hazardous Chemicals and Pesticides in International Trade (hereafter referred to as the Rotterdam Convention).[35] The second approach, generally the preference of the shipping industry, was to see the problem in more traditional maritime terms, as trade in ships regulated by the traditional jurisdictional rules of the law of the sea.

The 1989 Basel Convention was a response to growing awareness of the effects of international trade in toxic substances, particularly between the developed countries of the OECD and developing states and Eastern Europe. Media reports of incidents like the voyage of the *Khian Sea*, which spent nearly two years between 1986 and 1988 traveling the globe, looking for a place to dump 15,000 tons of Philadelphia incinerator ash, and the deaths and injuries caused in Koko, Nigeria, in 1988 by 8,000 of barrels of Italian hazardous waste deposited on the land of a Nigerian farmer helped pressure governments to act.[36]

The Basel Convention is built around four core objectives: to minimize the generation of hazardous waste, to dispose of it as close to its original source as possible, to reduce the movement of waste across international boundaries, and to ensure its disposal in an environmentally responsible way. State parties play a central regulatory role through a system of prior, informed, written consent. The "State of export" must ensure that both the "State of import" and the state through whose territory hazardous waste will pass are fully aware of the dangers it represents and have agreed to its transboundary movement before it can be exported.[37] Furthermore, the exporting state must not permit the export of hazardous waste "if it has reason to believe that the wastes in question will not be managed in an environmentally sound manner,"[38] and must be prepared to reimport the waste if it becomes evident that adequate management measures are not in place in the importing state.[39]

While the regime created by the Basel Convention lacks the institutional structure of a specialized agency such as the IMO, it does have an ongoing process through which the Conference of the Parties (CoP) can develop new rules. Two important changes have been made since the treaty came into force in 1992, both of which have potential relevance to the shipbreaking industry. The first was the 1995 adoption of an amendment to the convention known as the Basel Ban. This would prohibit the shipment of toxic waste from "Annex VII" to "non-Annex VII" parties, essentially establishing a prohibition on shipments of hazardous waste between developed and developing nations. Because the ban would include waste intended either for disposal or for recycling, it has been opposed, in part, by states hoping to develop waste recycling industries.[40] Though not in force, it has been the basis for regional efforts, including within the European Union, to make the transfer of hazardous waste to developing states illegal.[41] A second development was the negotiation of the Protocol on Liability and Compensation for Damage Resulting from Transboundary Movements of Hazardous Wastes and Their Disposal (hereafter referred to as the Liability Protocol),[42] which attempts to address the thorny issue of the liability faced largely by private parties who may be responsible for damage caused by hazardous waste shipped either under or in violation of the terms of the convention.[43] Like the ban amendment, the Liability Protocol is not yet in force, but the idea that generators of waste should be liable for the damage it causes is very much part of the political reaction to the problems posed by shipbreaking and consistent with the polluter pays principle. To the extent the Basel regime at least attempts to address this issue, it may be seen as offering the potential for effective regulation that other approaches may not.

The Stockholm and Rotterdam Conventions complement the Basel Convention by also adopting a prior informed consent approach to the substances they regulate. The persistent organic pollutants, such as polychlorinated biphenyls (PCBs), whose trade is controlled by the Stockholm Convention, and the PCBs and other chemicals regulated by the Rotterdam Convention are substances commonly found on ships whose presence could affect any shipbreaking trade.[44]

Those opposing the transfer of the *Clemenceau* to Alang argued that it would violate EU and Basel Convention rules. Even though the Basel Ban had yet to come into effect internationally, the European Union had implemented it internally,[45] suggesting that France could not legally export the ship to a non–OECD state. Even within the Basel framework, France, as the exporting state, was required to get the written consent of India and any state of transit before permitting the *Clemenceau* to leave France. France also had to be convinced that the ship would be dismantled in an environmentally sound way, a case that well-publicized media accounts of conditions at Alang suggested would be very difficult to make.[46]

France argued that neither the EU waste regulations nor the Basel Convention applied to shipbreaking and that it would not be appropriate to try to contend with the complex issues posed by shipbreaking within the Basel Convention framework. Article 1(4) states, "Wastes which derive from the normal operations of a ship, the discharge of which is covered by another international instrument, are excluded from the scope of this Convention."[47] From this perspective, waste issues associated with ships, even up to their arrival at shipbreaking yards, could be seen as governed by IMO rules, rather than the Basel Convention, and any "waste" associated with the actual breaking of the ship would be the responsibility of the ship recycler.[48] The *Clemenceau* presented the added complication of being a government-owned warship, which at least the French government thought rules of sovereign immunity should protect from the jurisdiction of Indian courts.[49]

Even if one accepts the view that Basel Convention rules could apply to ships, critics suggest that there would still be challenges in doing so, given the nature of the shipping and shipbreaking industries and the Basel Convention standards themselves. First, at what point does a ship become the equivalent of hazardous waste? Even if a vessel contained substantial amounts of hazardous materials, it would be difficult to imagine applying the Basel standards until the point comes to dismantle it. Yet the decision that a ship is on its "final voyage" is one often made fairly quickly, partly in response to changing market conditions, such as the price of steel. It would also be fairly easy for shipowners to disguise their true intent; once a ship leaves port it may be difficult to determine where it is really headed.[50] Second, in the case of shipbreaking, how does one identify the "export state"—the entity that plays such a key role under the Basel Convention, not only to approve waste transfers, but to judge the environmental appropriateness of the methods that will be used to manage it? This would normally seem to be the state from whose territory the waste is shipped. However, traditional rules of maritime law generally place regulatory responsibility in the hands of the flag state, not the last port from which the ship sailed. In any case, changing ship ownership and registration has become so easy and is such a common part of the process by which ships are sent to be recycled that keeping track of the relevant export state, even if tied to the flag of the vessel, would pose serious challenges. The fact that such a large percentage of the world's merchant fleet is registered under flags of convenience, where effective state control may be minimal, only compounds the problem.[51]

One can also question whether taking the Basel approach is good policy, especially if the ban on North-South waste trade is included. In the case of shipbreaking, the ban may be less limiting than it might seem, given the ease with which a ship's flag could be transferred to a non–Annex VII country whose export of the ship would not be prohibited. Yet to adhere to Basel rules, the new exporting state would still have to be convinced that the ship would be broken in environmentally responsible ways. Developing countries like India and Bangladesh, with the help of external funding, could develop more modern recycling facilities and thus comply with Basel's expectation of sound environmental practices.[52] However, this will likely depend on the willingness of developed countries to provide more financial support than has thus far been evident within the Basel framework. If the ban does work, there would likely be a significant gap between the number of ships that need to be recycled and the capacity of the approved shipbreaking yards to accommodate them. A policy leading shipowners to abandon or scuttle unwanted vessels would impose its own significant environmental costs.

The alternative to the Basel Convention at the time of the *Clemenceau* dispute was to rely on traditional rules of maritime and territorial jurisdiction, since no other treaty-based regime existed. As long as no clear transboundary impact was felt, either from the passage of the ship or from shipbreaking operations, the process was left up to the states most directly involved in the process: the flag state of the ship and the state on whose territory the breaking would take place. In response to the publicity surrounding conditions at Alang and other South Asian shipbreaking operations, the ILO and the IMO had begun work to improve the process, but nothing beyond non-binding guidelines was in place at the time that France was preparing to transfer the *Clemenceau* to India.

The Resolution

The *Clemenceau* dispute ended without any clear choice of legal regimes having been made. Further legal action in India was pre-empted by a 15 February 2006 decision of the French Conseil d'État, acting in response to a complaint from Greenpeace, to suspend the export of the *Clemenceau* and to have the case reviewed by lower courts.[53] This decision came at a time when the European Commission had begun an investigation to determine whether the transfer of the ship was consistent with EU law.[54] Hours later, and just before leaving for a state visit to India, France's President Jacques Chirac announced that he had ordered the *Clemenceau* returned to France. "On the issue of dismantling ships," Chirac declared, "which poses questions on a global dimension related to protection of the environment, France must act in the most exemplary way."[55] While environmentalists and most Indian trade unions claimed a great "bi-national victory,"[56] many who worked at

Alang saw the decision to recall the *Clemenceau*, in the words of one, as having "ruined the hopes of ship-breaking workers to earn handsome money."[57]

France's behavior in the case of the *Clemenceau* left, at best, an ambiguous precedent. Even while challenging the applicability of the Basel Convention, the French government provided the written assurances sought by Egypt, consistent with its position as the "transit" state. Both the French offer to take back any asbestos removed from the ship and the ultimate decision to repatriate the *Clemenceau* could also be viewed as acknowledging France's responsibility to reimport hazardous waste that could not be disposed of responsibly. When environmentalists cheered as the *Clemenceau* sailed back to France, they were celebrating not only the ship's return but also what they saw as affirmation of the direction that regulation of the shipbreaking industry should take.[58]

In July 2008, the French government announced an agreement to have the *Clemenceau*, which had been moored off Brest since its return from India, sent to Hartlepool for salvage.[59] Even this was marred by controversy. French environmentalists argued, as much on philosophical as legal grounds but in a way consistent with Basel Convention logic, that France should be responsible for managing its own hazardous waste. English activists also objected to accepting the risk posed by French waste. However, most major environmental groups saw the move as preferable to disposal at Alang, since the Hartlepool facility was far better able to recycle the ship responsibly.[60]

Post-Dispute Developments

Although the dispute between France and India over the *Clemenceau* effectively ended in 2006 with France's decision to repatriate the ship, the decision came in the midst of continuing debate over how shipbreaking should be regulated. As India was learning, there were economic costs to the more environmentally responsible position it was adopting on shipbreaking practices, as it was losing competitive position to neighboring states such as Bangladesh. National regulation alone would not be an adequate response. Moreover, the realities of the shipbreaking industry in situations where governments were not as directly involved as they were in the case of the *Clemenceau* demonstrated the need for effective international regulation.

Despite questions about the relevance of the Basel Convention, observers had suggested a number of ways to deal with the practical problems associated with applying the Basel rules to ships.[61] In 1999, Basel's CoP had begun discussing ship dismantling issues. Technical Guidelines for the Sound Management of the Full and Partial Dismantling of Ships[62] were adopted in 2002 as recommended practices for shipyards, particularly in developing countries. In 2003, a Basel working group took the significant but ambiguous step of declaring that "a ship may become waste, in accordance with Article 2 of the Basel Convention and that at the same time it may be defined as a ship under other international rules."[63] Members were invited to report to the Secretariat on how the Basel rules might be applied to the shipbreaking industry. Since then, the issue of ship recycling has remained somewhat uncomfortably on the Basel agenda.

More directly involved were the ILO, with its concern for workplace safety, and the IMO, whose long-standing interest in shipping made it a natural focus for shipbreaking issues. By 2000, ILO officials had visited Asian shipyards and begun calling for the organization to take an active role in developing standards to govern labor practices there.[64] In 2003, the ILO adopted a set of recommendations for Asian and Turkish shipyards, focusing on steps to enhance the capacity of national legal and administrative systems to provide appropriate oversight.[65] With the support of the shipping industry, the IMO took the lead in designing the actual legal framework to regulate shipbreaking. Despite the role played by the IMO's Marine Environment Protection Committee (MEPC) in drafting such important pieces of environmental legislation as the 1973/78 MARPOL agreement, environmentalists feared that industry interests would play too dominant a role in the IMO's deliberations. That the IMO was considering a Turkish and Greek request to remove Greenpeace's consultative status in response to the ship-boarding activities of some of its members at the same meeting that the IMO was approving new shipbreaking standards only made the political environment more difficult.[66] Environmentalists hoping for a quick response to what they saw as a pressing international problem were also concerned about the length of time it normally takes for IMO rules to come into force.

The "Guidelines on Ship Recycling,"[67] approved by the IMO Assembly in December 2003, would become the foundation for the 2009 Hong Kong Convention. Though only recommendations, they emerged from the MEPC in just over a year—a remarkably speedy process, given the complexity of the issues and the fact that the group drafting them was trying to coordinate its work with that of the Basel Convention and the ILO. The guidelines begin with the assumption that recycling ships is the best way to deal with aging vessels. They recommend the development of a "green passport" system that would require shipowners to maintain an inventory of all hazardous materials used in construction and anything added over the ship's lifetime. With their "makers to breakers"[68] approach, the guidelines require shipowners to be responsible in the selection of shipbreaking yards and to consult with regulatory authorities in the state where the recycling will take place. If it becomes apparent that the shipbreaking yard lacks the capacity to handle hazardous materials responsibly, the shipowner "should arrange for the removal of those materials to another appropriate facility or ensure that the facility obtains the technical capability to do so."[69] On the other hand, the guidelines make clear that it is ultimately the responsibility of the ship-recycling facilities and the states where they are located to ensure that ships are broken in a responsible manner.[70]

While the approach adopted in the guidelines mirrored some provisions of the Basel Convention, environmentalists led by Greenpeace and BAN were not impressed. In a 35-page critique, they characterized the guidelines as an "elaborate exercise to protect the shipping industry from responsibility by pretending that the Basel Convention, its obligations and decisions, has little scope over ships-as-hazardous-waste."[71] They also accused the IMO of shifting "ultimate responsibility . . . [to] the communities of workers and their families that toil in these ship recycling facilities, while the shipping industry, the recipient of the bounty of inexpensive ship disposal because of the absence of any health and safety infrastructure in these facilities, are meekly reminded by the IMO guidelines of their duty to help solve the problem."[72] Calling the concept of a "Green Passport . . . cynical in the extreme,"[73] they were particularly critical of the failure of the guidelines to support decontamination of ships before they are sent off for recycling and the refusal to treat end-of-life ships as "waste," both evidence of the IMO's desire to ignore "fundamental guiding principles embodied in the Basel Convention."[74] Reflecting a continuing skepticism that any North–South trade in ship recycling could be managed responsibly, Greenpeace argued that technical assistance provisions intended to enhance the shipbreaking capacity of developing countries would do nothing to respond to the real problems they face, such as the "lack of liability law . . . lack of a democratic climate for workers to organize or raise issues . . . and local corruption. . . . It is morally reprehensible for countries to pass the burden of their own toxic wastes to others simply because they are poor."[75]

Despite the criticism, the IMO worked to transform the guidelines into a binding international convention. In late 2005, the IMO Assembly approved a MEPC proposal to create a working group including representatives from both the ILO and the Basel Convention. What emerged was the Hong Kong Convention, adopted in May 2009 at a diplomatic conference in Hong Kong that attracted representatives from 63 nations, as well as delegates from the ILO, UNEP, and the EU. Eight NGOs, representing both shipping and environmental interests, were given consultative status. The convention was opened for signature in September 2009.[76]

The Hong Kong Convention is essentially a more formalized version of the IMO's guidelines. Its central responsibilities are directed at the state whose flag a ship flies or which operates "under its authority" and the state where ship-recycling facilities are located.[77] The convention establishes a regulatory framework to minimize the use of hazardous materials in the construction process, to develop an accurate inventory of the substances on board, and to ensure that a complete survey is made of every ship before it is sent for recycling. An annex includes 25 regulations and 6 appendices, which provide lists of hazardous materials requiring controls and standardized forms to implement the green passport system. A "ship recycling plan" is to be developed for each ship before it is broken, and all recycling facilities must be authorized by local officials under "standards that are necessary to ensure that Ship Recycling Facilities are designed, constructed and operated in a safe and environmentally sound manner. . . ."[78] Enforcement is left largely up to flag states and the states responsible for recycling facilities. Port states do have the right to inspect ships suspected of violations, but only to verify the existence of the required documentation.[79]

Reactions to the agreement varied, but the governmental representatives who had approved it were, not surprisingly, supportive. The Kenyan delegate termed the agreement an "important milestone . . . which will go a long way in alleviating the suffering of thousands of workers in the ship-recycling industry . . . [and] play a very important role in reducing the negative impact of the industry to the marine environment."[80] Others stressed that the compromise reached in Hong Kong was evidence that the IMO could respond quickly to a pressing environmental problem. Italy argued that the agreement provided "a firm and prompt reply to criticisms of 'IMO weak remedies,'" even while acknowledging that this was not the ultimate answer, but a "useful step forward to an effective legal regime."[81] The representative from the ILO applauded the IMO for its "excellent track record of collaboration . . . especially in areas of shared and overlapping competence"[82] and emphasized the need for continued cooperation as the IMO worked to implement the convention. The Basel Convention's representative offered a similar note of thanks but flagged what would soon become a point of potential conflict: whether the Hong Kong Convention "establishes an equivalent level of control as that established under the Basel Convention."[83]

Non-governmental participants were split. The International Chamber of Shipping (ICS), the chief lobbying organization for the shipping industry, called for early ratification of the agreement to give the industry the predictability needed to make investment decisions.[84] Friends of the Earth International called the convention a "profound disappointment," and "an obsolete relic that ignores long standing environmental and social principles. . . . Instead of real change, real responsibility, real action, we have been given an inventory, a plan and some guidelines."[85] The convention failed to offer a level of protection comparable to Basel, placed an unfair burden on developing countries, did not impose appropriate liability on the shipowners who benefited from the generation of toxic waste, did too little to encourage toxic-free ship design, and did not prohibit the "fatally flawed beaching method" for breaking ships.[86]

The Hong Kong Convention's most immediate challenge has been to become legally binding. The agreement has strict entry-into-force require-ments, since there was general recognition that it would be ineffective unless ratified by a critical number of major flag states and states with shipbreaking industries. The agreement will come into effect two years after 15 states have ratified it. However, the ratifying states must represent at least 40 per cent of the "gross tonnage of the world's merchant shipping," and states whose "combined maximum annual recycling volume . . . during the preceding 10 years constitutes not less than 3 per cent of the gross tonnage of the com-bined merchant shipping" of the parties.[87]

At a 2010 workshop in Izmir, Turkey, the IMO's Nikos Mikelis indicated the challenge ahead. In 2009, over 50 per cent of the world's fleet was flagged by Panama, Liberia, the Marshall Islands, Bahamas, Hong Kong, and Singapore. Moreover, 97 per cent of all ship recycling was taking place in only five states: China, India, Bangladesh, Pakistan, and Turkey. In the near term, it would take ratification by at least two of the top three recycling states to reach the required threshold.[88] There was some room for opti-mism, since 59 of the 63 countries represented in Hong Kong had accepted the Conference's Final Act.[89] Yet, as of 30 September 2015, the convention had been signed by only five states (France, Italy, Netherlands, St. Kitts and Nevis, and Turkey) and formally acceded to by only three (Congo, Nor-way, and France), whose combined merchant fleets then represented only 1.98 per cent of the world's tonnage.[90]

Why has it been so difficult to get states to formally accept an agree-ment that so many delegates seemed to embrace in 2009? The reasons vary by state, but among the chief obstacles remains the question that was at the center of the *Clemenceau* dispute: whether the rules of the Basel Conven-tion apply to ships. If they do, the issue is whether the standards of the Hong Kong Convention are consistent with them, since Basel's Article 11 requires that any waste-related agreements entered into by Basel parties "not derogate from the environmentally sound management of hazardous wastes and other wastes as required by this Convention."[91] After the Hong Kong Convention was signed, Basel's 10th CoP planned to address the compat-ibility issue at its 2011 meeting in Cartagena. The Basel Secretariat prepared a lengthy analysis of the two conventions,[92] but members of the CoP were clearly divided. The final conference report simply noted their differences and agreed to continue to study the matter.[93]

This issue has played out somewhat differently within the European Union. There is strong support for the Hong Kong Convention among some members, most notably France. However, the EU waste-shipment regulation, which implemented the Basel Convention and incorporated Basel's unratified ban on shipments of waste to non–OECD countries, presented a potential obstacle. In the absence of new EU rules specifically governing ships, the European Commission feared the Hong Kong Convention could conflict with the EU waste regulation; EU members were instructed to withhold ratification until this could be addressed. In December 2103, a new EU regulation on ship recycling was adopted, one designed to accelerate the implementation of the Hong Kong Convention with regard to the recycling of European ships, which would then not be covered by the waste-shipment regulation. It includes a process to ensure that EU ships would be recycled only at shipyards approved for inclusion on a European List and also goes beyond the Hong Kong Convention in specifically prohibiting the use of the beaching technique to dismantle European ships.[94] Because the new rules would not become fully effective for several years, the European Council decided in April 2014 to authorize EU members to ratify the Hong Kong Convention, thus paving the way for French ratification in May to be followed, it was hoped, by others.[95]

While members of the environmental community approved of some aspects of the new EU regulation, the founder of the NGO Shipbreaking Platform, Ingvild Jenssen, urged the European Union to do more to integrate the polluter pays principle into the new regime by including a "mandatory financial mechanism that ensures the internalization of costs" to encourage more responsible ship recycling.[96] Another Platform activist argued that European shipowners could easily avoid the restrictions by reflagging their vessels before sending them to South Asia.[97]

Developments in India suggested that the choice of legal regimes to govern shipbreaking was also far from resolved in ship-recycling states. In responding to a draft version of the Hong Kong Convention, representatives of the Indian shipbreaking industry had challenged the IMO's right to regulate shipbreaking. P.S. Nagarsheth, president of the Iron Steel Scrap and Shipbreakers Association of India, argued, "Once a ship is delivered to a ship recycler . . . once it is no more a floating structure, the role of the IMO should cease." Instead, ILO rules should govern shipbreaking operations and "the handling of hazardous waste should be based on Basel norms." Nagarsheth claimed that beaching was "the only economically viable method" of recycling ships, and appropriate as long as all hazardous materials had been removed before the ship arrived in India. He denounced the proposed convention as an unacceptable attempt by ship-owning countries to transfer all responsibility for the problem onto ship-recycling countries.[98]

In 2012, the Basel Convention was also invoked by opponents of a plan to recycle at Alang the infamous *Exxon Valdez*, reflagged several times and now renamed *Oriental Nicety*. Members of the New Delhi–based Toxics-Watch Alliance argued that the ship should not be allowed to enter Indian waters and should be sent back to the "country of origin," because the toxic materials on board put it in violation of the Basel Convention.[99] The Indian Supreme Court permitted the ship to be broken at Alang, since it accepted the argument that the hazardous waste had been removed. Noteworthy, however, was the Court's insistence that, if waste were to be discovered during recycling operation, disposal costs would be the shipowner's responsibility. More significantly, the Court ruled that, in future cases, "the concerned authorities shall strictly comply with the norms laid down in the Basel Convention."[100]

Reacting in 2013 to the Hong Kong Convention and the recycling regulation emerging from the European Union, the ToxicsWatch Alliance argued again that Basel Convention rules should govern ship recycling, blasting the Hong Kong Convention in language remarkably similar to that used earlier by Indian shipbreakers. It called the Hong Kong Convention a "regressive anti-environment, anti-labor" agreement and the IMO "callous towards the plight of the workers and . . . simply pandering to the whims and fancies of the shipowners from developed countries." It termed the EU's recycling regulation as a "breach of the European Union's legal obligations to uphold the Basel Convention," and called upon India and other recycling nations not to ratify the agreement.[101]

Analysis

The *Clemenceau* dispute was settled not through negotiation or the work of an international tribunal but by a unilateral decision by the French government to return the ship to France. France was under pressure at home and abroad from environmental organizations linking this dispute to the larger struggle to end destructive South Asian shipbreaking practices. Opponents of the transfer were aided by the fact that the *Clemenceau* was a huge physical object, one clearly connected to the sovereign power of France and thus impossible to disown. The ship itself, more than the hazardous substances on board, became the dispute's focal point and symbol.

While national governments played key roles in this dispute, the experience also reveals the constraints under which they were operating. One could

imagine a deal worked out quietly between the Indian and French governments, under which France would either arrange for removal of more of the
asbestos before the ship sailed, or assist in its decontamination at Alang and
repatriate the hazardous waste. However, under the glare of public scrutiny
and with legal challenges in both France and India, such an alternative was
politically impossible. While the dispute was not resolved in French or Indian
courts, judicial involvement narrowed the range of available options.

Perceptions of what "the law" required also played an important role
in defining the dispute's possible outcomes. International law was invoked
not only in courtrooms but by all the participants; indeed, law was central
to the language of the dispute. However, the battle over the *Clemenceau*
also revealed genuinely divergent perspectives about what international law
required and whether the rules of the Basel Convention and existing EU
legislation applied to ships. Even those who felt that the Basel Convention
should apply saw its implications quite differently. Shipbreakers focused on
the need for shipowners to preclean ships before sending them to South
Asian beaches. Environmentalists saw beaching ships at places like Alang
as inherently inconsistent with Basel's requirement of "environmentally
sound" waste disposal.

The *Clemenceau* dispute revealed the need for clearer rules governing shipbreaking and gave impetus to ongoing international efforts to develop them.
Both the substance of the new regime and the French role in supporting it
can fairly be traced to the *Clemenceau* dispute, as France saw an opportunity
to seize the moral and political high ground in negotiations underway both
in Europe and in the IMO. However, in deciding to repatriate the *Clemenceau*,
France may have inadvertently reinforced the perception of those hoping to
end South Asian shipbreaking practices that the framework provided by the
Basel Convention could, as both a practical and political matter, provide a
solid foundation for the new regime.

The most tangible products of recent negotiations are the Hong Kong
Convention and the EU ship-recycling regulation, both of which critics
see as deviating in significant ways from the Basel approach. Yet it was clear
from the outset that, were the IMO to take the lead role, it would have
to address problems such as the working conditions in, and the environmental impact of, South Asian shipyards—problems that went well beyond the
issues on which the IMO normally focuses. For all of its shortcomings, the
Hong Kong Convention must be seen as something of a surprise by those
convinced that the IMO had too limited a perspective to take on such a
broad set of concerns.

The Hong Kong Convention was, in Tony Puthucherril's words, a
"political compromise, . . . not the final solution,"[102] as even its most ardent

supporters would admit. Given the IMO's central role in the drafting process, the form that the compromise took was undoubtedly a product of the "maritime lens" through which the shipbreaking problem was viewed.[103] Nonetheless, there are important aspects of the convention that would seem to be a necessary part of any ship-recycling regime. These include the emphasis it places on limiting the use of hazardous materials in ship construction, monitoring the ship throughout its lifetime to keep track of any additional hazardous waste that may be added, developing a clear plan for the recycling of the ship at the end of its life, and ensuring that recycling takes place under environmentally safe conditions.

The Hong Kong Convention does have limitations, some of which may need to be addressed as the regime evolves. First, it does not apply to ships under 500 GWT or to warships. Thus, it would not have covered the *Clemenceau*, a point not lost on critics, although parties are to ensure that "such ships act in a manner consistent with this Convention, so far as is reasonable and practicable."[104] Second, in Puthucherril's words, the shipowner remains "an enigma," a key player in the shipbreaking process whose responsibilities and potential liability are never clearly spelled out.[105] The shipowner's status can shift very rapidly as the ship moves from active service to its last stage of life, since Regulation 1(8) of the convention declares that the term shipowner "also includes those who have ownership of the ship for a limited period pending its sale or handing over to a Ship Recycling Facility."[106] This may unwisely shift whatever responsibilities do exist to the people least likely to assume them and the ones often most difficult to hold accountable under a system of flag state enforcement.[107] Third, the convention does little to promote the precleaning of ships before they are transferred to be broken.[108] Regulation 8 simply requires that "ships destined to be recycled . . . conduct operations in the period prior to entering the Ship Recycling Facility in order to minimize the amount of cargo residues, remaining fuel oil and wastes remaining on board."[109] Finally, the ultimate success of the Hong Kong regime depends upon the ability of existing ship-recycling states to make substantial investments in facilities and to improve regulatory supervision to ensure that a system of "safe and environmentally sound" ship recycling can be created and maintained. While calling for "technical assistance and cooperation,"[110] the convention provides no tangible mechanism to make this happen.

A source of disagreement in the Hong Kong negotiations, and an issue that may become more relevant if key states choose not to sign the convention even as it comes into force, is the role of non-parties. The agreement makes it illegal for parties to send ships to be recycled in non-party states, even if the latter maintain acceptable shipbreaking facilities.[111] Even the Basel

Convention permits parties to enter into international agreements with non-parties to permit the transfer of hazardous waste, as long as these arrangements "do not derogate from the environmentally sound management of hazardous wastes and other wastes as required by this Convention."[112] The United States and others argued unsuccessfully that a comparable provision was needed in the Hong Kong Convention, not only to keep the agreement consistent with international trade rules but also to prevent a perverse incentive to transfer end-of-life ships to non-party registries if it became difficult to find available shipbreaking capacity within convention parties. Yet allowing such an exception might well have created a disincentive for recycling states to join the convention, and it was rejected in the final draft.[113]

Again assuming that the Hong Kong Convention comes into force, a continuing question is whether the evolving rules of the Hong Kong regime can be reconciled with provisions of the Basel Convention that at least many feel should take precedence in the event of conflict. There are clear areas of tension, particularly if the Basel parties fully ratify the ban on trade in hazardous waste between developed and developing countries and the Liability Protocol, which targets the "generators" of waste in a way that the Hong Kong Convention does not. These include the criminal sanctions associated with "illegal traffic" under Basel; the question of whether prior decontamination of ships is required by Basel; the focus in Basel on the "state of export" rather than the Hong Kong Convention's "flag state" orientation; and the state-based system of prior, informed consent required by Basel, which does not have an equivalent place—at least for states—in the way decisions are made about exporting ships for recycling under the Hong Kong Convention.[114]

Like most multilateral environmental agreements, the Hong Kong Convention has provisions that will allow the parties to narrow the distance between the two regimes. Article 15 of the convention makes clear that nothing undertaken in the agreement undermines "the rights and obligations of the Parties under other relevant and applicable international agreements," of which the Basel Convention could be one.[115] Moreover, Regulation 3 explicitly recognizes the need to take into account "the relevant and applicable technical standards, recommendations and guidance developed under the Basel Convention"[116] in framing the measures designed to implement the Hong Kong Convention. Perhaps most important is Article 1(2) stating that parties are not prevented from applying "more stringent measures consistent with international law" than those imposed by the convention if required "to prevent, reduce or minimize any adverse effects on the environment."[117] Thus, Basel parties could opt for stricter rules. Admittedly, tougher standards applied unilaterally by flag states could lead shipowners to register their vessels elsewhere, and competitive pressures may discourage recycling states from moving more quickly than the Hong Kong Convention requires. However, the framework does make such "extra-regime" measures possible if states feel the need to push regulatory efforts ahead more quickly than the Hong Kong parties are prepared to move—something the European Union is doing through its ship-recycling regulation. Finally, the convention itself can be amended if the parties agree. Article 18 provides two mechanisms for this, either through the initiative of individual states proposing changes, which would be approved by the MEPC and sent on to the membership as a whole, or by the convening of a special conference, which could approve changes and then send them out for state acceptance. With the convention not yet in force, it is premature to suggest what amendments would likely be considered, but concerns over such issues as the lack of rules for precleaning ships could be addressed in this way.

Shipbreaking poses difficult challenges for international environmental law. It has engaged the attention of different international regimes, each constrained by its organizational mandate and structure, which approach it within a framework of maritime law not easily adapted to the problems shipbreaking presents. In its current form, the Hong Kong Convention is only a partial response, and it is unclear what will happen during the critical period before the agreement comes into effect. Disputes continue over the breaking of individual ships, and the question of the relevance of the Basel Convention is raised repeatedly in national courts, called into action by energized NGOs unwilling to sit back and wait for the arrival of what they see as a flawed Hong Kong regime.

In the immediate future, the Hong Kong and Basel regimes will likely continue on separate, but parallel paths. Their general concerns are similar. Both emphasize the need to minimize the generation of hazardous waste, to monitor that waste and be aware of the dangers it represents, and to manage its disposal in environmentally sound ways. Given the realities of the contemporary shipping industry, the pressing need to deal soon with aging vessels, and the limited capacity of existing green recycling facilities, compromise is needed, one that goes beyond what is permitted by the strictest application of the Basel Convention to end-of-life ships.

Moving forward, part of the answer is to ensure that future ships be designed with a genuine "cradle to grave" approach and that their construction and operation incorporate a clearer sense of the ultimate costs—economic, human, and environmental—incurred when they are dismantled. To make this work, and to help provide the resources required to make safe recycling possible, policies are required to make those who derive the benefits from international shipping internalize those costs in the way they conduct their operations. Progress is also needed on an issue that neither the Basel nor Hong Kong regimes has adequately addressed: the creation of mechanisms to make available to South Asian countries resources to permit ships to be broken there safely. To deny these nations an opportunity to develop an important industry that generates jobs and recycled steel raises serious questions of economic justice, but environmental justice also calls for better protection of Asian workers and the South Asian environment. Both fairness and the logic of the polluter pays principle would argue for the development of a system in which a tax on ship construction could be used to help fund the ship-recycling process.

Even though it may be difficult to establish a ship-recycling fund in the near future, more modest efforts can be undertaken. Japan recently proposed a compromise to improve conditions at Indian ship-recycling yards by providing concrete flooring and drainage facilities for beach areas where ships are being broken. Although this would not likely meet the standards for the "built structures" mandated by the EU recycling regulation, it would entail new investments in Indian ship-recycling yards of around $200 million to which the Japanese government is apparently prepared to contribute. The NGO Shipbreaking Platform remains opposed to any approach that permits beaching of ships to continue, but this proposal at least suggests some movement to address a key weakness of the Hong Kong Convention.[118]

Notes

1   United Nations Environment Program (UNEP), "Convention on the Control of Transboundary Movements of Hazardous Waste and Their Disposal," Basel, signed 22 March 1989 (in force 5 May), Art. 1(3) [hereafter cited as "Basel Convention"].   http://www.basel.int/Portals/4/Basel%20Convention/docs/text/BaselConventionText-e.pdf.

2   International Maritime Organization (IMO), "Hong Kong International Convention for the Safe and Environmentally Sound Recycling of Ships," 19 May 2009, IMO Doc. SR/CONF/45 [hereafter cited as "Hong Kong Convention"]. http://ec.europa.eu/environment/waste/ships/pdf/Convention.pdf.

3   Katie Paul, "Exporting Responsibility: Shipbreaking in South Asia; International Trade in Hazardous Waste," *Environmental Policy and Law* 35, no. 4 (2004): 74–75.

4   Tony Puthucherril, *From Shipbreaking to Sustainable Ship Recycling: Evolution of a Legal Regime* (Leiden: Martinus Nijhoff, 2010), 41–43.

5   IMO, *International Shipping and World Trade: Facts and Figures* (London: IMO Maritime Knowledge Centre, 2009), 11.

6   Paul, "Exporting Responsibility," 74.

7   IMO, *International Shipping*, 16.

8   IMO, Marine Environment Protection Committee, "IMO Meeting Adopts Accelerated Single-Hull Tanker Phase-Out, New Regulation on Carriage of

Heavy Fuel Oil," 1–4 December 2003. http://www.imo.org/blast/mainframe. asp?topic_id=758&doc_id=3341.

9   Saiful Karim, "Environmental Pollution from the Shipbreaking Industry: International Law and National Legal Response," *Georgetown International Environmental Law Review* 22, no. 2 (2010): 185–240.

10   David Dodds, "Breaking Up Is Hard to Do: Environmental Effects of Shipwrecking and Possible Solutions under India's Environmental Regime," *Pacific McGeorge Global Business and Development Law Journal* 20 (2007): 211–12.

11   Matt Cohen, "U.S. Ship-Breaking Exports: Balancing Safe Disposal with Economic Realities," *Environs: Environmental Law and Policy Journal* 28, no. 2 (2005): 244–47. See also David Killion, "Trans-Atlantic Ghost Busting: The Failed Attempt to Dispose of the Chesapeake 'Ghost Fleet' in the United Kingdom," *University of Richmond Law Review* 42 (2008): 731–52.

12   See the illuminating story of the breaking of the Canadian cargo ship *Ferbec* at Alang, in Matthew McClearn, "Dark Voyage," *Canadian Business* 78, no. 20 (2005): 64–88. Another good description of the shipbreaking process can be found in William Langewiesche, "The Shipbreakers," *Atlantic Monthly* 286, no. 2 (2000): 31–49.

13   For an overview of some of the human and environmental effects of shipbreaking, see Puthucherril, *From Shipbreaking*, 33–38. See also Paul J. Bailey, "Is There a Decent Way to Break up Ships?," *ILO Discussion Paper* (2000) and Paul, "Exporting Responsibility," 75–76.

14   Will Englund and Gary Cohn Sund, "A Third World Dump for America's Ships, Part 3," *Baltimore Sun*, 9 December 1997.

15   NGO Shipbreaking Platform, http://www.shipbreakingplatform.org/.

16   As an example, see the story of the transfer and destruction at Alang of the Canadian cargo ship *Ferbec* in McClearn, "Dark Voyage."

17   Puthucherril, *From Shipbreaking*, 81.

18   Vaiju Naravane, "A Shipload of Trouble from France," *The Hindu*, 3 January 2006. See also "Killer Clemenceau: The Ecocrime That Almost Was," *Financial Express*, 29 August 2004.

19   Julio Godoy, "France: Legal Battle Fails: Asbestos-Laden Ship Sails for India," *Inter Press Service*, 3 January 2006.

20   Puthucherril, *From Shipbreaking*, 81.

21   Basel Action Network (BAN), "Comments on Statement of French Government on Clemenceau by the Basel Action Network on Behalf of the Greater Coalition Demanding Return of Clemenceau to France for Decontamination," 24 January 2006. http://www.ban.org/library/statement_of_french_government_ on_clemenceau.pdf.

22   Godoy, "France: Legal Battle Fails."

23   "Egypt Halts Convoy Tugging Clemenceau," *The Hindu*, 13 January 2006.

24   Heba Saleh, "Egypt Grants 'Toxic' Ship Passage," *BBC News*, 5 January 2006.

25   Puthucherril, *From Shipbreaking*, 65–66. See, more broadly, Armin Rosencranz and Michael Jackson, "The Delhi Pollution Case: The Supreme Court of India and the Limits of Judicial Power," *Columbia Journal of Environmental Law* 28 (2003): 223–54.

26   Puthucherril, *From Shipbreaking*, 65–67.

27   Supreme Court of India, "Research Foundation v. Union of India, and Others," Writ Petition (Civil) 657 of 1995, 14 October 2003, Writ.

http://www.elaw.org/content/india-research-foundation-v-union-india-others-wp-6571995-20031014-hazardous-wastes.

28   Ibid., para. 70.2(2).

29   Ibid., para. 68.

30   Puthucherril, *From Shipbreaking*, 73–77.

31   Zubair Ahmed, "Stay Out, India Tells Toxic Ship," *BBC News*, 6 January 2006.

32   Puthucherril, *From Shipbreaking*, 82.

33   "France Offers to Take Clemenceau's Toxic Waste," *Hindustan Times*, 27 January 2006.

34   UNEP, "Convention on Persistent Organic Pollutants," Stockholm, signed 22 May 2001 (in force 14 May 2004) [hereafter cited as "Stockholm Convention"]. http://chm.pops.int/TheConvention/Overview/TextoftheConvention/tabid/2232/Default.aspx.

35   UNEP, "Convention on the Prior Informed Consent Procedure for Certain Hazardous Chemicals and Pesticides in International Trade," Rotterdam, signed 10 September 1998 (in force 24 February 2004) [hereafter cited as "Rotterdam Convention"]. http://www.pic.int/TheConvention/Overview/TextoftheConvention/tabid/1048/language/en-US/Default.aspx.

36   David Hunter, James Salzman, and Durwood Zaelke, *International Environmental Law and Policy*, 4th ed. (New York: Foundation Press, 2011), 192–98. On the development of the Basel Convention and its basic provisions, see Pamela S. Chasek, David L. Downie, and Janet Welsh Brown, *Global Environmental Politics*, 5th ed. (Boulder, CO: Westview Press, 2010), 129–40.

37   "Basel Convention," Art. 6.

38   Ibid., Art. 4(d).

39   Ibid., Art. 8.

40   Chasek, Downie, and Brown, *Global Environmental Politics*, 132–34.

41   Karim, "Environmental Pollution," 194–95.

42   UNEP, Basel Convention, "Protocol on Liability and Compensation for Damage Resulting from Transboundary Movements of Hazardous Wastes and Their Disposal," Basel, signed 10 December 1999 (not in force) [hereafter cited as "Liability Protocol"]. http://archive.basel.int/meetings/cop/cop5/docs/prot-e.pdf.

43   For an overview of the Liability Protocol, see Sejal Choksi, "The Basel Convention on the Control of Transboundary Movements of Hazardous Waste and Their Disposal: 1999 Protocol on Liability and Compensation," *Ecology Law Quarterly* 28 (2001): 509–39.

44   Karim, "Environmental Pollution," 201–02.

45   European Council, "Council Regulation (EC) No 120/97 of 20 January 1997 amending Regulation (EC) No 259/93 on the Supervision and Control of Shipments of Waste within, into and out of the European Community," *Official Journal of the European Communities* L 022, 24 January 1997, 0014–0015.

46   Marcos A. Orellana, "Shipbreaking and Le Clemenceau Row," *ASIL Insights* 10, no. 4 (2006).

47   "Basel Convention," Art. 1(4).

48   Puthucherril, *From Shipbreaking*, 113–14.

49   It is debatable how persuasive that argument is when the ship is no longer operational, indeed under tow headed for dismantling. See Orellana, "Shipbreaking and Le Clemenceau Row."

50   Karim, "Environmental Pollution," 193. See also, McClearn, "Dark Voyage."

51   Puthucherril, *From Shipbreaking*, 115.

52   Karim, "Environmental Pollution," 193–95.

53   France, Conseil D'État, "Association Ban Asbestos France, Association Greenpeace France, Comité Anti-amiante Jussieu, Association Nationale de Défense des Victimes de l'Amiante v. République Française ("Le Clemenceau") Conseil d'État (6ème et 1ère section réunies), Suspension Decision of February 15, 2006, N° 288801." http://archive.basel.int/ships/relevcaselaw.html.

54   Gopal Krishna, "French Apex Court Rules, Clemenceau Recalled," *indiatogether. org*, 16 February 2006. See also Frederick Noronha, "Toxic Warship Not Allowed to Disrupt India-France Summit," *Environment News Service*, 20 February 2006.

55   Julio Godoy, "France: Court Stops Asbestos-Bearing Ship's Voyage to India," *Inter Press Service*, 16 February 2006.

56   Ibid.

57   Kushal Jeena, "Analysis: Despair as Clemenceau Returns," *UPI*, 20 February 2006.

58   Noronha, "Toxic Warship."

59   Charles Bremner, "Hartlepool to Break up France's Toxic Flagship Clemenceau," *The Times*, 2 July 2008.

60   Martin Wainwright, "Contaminated Aircraft Carrier Finds Final Resting Place in Hartlepool," *The Guardian*, 6 February 2009.

61   See, for example, Amy E. Moen, "Breaking Basel: The Elements of the Basel Convention and Its Application to Toxic Ships," *Marine Policy* 32 (2008): 1053–62.

62   UNEP, Conference of the Parties to the Basel Convention on the Control of Transboundary Movements of Hazardous Wastes and Their Disposal, "Technical Guidelines for the Environmentally Sound Management of the Full and Partial Dismantling of Ships," sixth meeting, Geneva, 9–13 December 2002, U.N. Doc. UNEP/CHW.6/23 (8 August 2002). http://www.basel.int/Portals/4/Basel%20Convention/docs/meetings/sbc/workdoc/techgships-e.pdf.

63   UNEP, Open-Ended Working Group of the Basel Convention on the Control of Transboundary Movements of Hazardous Wastes and Their Disposal [OEWG], "Report of the Open-ended Working Group of the Basel Convention on the Work of Its Second Session," Geneva, 20–24 October 2003, UN Doc. UNEP/CHW/OEWG/2/12 (16 December 2003), 17–18. http://www.basel.int/TheConvention/OpenendedWorkingGroup%280EWG%29/ReportsandDecisions/tabid/3413/Default.aspx.

64   See Bailey, "Is There a Decent Way."

65   International Labor Organization (ILO), "Safety and Health in Shipbreaking: Guidelines for Asian Countries and Turkey," ILO Doc. GB.289/205 (March 2004). http://www.ilo.org/wcmsp5/groups/public/---ed_protect/---protrav/---safework/documents/normativeinstrument/wcms_107689.pdf.

66   "UN Organization Seeks to Silence Greenpeace," *Greenpeace.org*, 17 November 2003.

67   IMO, "Guidelines on Ship Recycling," 5 December 2003, IMO Doc. A 23/Res.962. https://www.transportstyrelsen.se/globalassets/global/sjofart/dokument/guidelines_on_ship_recycling_resolution_962.pdf.

68   Ibid., para. 1.1.

69 Ibid., para. 8.1.5.

70 Ibid., para. 1.7. For a more detailed analysis of the IMO Guidelines, see Puthucherril, *From Shipbreaking*, 134–43.

71 Greenpeace International/BAN, "The IMO Guidelines on Ship Recycling Annotated," *ban.org*, 21 November 2003, 1.

72 Ibid., 1–2.

73 Ibid., 2. 2.

74 Ibid.

75 Ibid., 35.

76 For an overview of the drafting process, see Karim, "Environmental Pollution," 207–08.

77 "Hong Kong Convention," Art. 4, 4.

78 Ibid., Annex, Regulation 15, 23.

79 Ibid., Art. 8, 4.

80 IMO, International Conference on the Safe and Environmentally Sound Recycling of Ships, "Statements by Delegations and Observers at the Closing Session of the Conference," Hong Kong, 11–15 May 2009, IMO Doc. SR/CONF/INF.8, 7. http://www.sjofartsverket.se/pages/19514/sr-conf-inf8.pdf.

81 Ibid., 5.

82 Ibid., 12.

83 Ibid.

84 Ibid., 4–15.

85 Ibid., 14.

86 Ibid., 5.

87 Ibid., Art. 17, 9.

88 Nikos Mikelis, "Introduction to the Hong Kong Convention and Its Requirements," Ship Recycling and Technology Transfer Workshop, Izmir (Turkey), 14–17 July 2010, 17–22. http://www.imo.org/en/KnowledgeCentre/PapersAndArticlesByIMOStaff/Documents/Introduction%20to%20the%20Hong%20Kong%20Convention%20and%20its%20requirements%20-N.%20Mikelis.pdf. Because these numbers change annually, it is difficult to state precisely what mix of states would be most likely to form the required critical mass of ratifications.

89 Thomas Ormond, "Hong Kong Convention and EU Ship Recycling Regulation: Can They Change Bad Industrial Practices Soon?," *Jean Monnnet Working Paper Series* no. 5 (2013): 4–5.

90 IMO, "Status of Multilateral Conventions and Instruments in Respect of Which the International Maritime Organization or the Secretary-General Performs Depositary or Other Functions," 9 December 2014.

91 "Basel Convention," Art. 11.

92 UNEP, Basel Secretariat, "Environmentally Sound Dismantling of Ships," 11 July 2011, Doc. UNEP/CHW.10/18. http://archive.basel.int/meetings/cop/cop10/documents/18e.pdf.

93 UNEP, "Report of the Conference of the Parties to the Basel Convention on the Control of Transboundary Movements of Hazardous Wastes and Their Disposal on Its Tenth Meeting," Cartagena (Columbia), 17–21 October 2011, Doc. UNEP/CHW.10/28, 1 November 2011. http://archive.basel.int/meetings/cop/cop10/documents/28e.pdf.

94   European Union, "Regulation (EU) No. 1257/2013 of the European Parliament and of the Council of 20 November 2013 on Ship Recycling and Amending Regulation (EC) No. 1013/2006 and Directive 2009/16/EC," *Official Journal of the European Union*, L330/1, 10 December 2013. http://eur-lex.europa.eu/legal-content/EN/TXT/PDF/?uri=CELEX:32013R1257&qid=1418667603088&from=EN. See the requirement that all recycling take place on "built structures." Article 13c, 11. See also European Commission, "Adoption, Entry into Force, Application of the EU Ship Recycling Regulation." http://ec.europa.eu/environment/waste/ships/.

95   Nikos Mikelis, "EU Moves Ahead on Ship Recycling," *Maritime Executive*, 7 July 2014.

96   Ingvild Jenssen, "Making Sure the New EU Ship Recycling Regulation Works," *governmentgazette.eu*, 5 March 2014.

97   Ida Karlsson, "New EU Rules 'Fail' against Shipbreaking Dangers," *Inter Press Service*, 17 July 2013.

98   Vikram Kharvi, "Indian Ship Recyclers Oppose IMO Draft at Mumbai Workshop," *Shipping Today*, 2 March 2009.

99   Gopal Krishna, "Supreme Court Upholds Basel Convention But Allows Hazardous US Ship Exxon Valdez," *countercurrents.org*, 30 July 2012.

100   Supreme Court of India, "Research Foundation for Science, Technology and Natural Resource Policy v. Union of India & Ors.," I.A. Nos. 61 & 62 of 2012 in Written Petition C No. 657 of 1995, 30 July 2012, 14–15. http://ibasecretariat.org/india_Supreme_court_order_july30_2012.pdf.

101   Gopal Krishna, "Why India, Bangladesh and Pakistan Should Adhere to Basel Convention and Not Ratify Hong Kong Convention on Ship Breaking," *toxicswatch.org*, 12 September 2013.

102   Puthucherril, *From Shipbreaking*, 195.

103   Ibid., 189.

104   "Hong Kong Convention," Art. 3, 3.

105   Puthucherril, *From Shipbreaking*, 185–86.

106   "Hong Kong Convention," Art. 3, 3.

107   Puthucherril, *From Shipbreaking*, 186.

108   Ibid., 175.

109   "Hong Kong Convention," Reg. 8, 18.

110   "Hong Kong Convention," Art. 13, 7.

111   "Hong Kong Convention," Reg. 8, 18.

112   "Basel Convention," Art. 11.

113   Puthucherril, *From Shipbreaking*, 170–72.

114   For further discussion of these and other areas of potential conflict, see Puthucherril, *From Shipbreaking*, 175–80.

115   "Hong Kong Convention," Art. 15, 8.

116   Ibid., Reg. 3, 14.

117   Ibid., Art. 1(2), 2

118   Costa Paris, "Japan Offers Compromise to EU Ship-Breaking Rules: A Key Worry of Regulators Centers around the Practice of 'Beaching,'" *Wall Street Journal*, 13 March 2014.

8
Uruguayan Pulp Mills

Introduction

On 20 April 2010, the International Court of Justice (ICJ) handed down its decision in the Pulp Mills case,[1] a ruling designed to end a seven-year dispute between Argentina and Uruguay over the construction in Uruguay of a massive cellulose plant on the River Uruguay directly across from Argentina. Argentina claimed that Uruguay had violated international law in permitting the pulp mill's construction, both in the procedures used to assess its potential impact and in its judgment that the facility could be operated without harming the environment or the Argentine economy. The dispute escalated in 2006 when Argentine protestors blocked bridges over the river, interfering with trade between the two nations. The situation became so serious that Uruguay's president reportedly considered using military force to protect the mill from possible Argentine attack.[2]

A distinctive feature of the pulp mills dispute was the prominent role of the ICJ. As discussed in Chapter 4, until recently few environmental disputes have been heard by the Court or by any international tribunal. The decision to involve the ICJ was made unilaterally by the Argentine government. It could do so because in 1975 Argentina and Uruguay had signed the Statute of the River Uruguay,[3] which gives the Court compulsory jurisdiction in cases involving the application of the Statute if other forms of dispute settlement have failed. Their willingness to include this provision in the Statute reflected confidence that a long history of bilateral cooperation would normally prevent disputes from getting that far. Moreover, developing state practice involving international waterways generally, and the River Uruguay in particular, had resulted in a body of law that would be both predictable and fair and unlikely to result in the "winner takes all" outcomes often feared in court decisions.

This chapter focuses on the legal challenges brought by Argentina against the construction of the pulp mills and how the ICJ responded. It analyzes the Court's contribution, both to the resolution of the dispute and to the development of broader standards of state responsibility for preventing transboundary damage. It also discusses some of the issues courts face in adjudicating complex transboundary disputes. While the ICJ played the most prominent role in the pulp mills dispute, other adjudicative and administrative bodies were also drawn in. The Statute had created an administrative body to help manage the river; the extent of its involvement soon became a major point of contention. Since the World Bank was helping to finance the mills, project opponents also invoked the World Bank's complaint procedure to try to prevent construction. On the other side, when Argentine protestors began to disrupt Uruguayan trade (and indirectly the construction process), Uruguay filed a claim against Argentina using the dispute settlement process provided by a regional trade agreement, thereby adding another layer of institutional complexity to the dispute.

The Context

The Uruguayan project was an important step in the development of one of the most dynamic new industries in the Southern Cone of South America. With a climate conducive to the farming of fast-growing eucalyptus trees, low labor costs, and what environmentalists claim are lax environmental standards regarding the use of pesticides and herbicides, the region has seen tremendous growth in pulp and paper manufacturing.[4] It is an industry actually far more developed in neighboring Brazil, Chile, and Argentina, where the total acreage of managed forest for wood production was nearly double that of Uruguay's at the time of the dispute.[5] Given the comparative economic advantages of pulp production in this region compared to traditional European sources, the pulp industry has attracted extensive foreign investment from European companies like the Spanish firm Empresa Nacional de Celulosa España (ENCE) and Finland's Oy Metsä-Botnia Ab (Botnia). Both proposed to build plants in Uruguay. Because these investments have generated concern among European workers who fear the migration of jobs overseas,[6] it is not surprising that neither Spain nor Finland played a visible role in the dispute.

In 1987, the Uruguayan government began to place special emphasis on developing its forestry and pulp wood industry, passing new legislation designed to encourage wood production. Total acreage devoted to tree planting increased from 50,000 to 800,000 hectares.[7] Uruguay quickly attracted international attention because of its reputation for political stability and receptivity to foreign investment.[8] Beyond its access to the River Uruguay, Fray Bentos offered a site in an established industrial region, with good rail and road connections to both Uruguay and Argentina. ENCE had established a subsidiary in Uruguay as early as 1990. The company was familiar with the region and had good relations with the Uruguayan government.[9]

Argentina and Uruguay historically have had a good relationship, a product of their shared boundary and relative sizes. In terms of both population and GDP, Uruguay is roughly one-tenth the size of Argentina, and depends

Map 8.1 This map shows the location of the Fray Bentos pulp mill on the River Uruguay directly across from Argentina's province of Entre Rios, the center of public opposition to the new plant. It also indicates the Libertador General San Martin Bridge, one of the key transboundary bridges blockaded by project opponents.

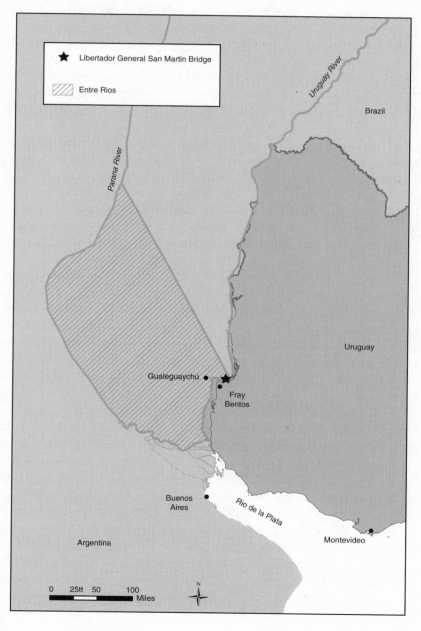

heavily upon Argentina both as a source of imports and as a market for Uruguay's largely agricultural exports. Together with Brazil and Paraguay, they were founding members in 1991 of the Southern Common Market (Mercosur),[10] an organization designed to promote the free flow of goods, labor, and capital throughout the region. Ties between the two nations have been strengthened by the fact that roughly 120,000 Uruguyans have moved to Argentina since 1960.

An earlier product of this close relationship was the 1975 Statute of the River Uruguay, the agreement at the heart of the pulp mills dispute. The River Uruguay begins in the southern mountains of Brazil and flows south forming the boundary between Argentina and Uruguay before joining with the Parana River to create the La Plata River basin as it empties into the southern Atlantic Ocean.[11] The Statute's primary purpose was to create a process of notification and communication to allow the parties to review projects that could damage the river or the interests of the other. A River Uruguay Administrative Commission (CARU) was established, consisting of ten delegates, five from each country.[12] In addition to its role in overseeing proposed projects, the Commission was given broad rule-making responsibilities covering areas such as navigation safety, resource conservation, and pollution control. Decisions of the Commission, which began work in 1978, are made by a concurrent vote of the two national delegations.

The Argentine banking crisis of 1998–2002 had profound effects in Uruguay and helped frame the political context for the 2003 pulp mills dispute. An earlier Argentine government had tried to curb the country's chronic hyperinflation by linking the Argentine peso to the US dollar. A difficult recession in the late 1990s forced the government to engage in massive borrowing to cover Argentina's substantial current account deficit. All of this came at a time when world markets were dealing with the Asian financial crisis discussed in Chapter 3, and there was limited confidence in the ability of the International Monetary Fund (IMF) to contain the growing problem of Third World debt. In December 2001, Argentina defaulted on almost $100 billion, the largest sovereign debt default in history and additional curbs were placed on Argentine banks. Unemployment in Argentina soared to over 25 per cent, and many Argentine factories went bankrupt, triggering widespread protests and fears of revolution. Local "assemblies" formed to protest Argentina's economic problems would soon become important players in the pulp mills dispute, both through direct action and by pressuring Argentine politicians to take decisive action to prevent their construction.[13]

While the crisis was centered in Argentina, Uruguay was also hard hit. Argentine investors, unable to access funds at home, began withdrawing heavily from accounts in Uruguay, triggering similar moves by foreigners.

By the end of July 2002, net assets in Uruguayan banks had plummeted by almost 38 per cent, including 51 per cent of all foreign-owned assets. A domestic credit crunch ensued. Combined with a drop in exports to Argentina, the result was a GDP contraction of 10.7 per cent in 2002.[14] Unemployment reached 20 per cent, and the percentage of those in poverty climbed to over 40 per cent. At the height of the crisis, Uruguay's frustrated president, Jorge Batlle, was forced to apologize to his Argentine counterpart after calling Argentinians "a bunch of thieves." Tensions were high, particularly since all of this came shortly after an outbreak of hoof-and-mouth disease (alleged by many to have come from Argentina) had hurt Uruguay's important cattle industry.[15] Riots broke out in Montevideo in August 2002, and a general strike was called as Uruguayans became increasingly dissatisfied with Batlle's free market policies.[16]

The regional economic crisis soon brought new, more leftist-oriented leadership to both countries. In Argentina, after a series of interim leaders, Néstor Kirchner was elected president in May 2003, promising tough negotiations with the IMF and a series of emergency measures to assist unemployed workers. When Uruguay authorized the first of the pulp mills in October 2003, President Kirchner had been in office for less than six months. In Uruguay, President Batlle would be replaced within the year by Tabaré Vázquez, leader of the Broad Front coalition, which took control of both houses of parliament.

The pulp mills dispute involved a variety of interests and participants, ranging from the Spanish and Finnish companies constructing the mills, along with their public and private sources of finance, to NGOs representing environmental, social justice, and labor constituencies. It took place in a regional context where political rivalries had developed between leftist Latin American governments connected with Venezuela's Hugo Chavez and more conservative regimes whose top priority was attracting foreign investment. The dispute had serious implications for Mercosur, and thus brought other members into the process of attempting to resolve what many felt should have remained a local problem managed bilaterally by the Argentine and Uruguayan governments.[17] As tensions escalated, participants approached both the Organization of American States and the Inter-American Commission on Human Rights. Church leaders, a Nobel Prize–winning novelist, and the king of Spain all offered to mediate.

The Dispute

In October 2003, the Uruguayan government announced its decision to permit the Spanish company ENCE to build a $600 million pulp mill near

Fray Bentos on the River Uruguay. While ENCE later decided to site the mill farther from the Argentine border, a second, much larger mill was proposed for construction nearby by the Finnish company Botnia. When constructed, the two plants would represent a $1.7 billion investment in Uruguay's economy. Funding would come from private sources and the World Bank, with $175 million being provided by the International Finance Corporation (IFC) and another $350 million backed by the Multilateral Investment Guarantee Agency (MIGA). This was easily the largest economic development project in Uruguay's history, amounting to approximately 10 per cent of Uruguay's GDP.[18] The total number of jobs to be created by the mills and the overall economic benefit of the project to the Uruguayan economy would become a source of disagreement.[19] However, this was a major undertaking and a project of tremendous significance to the Uruguayan government, particularly following the regional economic crisis.

Argentina objected to Uruguay's approval of the ENCE pulp mill, claiming that Uruguayan authorities had failed to consider and adequately weigh its potential impact in Argentina. While the technology to be employed by either ENCE or Botnia was substantially more advanced than that used at other regional pulp mills, the Elemental Chlorine Free (ECF) technique that Uruguay was permitting would lead to the emission of more dioxins than the Totally Chlorine Free (TCF) approach being mandated for use in the European Union.[20] The Argentine submission to the International Court of Justice later detailed the plants' likely effects not only on the river and its ecology, including downstream fisheries, but also on the regional airshed and economic interests downwind of the plant.

Environmental and economic concerns were intertwined. Since the plants were to be located just across the River Uruguay from a popular tourist area, Argentina worried about the impact on tourism caused by fumes from the factories as well as their visual effect. The sheer scale of the ENCE and Botnia plants contributed to the unprecedented concern they aroused. This also permitted Argentinians, while recognizing their own country's involvement in the pulp industry, to argue that something fundamentally different was being proposed across the border.[21] In more clearly political terms, this was a classic transboundary environmental dispute, even if the river on which the plants would be sited was to some extent a shared resource. From the Argentine perspective, the plants offered no direct benefits and a number of potential costs, or at least risks they found unacceptable.

Most Uruguayans saw things quite differently. To be sure, there had been domestic resistance from a major opposition party, Frente Amplio, and from environmental NGOs who had contacted Argentineans across the river in Gualeguaychú to coordinate efforts against the pulp mills.[22] The Uruguayan branch of Friends of the Earth had urged the World Bank not to approve financing for the project, although their concern was more clearly directed at the local effects of the eucalyptus plantations, and the huge amounts of water they consume, than the operation of the pulp mills themselves.[23]

However, in the tense political atmosphere after the Argentine banking crisis many Uruguayans viewed the mills in nationalistic terms.[24] In a poll taken at the end of 2005, 69 per cent of Uruguayans in the region around the plants favored their construction, while 19 per cent were opposed.[25] This was an economic development project being built on Uruguayan sovereign territory. Uruguay had a right to develop, and this was an important national initiative offering the prospect of much-needed jobs. If there were negative environmental consequences of the plants' operations, they would be felt in Uruguay as well, and the tradeoffs were acceptable. In the view of one potential mill-worker, "I'd rather die of pollution 20 years from now than die of hunger today from a lack of work."[26] Few Uruguayans seemed to share that fatalism, confident in the new European-imported technology to be used at the mills and backed by an IFC review suggesting that no serious environmental damage would result from the plants' operation.[27] More common was the sense that Argentina was being hypocritical in criticizing plants far cleaner than anything on the Argentine side of the border.[28] There was even hope that the new facilities at Fray Bentos would improve the health of the River Uruguay by processing pollution from dirty Argentine sources up-river. Moreover, Uruguayans suspected that Argentine opposition had more to do with Argentine jealousy that the plants were being built in Uruguay,[29] that the central issue was not environmental impact but competition for economic investment.[30]

Competing explanations are offered for what transformed a local disagreement into a full-blown international dispute that made its way to The Hague. Observers disagree about who was to blame and whether the escalation was caused by miscalculation or mismanagement by national officials or whether it resulted from a conscious decision by politicians to take advantage of the issue for domestic political reasons. Pakkasvirta suggests that underlying political and philosophical differences between the two nations, largely misunderstood by the media, contributed significantly to the dispute's persistence.[31] In any case, the steps taken and not taken in the roughly two years after Uruguay approved the ENCE mill set the stage for Argentina's decision to approach the ICJ. It is unlikely that the Court would have taken the case until Argentina could reasonably argue that direct negotiation had failed, something the behavior of the disputants would convincingly demonstrate.

Under Article 7 of the Statute of the River Uruguay, CARU was to be notified if either party "plans to . . . carry out any other works which [are] liable to affect navigation, the regime of the river or the quality of its waters." The Commission would have 30 days to determine in a preliminary way "whether the plan might cause significant damage to the other Party."[32] If so, CARU would contact the affected party, which would be required to indicate any objections within 180 days or effectively permit the other to proceed with the project. In case of objections, there would be another period of 180 days for the parties to try to resolve their differences, a process in which CARU would play a facilitating role. However, because both states were represented equally in CARU, and there was no provision in the Statute for resolving ties, the process would essentially become one of bilateral negotiation. Should this fail, either party could then invoke Article 60 and submit the matter to the ICJ. Until political differences between Uruguay and Argentina escalated during the banking crisis, CARU was generally effective in helping to resolve some difficult and potentially divisive river issues.[33]

The results in the pulp mills dispute were quite different, something Argentina successfully attributed during the ICJ litigation to Uruguay's failure to work within established Statute rules. CARU was not cut out entirely, but it was not the central player Argentina preferred and felt that the Statute intended. Representatives of ENCE did provide some information about the project to the president of CARU in 2002, at the time the company was submitting an environmental impact assessment (EIA) to Uruguayan authorities. CARU stayed involved, at various points requesting additional information from the Uruguayan government and sending a legal adviser to attend a public hearing in Fray Bentos. On 8 October 2003, the day before Uruguay issued its initial environmental authorization for the plant's construction, Uruguay informed CARU that a report on the project would be forthcoming. Soon after the authorization, CARU offered to review technical aspects of the proposal and held an "extraordinary session" on 17 October where Argentina complained about the Uruguayan action. CARU then suspended its work for more than six months. CARU played a similarly marginal role as planning for the Botnia project went forward during 2004. CARU officials met with Botnia representatives, sought information from the Uruguayan government, and attended a public hearing. In early February 2005, Botnia received initial Uruguayan authorization to begin construction of its mill and the nearby port terminal. CARU meetings continued to serve as a forum for Argentine complaints and requests that construction of both the ENCE and Botnia mills be postponed.[34]

As it became clear that Uruguay was bypassing the normal process of bilateral review, the dispute moved to the political level. On 10 October 2003, the day Uruguay issued the ENCE permit, the Uruguayan and Argentine presidents met at Batlle's presidential retreat at Anchorena Park in Colonia, Uruguay. Accounts of the meeting differ. Either Uruguay agreed not to go forward with the project until it had dealt with Argentina's environmental objections (Argentina's view) or Argentina admitted that, in principle, it was not opposed to the project and was willing to resolve their differences outside the CARU framework (Uruguay's view).[35] These conflicting interpretations could not be reconciled easily, and what Malamud appropriately terms a "dialogue of the deaf"[36] was now fully underway. Subsequent developments help explain both the Argentine decision to take the matter to the International Court of Justice and the relative ease with which the two governments ultimately decided to resolve the dispute based on the Court's decision.

The first significant political step after the apparent failure of the CARU process was taken in May 2005, when the Uruguayan and Argentine foreign ministers created a High Level Technical Group (GTAN), which was given the unenviable task of trying to resolve the dispute within 180 days. By now binational tensions had been heightened by the first of a series of blockades of key bridges over the River Uruguay. The protests were organized by members of local environmental Argentine assemblies, with significant support from local politicians, most notably Jorge Busti, Governor of the Province of Entre Rios directly across from Fray Bentos.[37] This was an easy issue for regional politicians to embrace; the situation of President Kirchner, with broader national responsibilities, was more complicated. With midterm legislative elections scheduled for October 2005, Kirchner traveled to the region in May and made speeches sharply criticizing the Uruguayan government and calling the relocation of the mills a "causa nacional."[38] This played well politically, and Kirchner's coalition won the election. However, Kirchner's involvement raised the stakes significantly both at home and abroad, as the Argentine position seemed to be shifting from one of demanding more information about the plants to insisting that they be built elsewhere. This was not conducive to bilateral compromise and also raised concerns within Argentina's own important pulp and paper industry about whether a broader shift in government policy was on the horizon.[39]

In this highly charged political environment, GTAN's failure was predictable. If this was to be a technical process, it was a sign of the troubles ahead that the Argentine minister used an early GTAN meeting to convey requests from the Entre Rios government that the plants be moved and construction suspended for 180 days.[40] GTAN held 12 meetings between 3 August 2005, and 30 January 2006, but was unable to reach agreement on even a single report to issue to the two governments. On 31 January, Uruguay announced that the process had failed; Argentina said the same on 3 February.[41] Argentina then took steps to submit its case to the International Court of Justice, amid

Uruguayan suspicions that the GTAN process had simply been a diplomatic exercise to justify Argentina's ICJ claim.[42]

Legal Issue: International Adjudication

International adjudication has a reputation for being a slow, procedurally rigid process. Uncertainty about how often imprecise rules of environmental law will be interpreted can encourage disputing states to rely instead on diplomatic procedures, over which they have more direct control. Moreover, the technical complexity of the scientific issues posed in environmental disputes may seem to make them inappropriate for legally trained judges to address.[43] There is also a history in which courts, even when brought into environmental disputes, have not been as helpful as the claimants had hoped. In 1974, Australia and New Zealand took their dispute with France over French atmospheric nuclear testing in the South Pacific to the International Court of Justice. France defied a provisional measure ordered by the Court to stop the tests while the case was being heard, and the ICJ ultimately dismissed the claims as moot after France announced it did not intend to continue atmospheric testing.[44] When France rescinded a self-imposed moratorium and resumed underground nuclear testing in 1995, Australia and New Zealand were unsuccessful in persuading the Court to reconsider the case based on its 1974 ruling.[45]

Nevertheless, an increasing number of environmental regimes now provide adjudicative and quasi-adjudicative processes as dispute settlement options. In 1993, the ICJ created an Environment Chamber designed to provide a forum with more environmental expertise. While the Chamber has yet to hear a case, the entire Court has issued important rulings with environmental dimensions in two other cases, the Gabčíkovo–Nagymaros dam dispute between Hungary and Slovakia (1997)[46] and the Antarctic Whaling dispute between Australia and Japan (2014).[47] Although the case was later withdrawn, in 2008 Ecuador brought a claim before the ICJ against Colombia concerning damage allegedly being caused in Ecuador by Colombia's aerial spraying of herbicides in boundary areas.[48]

Ironically, as discussed in Chapter 5, what some now fear is the proliferation of tribunals with overlapping areas of jurisdictional responsibility and the potential for competing judgments to emerge.[49] In the Sellafield MOX dispute, Ireland took its case against the UK to both the International Tribunal of the Law of the Sea and an OSPAR Arbitral Tribunal. Neither court reached a decision on the merits of the case, leading one observer to call efforts to litigate the MOX dispute "a huge waste of precision resources."[50] However, the inclusion of binding third-party dispute settlement provisions in so many international agreements suggests that governments do view adjudication as an important component of contemporary environmental regimes.

Argentina's formal ICJ claim was brought on 4 May 2006, along with a request that the Court order Uruguay to halt further construction of the mills while the case was being considered. While the ICJ litigation proceeded, developments in two other institutional frameworks indicated how complex the dispute had become.

First, the Argentine bridge protests continued. They had badly hurt the Uruguayan tourist industry during the summer season of 2005–06 and now threatened to make it difficult to get supplies to the construction site at Fray Bentos. Uruguay took the matter to Mercosur on 12 April 2006, arguing before an ad hoc tribunal that the failure of the Argentine government to control the protests violated Mercosur's free trade rules. In its 6 September ruling, the panel agreed that Argentina had violated the agreement, but it imposed no sanctions since members were not convinced that Argentina's inaction was intentional.[51] The protests did succeed in encouraging some private investors to pull out of the projects. The biggest victory came on 21 September 2006, when ENCE announced that it would not build at the original site on the River Uruguay, thus removing one source of bilateral friction. However, the ENCE president announced from Buenos Aires the selection of another Uruguayan site, shortly after meeting with President Kirchner. Uruguayan officials were not happy with the company's lack of consultation with Uruguay, which was, after all, the project's host state.[52] Uruguay then filed its own application with the ICJ, requesting that the Court order provisional measures requiring Argentina to end the bridge protests.

Second, under pressure from the Argentine government and the Center for Human Rights and the Environment, an Argentine-based NGO, for its financial support of the projects, the IFC agreed to commission a second impact assessment. The final report, released on 6 October 2006, reinforced the IFC's earlier conclusion that the plants could be operated safely,[53] although it did suggest changes to respond to some of the complaints. Opponents remained unconvinced, and an IFC announcement in November 2006 that it was prepared to grant the loan for the Botnia plant triggered more Argentine blockades.[54]

Despite efforts by a number of third parties, including the king of Spain, to bring about a mediated solution, both countries were now clearly focused on the ICJ, what one observer had earlier called the "worst possible scenario."[55] When Argentina and Uruguay began oral arguments before the Court on the merits of the Argentine claim in September 2009, there were two points on which they agreed.

The first was that the Court should have imposed provisional measures on the other, since each feared that its interests would be at risk during the time it would take the Court to decide the case. The ICJ found neither argument persuasive. With regard to the Argentine request that Uruguay be ordered to stop construction, the Court held that Argentina had failed to make a compelling case that the mills presented "an imminent threat of irreparable damage." Moreover, Uruguay would have to realize that, by moving ahead with the project, it "necessarily bears all the risks" that might result from a later decision on the merits that could, at least in theory, require the closure of the mills.[56] Similarly, the Court did not feel that there was an "imminent risk of irreparable prejudice" to Uruguay's rights that would justify an order requiring Argentina to end the bridge protests.[57]

The second area of agreement was that the Court had jurisdiction to hear the case, thus sparing the parties what could have been a long and costly procedural battle. Argentina clearly felt this was the case when it brought the matter to the Court. Initially, the need to move expeditiously through the process had been heightened by the fact that the Botnia pulp mill, already under construction, would become operational in November 2007. Any chance to prevent this, or at least make changes in its design, would be jeopardized by delays. Uruguay could have continued to challenge the Court's jurisdiction on the grounds that diplomatic efforts to resolve the problem had not been exhausted, but realistically there was no process that was likely to be effective. Uruguay also wanted the protests stopped; a positive decision, at least on the substantive question of the safety of the plant, could help defuse them. Moreover, prospects for the future development of the Uruguayan pulp and paper industry could be enhanced by a judicial ruling that this controversial industry could be operated in an environmentally responsible way.

Argentina argued that Uruguay had violated both its procedural and substantive obligations under the terms of the Statute of the River Uruguay. Procedurally, it had failed to follow the rules of Article 7 in approving the pulp mills without first going through a process of notification, information sharing, and negotiation through CARU. Substantively, Argentina challenged the steps taken by Uruguay to oversee the design and construction of the plants, an argument that now could include a preliminary assessment of the impact the Botnia plant was having on the quality of the River Uruguay. As a remedy for these violations, past and continuing, Argentina asked the Court to order the closure of the Botnia mill, and to require Uruguay both to pay compensation for the damage the mill had caused and to ensure that no future violations of Argentina's rights took place.[58]

Uruguay disputed all of Argentina's claims, requesting that the Court reject them and affirm Uruguay's right to operate the Botnia mill. Uruguay argued that it had behaved in a manner consistent with its procedural obligations under the Statute, albeit not through the CARU process, but through alternative arrangements Uruguay believed Argentina had accepted. Uruguay also insisted that there was no evidence of any harm being caused by the Botnia plant. Under no circumstances was there reason to close the plant; at most, compensation might be ordered if the Court found that damage had been done to Argentina.[59]

The Resolution

In its final decision, the Court embraced neither state's position fully. Depending on one's perspective, the outcome could be seen as either a victory or a defeat for both. The Court ruled that Uruguay had violated its procedural obligations to Argentina under the Statute. However, there was no evidence that the plant, as constructed, was violating Argentina's substantive rights, and the Court considered a declaratory judgment an appropriate and sufficient remedy for Uruguay's procedural violations. The Court also held that the parties had an obligation to continue working together within the framework provided by CARU.[60] In its ruling, the Court addressed a number of issues that have potential relevance beyond the pulp mills dispute.

The first relates to the Court's perception of the limits of its jurisdictional competence, how broad a range of environmental issues it could examine and what standards beyond the Statute it could use to judge Uruguay's behavior. Argentina had argued that the Court should consider a number of environmental harms, such as noise and visual pollution and the problem of "bad odors," in addition to the pulp mills' immediate effect on the river. It also contended that the Statute provided a "referral clause," which allowed the Court to consider other relevant international treaties such as the Convention on International Trade in Endangered Species and the Biodiversity Convention as appropriate legal standards. The Court sided with Uruguay, holding that the Statute restricted its focus to matters directly associated with the river's aquatic environment.[61] Moreover, the ICJ found no referral clause in the Statute and held that its focus had to remain on obligations imposed by the Statute itself.[62] On the other hand, both sides had stated, and the Court agreed, that it could use rules of general international law to interpret the Statute, many of whose provisions were phrased in less than precise terms.

A second issue raised in the case is the relationship between a state's procedural and substantive obligations under international law. Argentina argued that the two types of obligations were integrally connected, that the illegality of the process by which the mill was approved should affect its ability to continue to operate, at least without substantial changes. Although the Court recognized a "functional link" between the two types of obligations, it still found them analytically distinct, with different judgments to be made about the consequences of violating each. The Court ruled that Uruguay's procedural violations did not merit anything other than a statement of disapproval, even though the pulp mill was built as a consequence of their breach.[63]

The Court then focused on one of the central questions posed by the case: what are a state's procedural obligations when activities within its jurisdiction threaten to damage another state? While its attention was directed at CARU's role as intended in the Statute, the Court was interpreting the Statute very much within the broader world of customary international law. What emerged were three distinct procedural obligations, the duty to *inform*, the duty to *notify*, and the duty to *negotiate in good faith* with a state that might be affected detrimentally by a proposed project.

Uruguay defended its failure to contact CARU early in the process on the basis that it would have been inappropriate to do so before all the technical details about the project and its possible impact were known. Uruguay also argued that the meetings between company representatives of both ENCE and Botnia had provided adequate notification about the plans for the mills, and that the GTAN meetings, although not ultimately successful, fulfilled its responsibility to negotiate with Argentina.

The Court disagreed, holding that Uruguay had violated all three procedural duties. Customary international law requires a state to "use all the means at its disposal in order to avoid activities which take place in its territory, or in any area under its jurisdiction, causing significant damage to the environment of another State."[64] Informing is the first step, and Uruguay should have informed CARU of the potential effects of the pulp mills as soon as it had been given a plan for the development of the project.[65] The Court emphasized that this responsibility resides with the state and could not be channeled to private companies.[66] With regard to notification, the Court stressed the need for an adequate environmental impact assessment, one transmitted to a potentially affected state before any decision to approve the plan is made.[67] Unwilling to consider the GTAN process an appropriate substitute for CARU meetings, the Court also held that Uruguay had violated its obligation to negotiate by approving the project before the "period of negotiation" had ended.[68] On the other hand, due diligence did not require Uruguay to secure Argentina's prior approval of the project. After the negotiation period, Uruguay had the right to authorize construction as long as it took Argentina's interests into account.[69] Although the judges were divided,[70] the Court held that Uruguay could do so even if the ICJ had not yet been able to hear the case.

Turning to Uruguay's substantive obligations, an important preliminary issue was which state bore the burden of proof in deciding whether the operation of the pulp mills was lawful. Argentina invoked the precautionary principle, arguing that it was Uruguay's responsibility to prove the safety of the pulp mills or, at least, to share that burden equally with Argentina. Uruguay took the more traditional view, largely embraced by the Court, that the burden of proof is on the plaintiff.[71] In a separate opinion, Judge Greenwood objected not that the burden was on Argentina, but that the Court set the threshold for meeting it so high. Similar to the distinction in standards of proof used criminal and civil proceedings, Greenwood suggested that it would be appropriate in complex environmental cases to lower the threshold.[72] That settled, the Court then explained what it saw as Uruguay's three substantive obligations as it moved forward with the pulp mills project.

The first is the duty to provide for what Article 1 of the Statute called the "optimum and rational utilization" of the River Uruguay. The Court found this formulation essentially equivalent to equitable utilization, a principle that presumes there is no strict set of rules governing how a shared river is managed and how competing uses are to be accommodated. Instead, a balancing process, often involving an institution like CARU, attempts to provide each state on the waterway a fair share of the river's uses. A long-standing concern about this principle is the fear that environmental protection could be treated as simply one more value to be considered and potentially sacrificed in the face of competing uses. In the Pulp Mills case, the Court suggested that the balancing process associated with equitable utilization should be considered in somewhat different terms with the "rights and needs to use the river for economic and commercial activities on the one hand, and the obligation to protect it from any damage to the environment that may be caused by such activities, on the other."[73] This approach does suggest a special concern for environmental interests, especially when the threat to them could be serious.

The second substantive obligation is one of "due diligence," which should govern the conduct of the state before and after it authorizes a project with potential transboundary impact. Among the steps required of the state are the creation and implementation of a set of rules to govern the activity in question. The Court held that, under the Statute, these rules need not be established internationally by a body like CARU, as Argentina had suggested, but that they do "have to conform to applicable international agreements and to take account of internationally agreed technical standards."[74] Thus the regulations implemented nationally by Uruguay could be considered sufficient evidence of due diligence if not in violation of international rules and enforced on a regular basis.

Finally, the Court held that it is now the customary law duty of states to conduct an environmental impact assessment in situations "when there is a risk that the proposed industrial activity may have a significant adverse impact in a transboundary context, in particular, on a shared resource."[75] However, the Court rejected Argentina's claim that there are international standards, embodied in international agreements such as the Espoo Convention, that prescribe what an EIA should include. This could be determined nationally, although the state did have to consider the "nature and magnitude of the proposed development and its likely adverse impact on the environment" and "to exercise due diligence in conducting such an assessment."[76] Within these broad parameters, there is substantial room for disagreement about what constitutes an adequate process. The Court was clear that customary international law also does not require the state to consult potentially affected parties, as Argentina had argued.[77] In addition, Argentina had criticized Uruguay's willingness to allow the ENCE and Botnia pulp mills to employ the ECF bleaching process rather than the TCF process that many consider a cleaner technology. The Court did not go so far as to insist that a state permit only the "best available technology" (BAT) to be used. Instead, it stated that "careful consideration" must be given to the technology to be employed, although exactly who was to give that technology "careful consideration" was left unclear.[78] In the case of the Botnia mill, the ECF process was cited in a 2001 study as used in 80 per cent of world pulp production. With the burden of proof again placed on it, Argentina was able to provide "no evidence . . . that the Orion (Botnia) mill is not BAT-compliant."[79]

Post-Dispute Developments

The ICJ decision led directly to a negotiated settlement between Argentina and Uruguay. By 2010, two new leaders were in power, José Mujica, elected president of Uruguay in 2009, and Cristina Fernández de Kirchner, who had succeeded her husband in 2007. Shortly after the verdict, under pressure from the Argentine government, the citizens' assembly suspended the blockade of one of the bridges crossing the River Uruguay. In July 2010, the Argentine and Uruguayan foreign ministers met in Buenos Aires behind closed doors to discuss a proposed system of environmental monitoring for the river.[80] A formal agreement was signed on 30 August to create a joint scientific committee which would begin sampling water quality at various points along the river and report its findings to CARU. It would also have the right to visit the Botnia pulp mill 12 times a year to take water samples. Argentine Foreign Minister Hector Timerman declared, "I'm most pleased, because it will also be a model for similar situations in other parts of the world," and made clear that there was no longer a "need for protests regarding the issue."[81]

Evidence of the new spirit of cooperation was soon apparent. In October, Uruguay's Foreign Minister Luis Almagro announced that the Finnish company Stora Enso would be licensed to build another major pulp mill in Uruguay, this time near the La Plata River. However, Almagro insisted that the plant would be subject to strict Uruguayan supervision, as Uruguay had "implemented wide ranging supervision measures following the experiences we have had with other pulp mill projects."[82] Uruguayan Deputy Secretary of the Environment, Jorge Patrone expressed confidence that this project "would not create a new diplomatic conflict" with Argentina. While the development of the plant would take place within the framework of the La Plata River Treaty, he pledged that Uruguay's "environmental demands will be the same that we have set in place on the River Uruguay. Our demands are in sync with those set in place on a global scale, just like the ones put in place towards the former Botnia pulp mill."[83] One year after the settlement, Argentine Foreign Minister Timerman reaffirmed that relations were still very good. "Problems of the past have been solved and overcome for the benefit of both peoples. . . . Yes, we have many issues pending but because we have much integration to advance on."[84]

Despite this optimistic assessment, tensions between Argentina and Uruguay were rekindled in the fall of 2013 when Uruguay approved an increase in output from the Fray Bentos mill, now owned by another Finnish company, UPM-Kymmene. Uruguay defended the action as "in conformity with its international obligations," and argued that "joint monitoring unambiguously shows that the UPM plant does not contaminate."[85] Uruguayan Foreign Minister Luis Almagro also indicated that over a year earlier he had proposed to Timerman new rules to strengthen the regime governing the River Uruguay. Argentina initially threatened to reopen its case against Uruguay before the ICJ. However, that step has not yet been taken as Argentina appears content to use restrictions on exports through Uruguayan ports and currency controls that reduce Argentine tourism in Uruguay to signal Argentine displeasure with the Uruguayan decision.[86]

Analysis

As in most of the disputes described in the preceding chapters, the national governments of Argentina and Uruguay were the key players on an international level, indeed necessarily so in the formal proceedings before the International Court of Justice. It was their willingness to argue the case in The Hague and to treat the Court's decision seriously that gave its verdict practical effect. However, it was also a dispute that reflected the complex domestic political context in which each state's national policy was developed and the range of intergovernmental and nongovernmental actors involved in the pulp mills project.

Of the conflicts analyzed here, the pulp mills dispute is the one in which international adjudication was most decisive. The primary benefit seems to have been in taking a dispute apparently unresolvable on a diplomatic level, in part given political forces at work in both countries by late 2005, into an entirely different arena. In an interview in March 2010, shortly before the ICJ decision was handed down, Uruguayan Foreign Minister Luis Almagro suggested that nothing could be done politically until the "Gordian knot" represented by the ICJ litigation was undone.[87] Whether the knot was actually a legal or political one is unclear, but litigation before a respected international tribunal provided both national governments a face-saving way to back down from positions that had become increasingly polarized.

Adjudication can provide answers to key questions, without which it is impossible to move forward diplomatically. Until the issue of Uruguay's right to build the mill at Fray Bentos could be resolved, it is difficult to see how the two sides could have a reached a negotiated settlement. Similarly, Argentina's sense that Uruguay was violating a treaty obligation in not working through the CARU process apparently needed judicial vindication before the Argentine government could feel comfortable accepting the new CARU-supervised system of joint monitoring. The Court's endorsement of CARU as a transboundary institution could be seen as tangible recognition of at least part of Argentina's position. It was helpful that the final ICJ decision was one in which each state could claim at least partial victory.

Moving the dispute into a judicial arena helped lower the level of nationalistic rhetoric and required both governments to frame their positions in more responsible terms in front of an increasingly global audience. As the debate shifted to matters of legal principle, Argentine protestors had to acknowledge that there was at least some level of hypocrisy in opposing a mill in Uruguay that would almost certainly be less environmentally damaging than those already operating in Argentina.[88] That the ICJ was not the only third party involved also contributed to the success of the overall dispute settlement process. Having the Mercosur tribunal available to Uruguay when Argentina was approaching the ICJ unilaterally put each state in a position to argue the legitimacy of international adjudication to important domestic constituencies. The Mercosur process also put Argentina on the defensive about its failure to control the blockades and may have helped move the government to a position where it was more ready to confront the protestors once the ICJ decision was handed down. The fact that the IFC was prepared to undertake a second project assessment also likely helped convince the Court, and perhaps even some reluctant Argentinians, that the plant was not as much of an environmental threat as some had feared.

International adjudication does have limitations, which were also evident here. As in the MOX dispute, the process encouraged both sides in the short run to articulate one-sided views of the issues, something that may have only reinforced the sense of right felt by non-governmental actors on both sides of the border. Even though both states accepted the Court's jurisdiction, the judicial process took time, as the parties prepared, articulated, and defended complicated legal arguments. Given the technical complexity of the issues posed by the project, the fact that the Court reached a verdict as quickly as it did in the Pulp Mills case is actually encouraging. What delay resulted was also not necessarily a bad thing. Slowing down the dispute effectively created a "cooling off" period, at least in terms of direct bilateral negotiations, and permitted domestic factors to help moderate national positions. Representatives of Argentina's pulp and paper industry had the opportunity to be heard about the broader policy implications of the Argentine position, and the two leaders who took office while the case was being decided seemed ready to adopt more conciliatory positions in a dispute that had lasted almost seven years. Even the fact that each state lost its bid to have the Court impose provisional measures against the other may have helped both governments realize the likely limits of what could be achieved internationally.

To have any positive impact, the Court's ruling had to be perceived by Argentina and Uruguay as consistent with their respective national interests. Ending the dispute required a process of bilateral negotiation between governments willing to compromise and ready to take the steps to get domestic constituencies to respect the agreement. The decision also had to provide a reasonable basis for managing economic development along the river. It was thus no substitute for the ongoing work of CARU, an institution with the technical expertise and potential to sort through the complex issues posed by transboundary resource management.

Beyond its role in helping settle the pulp mills dispute, the Court's ruling also offered a clearer sense of how far international environmental law has evolved in developing rules to prevent transboundary environmental damage and of areas where further development is needed. Three points deserve emphasis.

First, there is the issue of the role courts should play in transboundary environmental disputes. While the Court's involvement here should be encouraging to those who favor the expanded use of international adjudication, the International Court of Justice also recognized its limits. Its responsibility was to define clearly the hard law relevant to the dispute and to apply it fairly.

The Court served as an interpreter of the law, not its source, and it stressed the importance of having the parties resolve their substantive differences within the CARU process. For those hoping to see the Court play a more assertive law-development role, or to be more actively engaged in helping forge a final settlement between the parties, this somewhat cautious response could be disappointing. However, as in the MOX dispute, the Court's willingness to respect the limited authority the parties conferred on it under the Statute of the River Uruguay should reassure states considering the possibility of giving the ICJ compulsory jurisdiction in similar agreements. It may also help allay the fears of those who worry about potential competition and conflict when multiple adjudicative bodies become involved in a single dispute.

Second, although the Court's decision might be seen simply as an interpretation of a specific treaty, it does have broader relevance. The ICJ made extensive reference to customary international law in analyzing the parties' procedural and substantive obligations. It made clear that states have a general duty to initiate a process of transboundary consultation and negotiation before making major development decisions with transboundary implications, and to conduct a prior environmental impact assessment process that takes those risks seriously. On the other hand, the Court would not accept the argument that there are international standards for environmental impact assessment other than those that states accept by treaty. Similarly, its refusal to permit the precautionary principle to shift the burden of proving the safety of the pulp mills onto Uruguay suggests that this emerging principle may be less firmly embedded in customary international law than some would like, at least when applied in an adjudicative setting. The judicial restraint the ICJ showed should put the responsibility back on political leaders to give these legal concepts greater clarity.

A third, more troubling implication of the Court's decision was the limited support it offers to efforts to develop rules to *prevent* pollution, rather than relying on regimes of compensation and liability to be invoked once damage has already been done. As discussed in Chapter 2, this is a dimension of state environmental responsibility that deserves greater emphasis. Two aspects of the Court's decision are relevant in this regard. First, it reaffirmed Uruguay's right to permit construction of the plant once the required period of negotiation had passed, but before Argentina had been able to take the matter to the Court. It has long been understood, at least in a riparian context, that a potentially affected state does not have the right to veto uses of the river by others, for instance simply by refusing to take seriously any proposed changes. However, when there is an international tribunal available to rule on a controversial project, it is at least debatable whether states should still be able move ahead with proposed projects before the case can be heard. Second, there is the fact that the penalty imposed against Uruguay was so light. This was a matter on which members of the Court disagreed,[89] and for good reason, at least when one looks beyond this case. If such limited consequences follow from what was held to be a clear violation of procedural rules, one wonders what sense of obligation these procedural norms will really be seen to impose. To be sure, the range of available sanctions was limited, and few really expected the Court to shut down the plant once it was built. However, by refusing Argentina's request for a provisional order to stop construction until the case could be heard, the Court left itself few options. Argentina's fear that permitting Uruguay to build the plant would create a *fait accompli* does not seem to have been misplaced.

What the ICJ provided in the pulp mills dispute was not a resolution of the dispute but a legal foundation on which one could be negotiated. The recent flare-up in tensions over the expanded output from Fray Bentos is a reminder of the limited impact any international adjudicative body can have if political leaders are unwilling to implement its decisions and to develop the rules its judgment may suggest are needed.

Notes

1   International Court of Justice (ICJ), "Case Concerning Pulp Mills on the River Uruguay: Argentina v. Uruguay (Judgment of 20 April 2010)" *ICJ Reports* no. 7 (2010): 14 [hereafter cited as ICJ, "Pulp Mills Judgment"]. http://www.icj-cij. org/docket/files/135/15877.pdf.

2   "Pulp Mill Row Raised Fears of Argentina-Uruguay War: Report," *UPI.com*, 14 October 2011.

3   Argentina and Uruguay, "Statute of the River Uruguay," Salto, 26 February 1975 (entered into force 18 September 1976), *United Nations Treaty Series*, no. 21425 (1982): 347 [hereafter cited as "Statute"]. http://www.internationalwaterlaw. org/documents/regionaldocs/Uruguay_River_Statute_1975.pdf.

4   Roberto Luchi and Ariel Llorente, "Rules of Entanglement: The River Uruguay's Pulp Mills International Dispute, a Case Study," (IAE, Esculea de Dirección de Nogocios, Universidad Austral, 2008), 2–3.

5   Carlos Malamud, "Pulp Mills Divide the River Plate," (Elcano Royal Institute, 2006), 3. http://www.realinstitutoelcano.org/analisis/944/944_Malamud.pdf. Malamud's 2006 study indicated that, even with the growth in Uruguayan forest production, Uruguay had only 800,000 hectares of planted forest compared to Argentina (1.5 million hectares), Chile (2.1 million hectares), and Brazil (5 million hectares). Brazil also dominated in terms of the capacity to process the wood with 241 pulp and paper mills. Chile had 13 and Argentina 10.

6   Jussi Pakkasvirta, "From Pulp to Fiction?: Fray Bentos Pulp Investment Conflict through the Finnish Media," *Cooperation and Conflict* 43 (2008): 426. This, in part, helps explain the very quiet role played by the Finnish government in supporting Botnia's interests in the dispute.

7   Malamud, "Pulp Mills Divide the River Plate," 3.

8   Sebastian Krapohl and Julia Dinkel, "From Finnish Pulp Mills and Blocked Bridges: The Escalation of Conflict and the Weakness of Judicialization in MERCOSUR." Paper presented at the European Consortium for Political Research General Conference, Reykjavík, 2011. http://ecpr.eu/Filestore/PaperProposal/bb2a7ab9-f8a2-4a30-8b85-e54f82b008ef.pdf.

9   Malamud, "Pulp Mills Divide the River Plate," 3–4.

10   Argentina, Brazil, Paraguay, and Uruguay, "Treaty Establishing a Common Market," Asunción, 26 March 1991 (entered into force 29 November 1991), *International Legal Materials* 30 (1991): 1041–63. http://www.jstor.org/stable/20693593.

11   The Statute was actually the product of a broader pattern of regional cooperation among the La Plata River basin riparians that began in 1969 with the signature of the La Plata River Basin Treaty. Brazil, Argentina, Bolivia, Paraguay, Uruguay, "Treaty of the La Plata River Basin," Brasilia, 23 April 1969 (entered into force 14 August 1970), *United Nations Treaty Series*, no. 1250 (1973): 10–13. http://www.internationalwaterlaw.org/documents/regionaldocs/La_Plata-1969.pdf.

12   See CARU, "The River Uruguay Executive Commission," http://www.caru.org.uy/web/pdfs_publicaciones/The-River-Uruguay-executive-commission-Uruguay-Paysandu.pdf.

13   Marcela Valente, "Argentina's New Neighborhood Assemblies: The Seed of a New Form of Citizen Participation," *Inter Press Service*, 25 March 2002.

14   Luis de la Plaza and Sophie Sirtaine, "An Analysis of the 2002 Uruguayan Banking Crisis," in *World Bank Policy Research Working Paper No. 3780* (Washington, DC: World Bank, 2005), 8–11.

15   Thomas Catan, "Uruguay President Apologises to Argentina," *ft.com*, 4 June 2002.

16   Heather Stewart, "Uruguay Riots Fuel Fear of Financial Meltdown," *The Guardian*, 2 August 2002.

17   See, for example, Celia Szusterman, "Pulp Friction: The Argentina-Uruguay Conflict," *openDemocracy*, 30 January 2008.

18   Cymie R. Payne, "Pulp Mills on the River Uruguay: The International Court of Justice Recognizes Environmental Impact Assessment as a Duty under International Law " *ASIL Insights* 14, no. 9 (2010).

19   See Pakkasvirta, "From Pulp to Fiction?," 421–46. For another view, see Malamud, "Pulp Mills Divide the River Plate."

20   That European companies moving their operations to Uruguay would not face these new restrictions was not lost on commentators. See, Marcela Valente, "Pulp Mill Agreement Eases Tension, Not Residents' Fears," *Inter Press Service News Agency*, 25 July 2005.

21   Marcela Valente, "Double Standards on Pulp Mills," *Inter Press Service News Agency*, 27 October 2005.

22   Ramiro Berardo and Andrea K. Gerlak, "Conflict and Cooperation Along International Rivers: Crafting a Model of Institutional Effectiveness," *Global Environmental Politics* 12, no. 1 (2012): 107.

23   Dario Montero, "Bridges Close as Credit Lines for Pulp Mill Open," *Inter Press Service News Agency*, 22 November 2006.

24   Daniel Kazhdan, "Precautionary Pulp: Pulp Mills and the Evolving Dispute between International Tribunals over the Reach of the Precautionary Principle," *Ecology Law Quarterly* 38 (2011): 542–43.

25 Malamud, "Pulp Mills Divide the River Plate," 6.
26 Dario Montero, "Pulp Mills Pit 'Greens' against Labor," *Tierramérica*, 15 February 2006.
27 Johanna Pohjola, "Botnia Pulp Factory Centre of Dispute between Argentina and Uruguay," *Helsingin Sanomat*, 2 January 2006.
28 Marcela Valente, "Double Standards on Pulp Mills," *Inter Press Service News Agency*, 27 October 2005.
29 Krapohl and Dinkel, "From Finnish Pulp Mills," 19–22.
30 Malamud, "Pulp Mills Divide the River Plate," 6.
31 Pakkasvirta, "From Pulp to Fiction?"
32 "Statute," Art. 7, 341.
33 Kazhdan, "Precautionary Pulp," 542.
34 ICJ, "Pulp Mills Judgment," paras. 24–44, 30–39.
35 ICJ, "Pulp Mills Judgment," para. 32, 36.
36 Malamud, "Pulp Mills Divide the River Plate," 3.
37 Michael K. Lee, "The Uruguay Paper Pulp Mill Dispute: Highlighting the Growing Importance of NGOs and Public Protest in the Enforcement of International Environmental Law," *Sustainable Development Law and Policy* 7 (2006): 71–73.
38 Luchi and Llorente, "Rules of Entanglement," 13.
39 Malamud, "Pulp Mills Divide the River Plate," 7–8.
40 Ibid., 4–5.
41 ICJ, "Pulp Mills Judgment," para. 40, 28.
42 Dario Montero, "Pulp Mill Conflict Hits Tourism," *Inter Press Service News Agency*, 2 January 2006.
43 See, generally, Patricia W. Birnie and Alan E. Boyle, *International Law and the Environment* (Oxford: Oxford University Press, 2002), 179–85.
44 ICJ, "Nuclear Tests Case: New Zealand v. France (Judgment of 24 December 1974)," *ICJ Reports* (1974): 457–78. http://www.icj-cij.org/docket/files/59/6159.pdf.
45 ICJ, "Request for an Examination of the Situation in Accordance with Paragraph 63 of the Court's Judgment of 20 December 1974 in the Nuclear Tests: New Zealand v. France (Order of 22 September 1995), *ICJ Reports* (1974): 288–308. http://www.icj-cij.org/docket/files/97/7555.pdf.
46 ICJ, "Case Concerning Gabčíkovo-Nagymaros Project: Hungary and Slovakia (Judgment of 25 September 1997)," http://www.icj-cij.org/docket/files/92/7375.pdf.
47 ICJ, "Whaling in the Antarctic: Australia v. Japan, New Zealand Intervening (Judgment of 31 March 2014)," http://www.icj-cij.org/docket/files/148/18136.pdf.
48 ICJ, "Ecuador Institutes Proceedings against Colombia with Regard to a Dispute Concerning the Alleged Aerial Spraying by Colombia of Toxic Herbicides over Ecuadorian Territory," press release, 1 April 2008.
49 See, generally, Chester Brown, "The Proliferation of International Courts and Tribunals: Finding Your Way through the Maze," *Melbourne Journal of International Law* 3 (2002): 453–75.
50 Nikolaos Lavranos, "The Epilogue in the MOX Dispute: An End without Findings," *European Energy and Environmental Law Review* 18 (2009): 184.

51   C. Leah Granger, "The Role of International Tribunals in Natural Resource Disputes in Latin America," *Ecology Law Quarterly* 34 (2007): 1342–43.
52   Luchi and Llorente, "Rules of Entanglement," 17.
53   "World Bank Group Releases Final Cumulative Impact Study," *IFC News*, 12 October 2006." For the full report, see International Finance Corporation, "IFC in Uruguay," (2006).
54   Montero, "Bridges Close."
55   "Pulp Mill Conflict Hits Tourism."
56   ICJ, "Case Concerning Pulp Mills on the River Uruguay: Argentina v. Uruguay (Request for Indication of Provisional Measures, Order of 13 July 2006)," paras. 73–78, 132–33. http://www.icj-cij.org/docket/files/135/11235.pdf.
57   ICJ, "Case Concerning Pulp Mills on the River Uruguay: Argentina v. Uruguay (Request for Indication of Provisional Measures, Order of 23 January 2007)," para. 50, 16. http://www.icj-cij.org/docket/files/135/13615.pdf.
58   ICJ, "Pulp Mills Judgment," paras. 22–23, 28–30.
59   Ibid., paras. 23–24, 28–31.
60   Ibid., paras. 267–81, 102–6.
61   Ibid., paras. 52–53, 41–42.
62   Ibid., para. 63, 46.
63   Ibid., para. 79, 49.
64   Ibid., para. 101, 55–56.
65   Ibid., para. 105, 56–57.
66   Ibid., para. 110, 58.
67   Ibid., paras. 120–21, 60.
68   Ibid., para. 149, 67–68.
69   Ibid., para. 152, 68.
70   Panos Merkouris, "Case Concerning Pulp Mills on the River Uruguay (Argentina v. Uruguay): Of Environmental Impact Assessments and 'Phantom Experts,'" *Hague Justice Portal* (2010): 7.
71   ICJ, "Pulp Mills Judgment," para. 162, 71.
72   ICJ "Case Concerning Pulp Mills on the River Uruguay: Argentina v. Uruguay (Judgment of 20 April 2010, Separate Opinion of Judge Greenwood)," para. 26, 7. http://www.icj-cij.org/docket/files/135/15889.pdf.
73   ICJ, "Pulp Mills Judgment," para. 175, 74.
74   Ibid., para. 197, 79–80.
75   Ibid., para. 204, 82–83.
76   However, the Court did say that Uruguay had consulted affected groups. Ibid., para. 205, 83–84.
77   Ibid., paras. 216–19, 87–88.
78   Ibid., para. 223, 88–89.
79   Ibid., paras. 223–25, 88–89.
80   "Argentina and Uruguay Making Progress over Pulp Mill Conflict," *infosurhoy*, 14 July 2010.
81   "Uruguay/Argentina Implement the End of the Pulp Mill Dispute," *MercoPress*, 31 August 2010.
82   "Uruguay Authorizes Stora Enso to Build a Pulp Mill Next to the River Plate," *MercoPress*, 13 October 2010.
83   "Uruguay Hopes New Pulp Mills Won't Create Rifts with Argentina," *BuenosAiresHerald.com*, 27 January 2012.

84 "Argentina Says the Pulp Mill Conflict with Uruguay Is Over and 'Buried,'"
    MercoPress, 23 August 2011.
85 "Pulp Mill Dispute: Uruguay Rejects Argentine Ultimatum and Doubles the
    Bet," *MerocPress*, 17 October 2013.
86 "Strained Argentina–Uruguay Relations Threaten to Alter Regional Trade
    Flows," *ihs.com*, 28 January 2014.
87 "Uruguayan Foreign Minister on Paper Mill," *BBC News*, 19 March 2010.
88 Valente, "Double Standards on Pulp Mills."
89 See Merkouris, "Case Concerning Pulp Mills."

9

From Conflict to Law

Introduction

Each of the six transboundary disputes discussed in this book is a product of the unique circumstances in which it occurred. One cannot understand the willingness of Indonesia's neighbors to accept Indonesian delays in ratifying the ASEAN Haze Agreement without recognizing that the country was devastated in 2004 by a massive tsunami, which killed more than 230,000 people and made all other regional issues, including transboundary air pollution, pale by comparison. Romania was able to escape liability for the Baia Mare cyanide spill, in part, because the European Union faced much bigger challenges in managing the accession aspirations of a number of Eastern European nations making the transition from centrally planned to free-market economies. Even where disputes took place under similar conditions, their effects could be quite different. The global financial crisis of the late 1990s provided Indonesia with an excuse to ask for understanding and assistance from its neighbors as it struggled to contain the fires. The same event likely encouraged Uruguay, which felt itself a victim of Argentina's economic policies, to take a tougher line about its right to develop its pulp industry according to Uruguayan priorities.

There are obvious dangers in attempting to draw broad conclusions from what are ultimately six case studies. However, they do offer a basis for some observations about the nature of transboundary environmental disputes, the relevance of international law in their management, and the ways in which international environmental law may be developed as a result of these experiences.

Transboundary Environmental Disputes

The six disputes support much of what has been written about the growing importance of environmental issues and the seriousness with which national governments approach them. What might once have been seen as matters of low politics, to be handled on a technical level with a minimum of public attention, now seldom escape the glare of public scrutiny. Six points deserve emphasis.

National governments are key players but face different political constraints. National governments were directly involved in all of the disputes, although they engaged them with varying degrees of enthusiasm and control over the directions they took. Canada and Ireland had solid public support for the tough positions they adopted in their respective battles over turbot and MOX and few direct external constraints. The only domestic danger came from appearing to concede too much as they negotiated political settlements. While the Spanish public strongly supported the cause of the Spanish fishing industry, the European Union's expanding role in fisheries management and the need to maintain a common EU policy compromised what Spain could hope to achieve. In the MOX dispute, disagreement within the United Kingdom over the viability of the MOX industry complicated the government's international position and made its economic justification for the MOX plant, at best a peripheral Irish concern, more central to the dispute and something the British had to defend internationally. The *Clemenceau's* status as a state-owned warship inevitably placed the French government in the middle of all decisions about how it would be broken. Political and legal challenges both at home and abroad led the government, concerned about its tarnished public image, to reverse course and repatriate the vessel, despite its earlier claim that it had every right to have the ship recycled at Alang. In reacting to the haze from the Indonesian brush fires, Indonesia's neighbors had to keep in mind that some had been set on land owned by Malaysian and Singaporean nationals.

With national governments playing such central roles, the power relationships between them were relevant but not as important as realists might anticipate. Despite Uruguay's alleged fear that Argentina was considering an attack on Fray Bentos, military force was generally of limited significance in these cases. However, in the turbot dispute, Canada did have the advantage of being geographically closer to the fisheries being regulated. Canadian authorities were in a position to act quickly and decisively in arresting the *Estai* and could credibly threaten further seizures, putting the burden on Spain to escalate the conflict militarily. Potentially more significant were disparities in physical size and economic power. Despite a smaller per capita GDP, Indonesia dwarfed its neighbors on a regional scale, and Argentina had comparable advantages over Uruguay. The differences between Ireland and the United Kingdom and between Hungary and Romania were also significant, but did not appear to be a decisive factor in the way the governments managed their differences. There was no consistent pattern of weaker states deferring to those that were stronger. Hungary's recognition of Romania's struggling transitional economy and the challenges the government faced in regulating its mining industry actually appear to have softened Hungary's demands for compensation.

International organizations matter, and regional organizations matter more. International organizations played important roles in most of the disputes and were often crucial in helping level the playing field between disputants. Regional organizations, closer to the problem and often with more immediate influence, tended to be those most visibly engaged, although their impact was felt differently in each.

The European Union was involved directly in three of these disputes; its role varied, in part, because of differences in its relationship with the disputing states. In the turbot case, the organization became a strong advocate supporting member states Spain and Portugal against non-member Canada, although internal differences among EU members limited the organization's ability to act as decisively as the early rhetoric of Fisheries Minister Emma Bonino had suggested. EU involvement was less clear in the MOX dispute, since both Ireland and the United Kingdom were members and because the extent of EU regulatory authority over nuclear energy was still a point of disagreement among EU members. However, the European Commission's affirmation of the safety of the MOX plant and the limited threat it posed to Ireland most likely strengthened Britain's case before both the OSPAR and ITLOS tribunals. The organization's influence was most evident during the Baia Mare dispute, because while neither Hungary nor Romania was a member, their shared desire to join gave both an incentive to behave responsibly. After originally insisting that Romania embrace the polluter pays principle, EU officials seemed to shift their focus from emphasizing liability to promoting an amicable end to the dispute. However, the European Union did provide investigators to determine the cause of the spill and the nature of the threat the cyanide posed. This was a crucial contribution at a time when people along the Danube were frightened and unwilling to trust the word of local government officials. While the European Union was not directly involved in the *Clemenceau* dispute, EU legislation designed to implement the Basel Ban was used in French courts to challenge the ship's transfer.

Other regional organizations with less direct regulatory power provided institutional frameworks in which key dimensions of several disputes were set. For all of its weaknesses, NAFO had determined a total allowable catch of turbot, and it was NAFO rules that Canada claimed to be enforcing. Spain and the European Union justified their refusal to accept Canadian enforcement by claiming that it was a violation of their NAFO-protected right to opt out of what they considered unfair fishing quotas. Ireland saw OSPAR as not only a tribunal in which to challenge the United Kingdom's information-sharing but also an organization genuinely concerned about the radioactive pollution that Ireland believed British nuclear activities at Sellafield were generating. With a very different organizational culture than that of the European Union, ASEAN nevertheless offered a mediating presence and ultimately an institution within which Indonesia was willing to work with neighbors to address the haze issue.

Although generally less directly involved than their regional counterparts, global organizations were also influential. Under the leadership of Klaus Töpfer, UNEP, which had anything but an activist reputation, took an unusually strong position in responding to the Southeast Asian haze problem. Aided by Indonesia's vulnerability during the financial crisis, Töpfer was able to get Indonesian officials to recognize the seriousness of the fires and the reasons for international concern about their impact on broader global environmental interests. UNEP also played a supporting role in the EU mission to assess conditions in the Danube after the Baia Mare accident. In the case of the Uruguayan pulp mills, World Bank funding brought global attention to the dispute, and its review process offered international backing to the argument that the mills could be operated safely. United Nations–sponsored negotiations on straddling fish stocks and the ongoing work on shipbreaking practices by the IMO, the ILO, and the parties to the Basel Convention created a larger context for the turbot and *Clemenceau* disputes respectively.

NGOs play crucial roles. While intergovernmental organizations generally had more direct control over the course of events in these disputes, NGOs were also actively engaged in all of them, keeping the public aware of problems that governments might be tempted to downplay and pushing for more effective action. Aided by the ease of communication provided by the Internet, NGOs forged important transnational collaborations, as in the MOX dispute when a coalition of NGOs challenged the passage of ships carrying nuclear cargoes through the Irish Sea. Nowhere was NGO impact more evident than in the case of the *Clemenceau*. A key member of the NGO Shipbreaking Platform, Greenpeace had been working on shipbreaking through its 50 Toxic Ships campaign, and the organization was well placed to take the lead in challenging French plans to transfer the ship. The dramatic boarding of the *Clemenceau* brought widespread publicity and added to the pressures on the French government.

In Argentina, NGOs operating on a local level helped to mobilize public opposition to the Uruguayan pulp mills through the bridge blockades that did so much to bring the dispute to a head. Although civil society was less developed in Romania at the time of the Baia Mare cyanide spill, Hungarian NGOs, supported by other European groups, kept pressure on the two governments to address the liability issues that seemed to be given declining emphasis as the dispute wore on. In the case of the Indonesian haze, NGOs provided crucial information about the sources and extent of the fires. The World Wildlife Fund helped keep attention focused on the threats posed to important habitat and endangered species and on the fires' broader impact on global carbon emissions.

Adjudication has become more prevalent but is seldom determinative. In the last two decades, states have been far more willing to include third-party dispute settlement provisions in international environmental agreements and, more importantly, to actually use them in the course of transboundary disputes. Spain attempted unsuccessfully to bring the International Court of Justice into the turbot case, but in the process was able to give its objections to the Canadian actions a sharper legal edge. In the MOX dispute, multiple tribunals were engaged. While none ever fully accepted jurisdiction, they provided arenas in which Ireland could vent its frustrations with British practices at Sellafield, while the United Kingdom was forced to defend publically what it felt were perfectly acceptable environmental impact assessment and consultation practices. Adjudication was undoubtedly most influential in the Uruguayan pulp mills dispute. Even here, the ICJ's decision essentially helped to establish the conditions required for a political settlement by acknowledging Uruguay's procedural violations but refusing to order the pulp mills closed.

International adjudication has limitations. As in the MOX case, it may force states to focus on issues peripheral to the dispute. The adversarial process employed in international litigation can harden national positions, making political compromise difficult. Critics may see resorting to adjudication as a way for governments to delay taking the steps to reach an unwanted agreement while appearing to be acting decisively. Others remain concerned about the potential for conflict between competing tribunals. On this point, the relatively conservative jurisdictional approaches taken by the various tribunals in the MOX dispute and the International Court of Justice in the Pulp Mills case suggest that this problem may not be as serious as some fear.

It is important not to ignore the increasingly prominent place of domestic courts in litigating environmental issues with international dimensions. Their role was most evident in the case of the *Clemenceau*, where Indian courts forced both national governments to look more closely at the impact of Indian shipbreaking practices generally and the disposal of the *Clemenceau* in particular. Actions in French courts by opponents of the transfer also likely reinforced the government's decision to repatriate the ship. In the Baia Mare case, the undeveloped nature of tort law in Hungary and Romania was a key reason the Hungarian government and private citizens injured by the spill were unable to pursue liability claims more effectively. Tort reform could enhance the potential role of domestic courts in cases like the Baia Mare spill, where serious damage is done and compensation seems appropriate.

Dispute settlement requires a basis for compromise or a fundamental change in position. The six disputes varied in the potential they offered for genuine compromise. In the turbot case, to the extent the question was the legitimacy of Canada's unilateral actions, the parties faced clear and likely unbridgeable differences. However, the dispute was at least partly over fish whose division between NAFO members could be reapportioned as part of the agreement. In the *Clemenceau* dispute, the size and visibility of the ship made any form of compromise difficult once the dispute became so public. Bringing the ship back to France became the only solution, one chosen by France, albeit from among few other options if Indian courts would not permit the ship to enter Indian waters. As long as Ireland and Argentina insisted that the MOX and pulp mill plants to which they objected simply not be built, a negotiated settlement was impossible. Given the fundamental concessions they made in reframing their objectives, it was important that new processes of joint consultation and monitoring were negotiable options to permit both governments to make plausible arguments that, in the end, they had achieved something worthwhile.

Transboundary environmental disputes are persistent. There is no better evidence of this than the Trail Smelter dispute, seemingly resolved by arbitration in the early 1940s. In recent years, the smelter's current owner, Teck Resources, Ltd., has faced claims in US courts concerning the transboundary harm allegedly being caused in the United States by metal waste that the smelter has been depositing into the Columbia River. In the case of the Indonesian fires, the fact that Indonesia has only so recently ratified the Haze Agreement has made this a matter of continuing regional concern, and the 1997–98 fires remain the yardstick by which all subsequent haze events have been measured. While Argentina has accepted the existence of the Fray Bentos mill, disagreement persists about the effect that increasing the mill's output could have on the Uruguay River.

Even when the immediate source of disagreement no longer exists, the factors that led to the dispute can have lingering effects on public attitudes and government behavior. Long after the Aurul mine closed, memories of the Baia Mare cyanide spill have generated substantial local opposition in Romania to plans to develop the Roşia Montană mine. The suggestion that the United Kingdom was even considering construction of a new MOX plant to recycle nuclear waste brought sharp reaction from Irish politicians recalling the battle over the Sellafield MOX Plant.

Law Shapes the Disputes

International law was invoked by disputants in all six case studies, sometimes formally before courts, more often in public statements, as government representatives justified their own behavior and challenged the actions of others. Law provided the "language of dispute," as few were willing to defend their positions on purely political or economic grounds; it mattered to all that their actions be perceived as lawful. While they insisted that existing legal norms provided inadequate protection for straddling fish stocks, Canadian officials worked hard to justify what they recognized as unilateral actions, arguing that their extended enforcement actions were designed to protect a common interest in conserving turbot stocks. Even the Indonesian and Romanian governments, which actively discouraged neighbors from assigning blame, still acknowledged the need to take some form of responsibility for the damage caused by activities on their territory, whether through apologies, punishment of those seen as directly responsible, or offers to cooperate to prevent future incidents.

Not only governments framed the disputes in legal terms. Whether emphasizing the polluter pays principle after the Baia Mare cyanide spill or challenging the legality of Canadian unilateralism in the turbot case, representatives of the European Union used rules of international law both to criticize and to indicate what steps disputing states should take. UNEP officials generally avoided suggestions that Indonesia itself was in violation of international law, preferring to emphasize ways to enhance Indonesia's capacity to control the brush fires. However, UNEP's Töpfer made clear that domestic legal reforms to make the punishment of violators possible should be an important part of the overall Indonesian response strategy. NGOs also frequently made reference to international law in criticizing state behavior. It is hardly surprising that an organization representing Hungarian lawyers would push for Romanian liability in response to the Baia Mare accident. However, even NGOs with far more activist reputations, like Greenpeace, were quick to refer to international legal norms, whether challenging shipments of nuclear materials to Sellafield or arguing that the Basel Convention's rules governing transboundary waste made it illegal to send the *Clemenceau* to Alang.

While each dispute posed questions of law specific to its context, three observations seem justified about what they say generally about the state of existing international environmental law as perceived by those most directly involved and as it affected state behavior.

Territorial sovereignty remains a powerful force. For all the factors involved in these disputes, it is difficult not to recognize the continuing importance of the principle of territorial sovereignty in determining the eventual outcome of each. In Indonesia, despite substantial international concern and pressure to change basic land-use practices, fire continues to be used to dispose of brush; in recent years there have been several periods of significant transboundary haze. In Romania, the Aurul mine was allowed to reopen without full implementation of the new regulatory procedures many had expected to see put in place, and the MOX plant began operation in Sellafield despite Irish protests. Both facilities were eventually shut down, but they succumbed to economic forces, not legal pressures. In the case of the *Clemenceau*, a key factor in France's decision to repatriate the ship was awareness of growing opposition in India, the state on whose territory the ship would be broken. Once constructed on Uruguayan soil, the Fray Bentos mill was allowed by the International Court of Justice to continue operation despite the procedural violations Uruguay committed in approving it. Since then, the boundary separating Uruguay and Argentina has made it difficult for Argentine officials to have the degree of oversight over the plant's level of pulp production they feel is warranted. Even in the turbot dispute, nominally over Canadian regulatory authority beyond Canadian waters, Canada's hand was undoubtedly strengthened by the efforts it had been taking within Canadian waters to conserve turbot stocks, efforts rendered ineffective without cooperation from those fishing beyond its territory.

Governments look forward, not back. The disputes studied here reinforce the observation that states seldom attempt to bring formal claims for past environmental damage, preferring to manage existing problems and focus on the development of new rules and procedures to prevent future ones. This obviously made sense in the MOX dispute, where the SMP had not yet been built, and in the Pulp Mills case, where the Fray Bentos plant, though operational, had yet to produce a level of damage likely to trigger Uruguayan responsibility and justify claims for compensation. Yet it was also true throughout the Indonesian haze dispute and became the reality even in the Baia Mare case where issues of liability were so clearly raised and with the Hungarian public, angry NGOs, and the European Union all arguing that someone should be held accountable for the damage.

Governments dispute the precise content of norms, not their existence. It is somewhat surprising that in most of these disputes there was relatively little disagreement about the basic rules that should apply. An exception was the turbot dispute, in which Spain and the European Union challenged Canada's authority to exercise enforcement jurisdiction beyond the Canadian EFZ. However in the others, even when the norms potentially in dispute had emerged only recently and might seem to be of questionable authority, the debate was over when and how they should apply.

Indonesia never made the case that it should not have prevented the haze pollution, only that the priority when the fires were still burning should be to put them out rather than assign blame. Romania found it difficult to deny that liability was important, even accepting the applicability of the polluter pays principle, but suggested that much of the liability should be borne by private parties, most notably Esmeralda. Both states embraced the spirit behind the principle of common but differentiated responsibilities, but neither claimed explicitly that its own level of development or state of economic transition justified a level of differential treatment that would relieve the state from the responsibility to prevent transboundary damage. In the MOX case, the United Kingdom agreed that environmental impact assessment and bilateral consultation were important. The British also recognized the value of the precautionary principle in their brief before the OSPAR tribunal, but only when the plant represented a genuine risk to Ireland, something they felt the facts simply did not support. Similarly, Uruguay acknowledged the need to conduct an environmental impact assessment of the proposed pulp mill but disagreed with Argentina about the content and timing of that assessment. Uruguay also felt that the two states had agreed to an alternative consultation process outside the CARU framework and that Uruguay's obligation to share information about the project with Argentina could be satisfied by the company constructing the plant.

Disputes Shape the Law

Even as international environmental law had an important place in the course of these disputes, the disputes themselves helped promote changes in the law. This appears to have been a conscious goal of the Canadian government in the turbot dispute, which helps to explain both how and when it acted. However, disputes can have a less direct impact, identifying areas where the rules really are unclear or less restrictive than might seem appropriate and, therefore, where legal reform is essential.

The MOX and pulp mills disputes reflected genuine disagreement about what the rules regarding transboundary consultation and information-sharing actually required. In the Pulp Mills case, the International Court of Justice held that there were no internationally accepted standards of environmental impact assessment beyond those established by treaty and that the broad, inclusive process of transboundary consultation many people felt was needed was simply not required as a matter of contemporary customary state practice. Moreover, while the Court accepted the existence of the precautionary principle, the way it placed the burden of proof on Argentina to prove the risks posed by the Fray Bentos plant suggests that much more must be done to make this an effective legal principle. The Baia Mare cyanide spill revealed the weakness of the liability mechanisms, not only in Eastern Europe but more broadly, and the MOX dispute reinforced concerns about the particular limitations of the liability regimes governing nuclear materials.

The *Clemenceau* dispute raised fundamental questions about the adequacy of existing international law regarding shipbreaking, as it helped sharpen the debate over whether the Basel Convention could be applied to end-of-life ships.

How foreign corporations should be integrated into transboundary environmental regimes was an issue identified, though unresolved, in several disputes. Participants in the Baia Mare dispute acknowledged the key role played by Esmeralda, but what kind and level of responsibility this Australian company, and perhaps even the Australian state, should bear was not at all clear, given the legal distance between the corporation and the actual cyanide spill, the connections of the Aurul project to the Romanian government, and the procedural challenges of taking action directly against the company. In the pulp mills dispute, the Court held that the companies involved could not be the primary means of informing Argentina about the details of their projects, but what their role should be and whether there was any home state responsibility to oversee their operations abroad were questions that remained unanswered. Given the importance of foreign investment to permit countries like Uruguay to undertake major development projects such as that at Fray Bentos, and the challenges developing countries face in providing effective regulation, these questions deserve closer scrutiny. Recent indications that Singapore may be willing to play a more assertive role in regulating, or at least holding accountable, Singaporean-owned companies engaged in illegal burning in Indonesia suggest one direction in which states may be headed, but not without raising serious concerns about the extent to which this could interfere with a state's territorial sovereignty.

The case studies analyzed here suggest the kinds of changes these disputes have encouraged, the conditions under which reforms are most likely, as well as the challenges faced in realizing them.

Reforms emphasize prevention, not liability. Just as during disputes, in their aftermath states have normally focused on developing procedures designed to prevent their recurrence. Some reforms have been tailored fairly narrowly to respond to the particular problems just encountered. Argentina and Uruguay agreed to give CARU a more direct role in monitoring the River Uruguay, with the support of a new bilateral scientific committee. After the MOX dispute, Ireland and the United Kingdom established a more regular process of bilateral consultation and arranged for site visitations to Sellafield to enhance Irish confidence in the safety of operations there. The dispute also had the effect of encouraging the European Commission to become more involved in monitoring the British nuclear program. Combined with the legislative work being done by the Commission to implement the environmental impact assessment obligations of the Espoo Convention and the public participation requirements of the Aarhus Convention, the effect has been to help clarify the nature of state procedural responsibilities that were at the heart of several of these disputes.

The turbot dispute led directly to changes in the UN Straddling Fish Stocks Convention, designed to enhance the ability of regional organizations like NAFO to enforce catch restrictions against individual fishing vessels. To the extent that these rules are implemented in practice, they can help prevent the overfishing that has been the source of serious international disagreement. Assuming it comes into force, the Hong Kong Convention represents an important step in the direction of developing a new generation of ocean-going vessels far greener in design than their predecessors. With careful monitoring of cargoes, and thoughtful and transparent plans for the ships' eventual recycling, the new green passport system has the potential to minimize the damage to the environment and the injury to workers employed in what will hopefully be far safer shipbreaking facilities. In the process, it may diminish the need for the liability protection that neither it nor the Basel Convention yet provides.

Improved liability standards have not been entirely forgotten, certainly not by those who consider them necessary not only to compensate victims of environmental damage but also to provide incentives to encourage states and private companies to take their prevention obligations seriously. The European Union completed its work on the Liability Directive in 2004. Given the timing and nature of the discussion surrounding its adoption, it seems evident that the Baia Mare experience had an effect on the directive's final form. The recent decision by the Indian Supreme Court to hold shipowners responsible for the costs of hazardous waste found during the shipbreaking process suggests that at least that dimension of the liability associated with ship recycling is being acknowledged by one of the key states involved in the process.

Reforms are more likely where ongoing institutional initiatives exist. The odds that positive changes will emerge in the aftermath of a transboundary dispute are enhanced by the presence of an organizational framework in which issues related to those at the center of the dispute are being addressed. The turbot dispute is the most obvious example, since Canada's carefully choreographed confrontation with the European Union coincided with the opening of a key session of the UN Conference on Straddling Fish Stocks and Highly Migratory Fish Stocks. As the conference was still negotiating the rules governing enforcement provisions to protect straddling fish stocks, Canada was well placed to use its experience with the *Estai* to illustrate the importance of an enhanced coastal-state role. The *Clemenceau* dispute arose when discussions about shipbreaking were already underway within the IMO, the ILO, and the Basel Convention. By the time of the actual negotiation of the Hong Kong

Convention, the ship was being dismantled in England and the dispute about its disposal was effectively over. However, perhaps anxious to repair its international reputation, France became one of the leaders in efforts to develop the new agreement and was the first EU member to ratify it.

Ongoing work on transboundary issues by the UNECE and the European Union have provided opportunities to address some of the procedural issues that arose in the Baia Mare and MOX disputes. Both the Espoo and Aarhus Conventions provide for regular meetings of the parties, and the development of the Strategic Environmental Assessment protocol offers a good example of the improvements that can be made as problems are identified. The European Union's implementation of UNECE obligations and additional work in areas of particular European concern, such as the implementation of the Basel Ban, provide institutional mechanisms through which EU members can attempt to negotiate needed changes. In the MOX dispute, OSPAR—an organization presumably sympathetic, given its desire to reduce radioactivity in Convention waters—served as a forum for Irish grievances about Sellafield and the MOX plant. Although OSPAR had no power to compel the United Kingdom to do anything, an OSPAR ministerial meeting became the place where the British, under attack by Ireland for the SMP project, could attempt to show their good faith by promising to phase out radioactive emissions. The commitment thus made, it has remained part of the United Kingdom's strategy on radioactive releases, even at a time when Britain has decided to make nuclear power a more important part of its overall energy policy. In the case of the Indonesian fires, the fact that ASEAN had been working on the transboundary haze problem for several years before the 1997–98 fires made it the natural body in which to develop the Haze Agreement.

The incentive to implement reforms fades quickly. Despite pressures generated during these disputes to improve the rules governing transboundary issues, and however genuine the initial desire to act, a common challenge has been to put proposed reforms into practice. The problem is certainly not unique to transboundary disputes. Whether responding even to widely recognized threats such as climate change or to dramatic events like the *Torrey Canyon* oil spill, the international community faces a process of treaty drafting and ratification that seldom permits a quick response. This is particularly true in dealing with issues like shipbreaking, where reaching broad global agreement—a process that inevitably brings into the new regime states with very different political and economic interests—seems important. If the proposed changes really are substantial, they can generate significant opposition from powerful domestic constituencies. The incentive for national leaders to expend the energy and political capital to overcome these forces can easily weaken as memories of the dispute fade and other issues begin to take priority. This makes all the more crucial the presence of ongoing institutional frameworks in which reforms can be promoted, combined with continued pressure from key governments and committed NGOs.

In the cases discussed here, it is important to remember that the UNECE's Liability Protocol, although signed by 24 states in 2003 after the Baia Mare spill, has been ratified by only 1 of the 16 states needed for the agreement to come into force. The 2009 Hong Kong Convention on ship recycling faces a similar challenge. It seems clear that neither agreement has attracted the degree of organizational or public support required to move the ratification process forward. The 2002 ASEAN Haze Agreement, although it went into force in just over a year, has only recently acquired Indonesia as a full party, a key step in making it effective. Continuing pressure from its neighbors within ASEAN finally convinced the Indonesian government to exert the political pressure needed domestically to bring about the agreement's ratification. Even in the case of the seizure of the *Estai*, which of all the disputes seemed to lead most quickly to tangible reforms on both the global and regional levels, there remains substantial doubt about the extent to which this has actually improved fishing practices in the Northwest Atlantic. Sustaining a commitment to improved enforcement has been a challenge. Only Canadian insistence on the need for further NAFO changes and the implied threat of further unilateral action seem to have kept the process of reform alive.

Law from Conflict

International environmental law is best developed when states recognize the value of creating rules and procedures that address environmental problems before they become sources of international dispute. Cooperation succeeds and conflict is avoided. Yet the record of state behavior suggests that too often such proactive collaboration simply does not take place.

The good news is that law is applied, its limitations uncovered, and better law developed even in times of conflict. The disputes studied here reaffirm the value of law and legal processes in helping states manage their differences, and point to the importance of maintaining active organizational frameworks into which disputants can channel their dissatisfaction when they find the existing law inadequate. Ongoing institutional cooperation offers the best hope of drawing from the environmental disputes that will inevitably arise the opportunity to develop rules and procedures that will make future disputes less likely. However, in the end, what is needed is the persistence of committed governments and individuals to use the pressure for reform generated by transboundary disputes to develop a more robust and effective body of international environmental law.

Bibliography

General Works

Andonova, Liliana B., and Ronald B. Mitchell. "The Rescaling of Global Environmental Politics." *Annual Review of Environment and Resources* 35, no. 1 (2010): 255–82. http://dx.doi.org/10.1146/annurev-environ-100809-125346.

Aneiros, Adela Rey. "Spain, the European Union, and Canada: A New Phase in the Unstable Balance in the Northwest Atlantic Fisheries." *Ocean Development and International Law* 42, no. 1–2 (2011): 155–72. http://dx.doi.org/10.1080/0090 8320.2011.542109.

Akcil, Ata. "A New Global Approach of Cyanide Management: International Cyanide Management Code for the Manufacture, Transport, and Use of Cyanide in the Production of Gold." *Mineral Processing and Extractive Metal Review* 31 (2011): 134–49.

Arevalo, Luis Barrioneuvo. "The Work of the International Law Commission in the Field of International Environmental Law." *Boston College Environmental Affairs Law Review* 32, no. 3 (2005): 493–507.

Austin, David, and Anna Alberini. "An Analysis of the Preventive Effect of Environmental Liability: Environmental Liability, Location and Emission Substitution: Evidence from the Toxic Release Inventory." Study commissioned by DG ENV of the European Commission. 30 October 2001. http://ec.europa. eu/environment/legal/liability/pdf/preventive_final.pdf.

Axelrod, Regina S. "The European Commission and Member States: Conflict over Nuclear Safety." *Perspectives* 26 (2006): 5–22.

Bailey, Paul J. "Is There a Decent Way to Break up Ships?" *ILO Discussion Paper* (2000).

Barber, Charles Victor, and James Schweithelm. *Trial by Fire: Forest Fires and Forestry Policy in Indonesia's Era of Crisis and Reform.* Washington, DC: World Resources Institute, 2000.

Bauer, Joanne R., and Daniel A. Bell, eds. *The East Asian Challenge for Human Rights.* Cambridge: Cambridge University Press, 1999.

Beck, Robert J. "International Law and International Relations: Prospects for Interdisciplinary Collaboration." In *International Rules: Approaches from International Law and International Relations*, edited by Robert J. Beck, Anthony C. Arend, and Robert D. Vander Lugt, 3–30. New York: Oxford University Press, 1996.

Beesley, J. Alan. "The Canadian Approach to International Environmental Law." *Canadian Yearbook of International Law. Annuaire canadien de Droit international* 11 (1973): 3–12.

Berardo, Ramiro, and Andrea K. Gerlak. "Conflict and Cooperation along International Rivers: Crafting a Model of Institutional Effectiveness." *Global Environmental Politics* 12, no. 1 (2012): 101–20. http://dx.doi.org/10.1162/ GLEP_a_00099.

Birnie, Patricia W., and Alan E. Boyle. *International Law and the Environment.* Oxford: Oxford University Press, 2002.

Bodansky, Daniel. *The Art and Craft of International Environmental Law*. Cambridge, MA: Harvard University Press, 2010.

Bodo, Peter, and Robert Nemeskeri. *Emergency Preparedness Plan: Non-Governmental Organizations in Case of Pollution Accidents*. Szentendre, Hungary: Regional Environmental Center for Central and Eastern Europe, December 2001.

Boehm, H.-D.V., and F. Siegert. "Ecological Impact of the One Million Hectare Rice Project in Central Kalimantan, Indonesia, Using Remote Sensing and GIS: Land Use Change and (Il)-legal Logging in Central Kalimantan, Indonesia." Paper presented at the 22nd Asian Conference on Remote Sensing, Singapore, 5–9 November 2001.

Bratspies, Rebecca M., and Russell A. Miller, eds. *Transboundary Harm in International Law: Lessons from the Trail Smelter Arbitration*. Cambridge: Cambridge University Press, 2006. http://dx.doi.org/10.1017/CBO9780511511394.

Brown, Chester. "The Proliferation of International Courts and Tribunals: Finding Your Way through the Maze." *Melbourne Journal of International Law* 3 (2002): 453–75.

Brunnée, Jutta, and Stephen J. Toope. *Legality and Legitimacy in International Law: An Interactional Account*. Cambridge: Cambridge University Press, 2010. http://dx.doi.org/10.1017/CBO9780511781261.

Bunyard, Peter. "Making a Mess of MOX." *Ecologist* 32, no. 1 (2002): 65–68.

Burke, William T. "The Law of the Sea Convention Provisions on Conditions of Access to Fisheries Subject to National Jurisdiction." *Oregon Law Review* 63 (1984): 73–119.

Caldwell, Lynton Keith. *International Environmental Policy: Emergence and Dimensions*. 2nd ed. Durham, NC: Duke University Press, 1990.

van Calster, Geert, and Leonie Reins. "The ELD's Background." In *The EU Environmental Liability Directive: A Commentary*, edited by Lucas Bergkamp and Barbara Goldsmith, 9–30. Oxford: Oxford University Press, 2013.

Cardozo, Michael. "Bridging the Gap between Political Scientists and Lawyers." *Proceedings of the Annual Meeting (American Society of International Law)* 81 (1987).

Chasek, Pamela S., David L. Downie, and Janet Welsh Brown. *Global Environmental Politics*. 5th ed. Boulder, CO: Westview Press, 2010.

Choksi, Sejal. "The Basel Convention on the Control of Transboundary Movements of Hazardous Wastes and Their Disposal: 1999 Protocol on Liability and Compensation." *Ecology Law Quarterly* 28 (2001): 509–39.

Churchill, Robin, and Joanne Scott. "The MOX Plant Litigation: The First Half-Life." *International and Comparative Law Quarterly* 53, no. 3 (2004): 643–76. http://dx.doi.org/10.1093/iclq/53.3.643.

Cohen, Matt. "U.S. Ship-Breaking Exports: Balancing Safe Disposal with Economic Realities." *Environs: Environmental Law and Policy Journal* 28 (2005): 237–68.

Coplin, William D. *The Functions of International Law: An Introduction to the Role of International Law in the Contemporary World*. Chicago: Rand McNally, 1966.

Corbett, Percy Ellwood. *Law in Diplomacy*. Princeton, NJ: Princeton University Press, 1959.

Cotton, James. "The 'Haze' over Southeast Asia: Challenging the ASEAN Mode of Regional Engagement." *Pacific Affairs* 72, no. 3 (1999): 331–51. http://dx.doi.org/10.2307/2672225.

Currie, Duncan E.J. "The Problems and Gaps in the Nuclear Liability Conventions and an Analysis of How an Actual Claim Would Be Brought under the Current

Existing Treaty Regime in the Event of a Nuclear Accident." *Denver Journal of International Law and Policy* 35, no. 1 (2006): 85–127.

Day, Douglas. "Tending the Achilles' Heel of NAFO: Canada Acts to Protect the Nose and Tail of the Grand Banks." *Marine Policy* 19, no. 4 (1995): 257–70. http://dx.doi.org/10.1016/0308-597X(95)00020-7.

DeSombre, Elizabeth, and Samuel Barkin. "The Turbot War: Canada, Spain and Conflict over the North Atlantic Fishery." In *Pew Case Studies in International Affairs*, Case Study No. 226. Washington, DC: Institute for the Study of Diplomacy, 2000.

Dodds, David. "Breaking Up Is Hard to Do: Environmental Effects of Shipwrecking and Possible Solutions under India's Environmental Regime." *Pacific McGeorge Global Business and Development Law Journal* 20 (2007): 207–36.

Dunoff, Jeffrey L., and Mark A. Pollack. "Reviewing Two Decades of IL/IR Scholarship: What We've Learned, What's Next." In *Interdisciplinary Perspectives on International Law and International Relations: The State of the Art*, edited by Jeffrey L. Dunoff and Mark A. Pollack, 626–53. New York: Cambridge University Press, 2012. http://dx.doi.org/10.1017/CBO9781139107310.031.

Earl, Greg. "Indonesia Turns Serious at Last in Scorching Issue." *Australian Financial Review*, 6 October 1997.

Economy and Environment Program for Southeast Asia (EEPSEA) and Worldwide Fund for Nature (WWF). "The Indonesian Fires and Haze of 1997: The Economic Toll," research report. Ottawa: International Development Research Centre, 1997.

Englund, Will, and Gary Cohn Sund. "A Third World Dump for America's Ships, Part 3." *Baltimore Sun*, 9 December 1997.

European Environmental Bureau. "EEB Analysis of the White Paper on Environmental Liability." February 2000. http://www.eeb.org/publication/2000/white_paper_on_environmental_lia.html.

Falk, Richard A. *The Status of Law in International Society*. Princeton, NJ: Princeton University Press, 1970.

Fitzmaurice, Malgosia. "OSPAR Tribunal: Dispute Concerning Access to Information under Article 9 of the Ospar Convention (Ireland v United Kingdom and Northern Ireland)." *International Journal of Marine and Coastal Law* 18, no. 4 (2003): 541–58. http://dx.doi.org/10.1163/157180803322711010.

Franck, Thomas M. *Fairness in International Law and Institutions*. Oxford: Clarendon Press, 1995.

Gilardi, Fabrizio. "Transnational Diffusion: Norms, Ideas, and Policies." In *Handbook of International Relations*, edited by Walter Carlsnaes, Thomas Risse, and Beth Simmonds, 453–77. Thousand Oaks, CA: Sage Publications, 2012.

Goldhaber, Michael D. *A People's History of the European Court of Human Rights*. New Brunswick, NJ: Rutgers University Press, 2007.

Goldsmith, Jack L., and Eric A. Posner. *The Limits of International Law*. Oxford: Oxford University Press, 2005.

Granger, C. Leah. "The Role of International Tribunals in Natural Resource Disputes in Latin America." *Ecology Law Quarterly* 34 (2007): 1297–347.

Hall, Terry. "'Carried by the Wind out to Sea'—*Ireland and the Isle of Man v. Sellafield*: Anatomy of a Transboundary Pollution Dispute." *Georgetown International Environmental Law Review* 6 (1994): 639–81.

Hassan, Daud. "International Conventions Relating to Land-Based Sources of Marine Pollution Control: Applications and Shortcomings." *Georgetown International Environmental Law Review* 16 (2004): 657–77.

Helfer, Laurence R., and Erik Voeten. "International Courts as Agents of Legal Change: Evidence from LGBT Rights in Europe." *International Organization* 68, no. 1 (2014): 77–110. http://dx.doi.org/10.1017/S0020818313000398.

Henkin, Louis. *How Nations Behave: Law and Foreign Policy*. New York: Columbia University Press, 1979.

Hey, Ellen, Ton IJlstra, and Andre Nollkaemper. "The 1992 Paris Convention for the Protection of the Marine Environment of the North-East Atlantic: A Critical Analysis." *International Journal of Marine and Coastal Law* 8, no. 1 (1993): 1–76. http://dx.doi.org/10.1163/157180893X00215.

Howe, Brendan, and Matthew Kerby. "The Canada-EU Turbot War and the Cybernetic Model of Decision-Making." *Round Table* 98, no. 401 (2009): 161–79. http://dx.doi.org/10.1080/00358530902757883.

Hudson, Chris. "The Role of International Law in the Protection of the Danube River Basin." *Colorado Journal of International Environmental Law and Policy* 12 (2001): 367–98.

Hunter, David, James Salzman, and Durwood Zaelke. *International Environmental Law and Policy*. 4th ed. New York: Foundation Press, 2011.

Jones, David Seth. "ASEAN and Transboundary Haze Pollution in Southeast Asia." *Asia Europe Journal* 4, no. 3 (2006): 431–46. http://dx.doi.org/10.1007/s10308-006-0067-1.

Kaplan, Morton A., and Nicholas Katzenbach. *The Political Foundations of International Law*. New York: John Wiley and Sons, 1961.

Karim, Saiful. "Environmental Pollution from the Shipbreaking Industry: International Law and National Legal Response." *Georgetown International Environmental Law Review* 22, no. 2 (2010): 185–240.

Katzenstein, Peter, and Rudra Sil. "Eclectic Theorizing in the Study and Practice of International Relations." In *The Oxford Handbook of International Relations*, edited by Christian Reus-Smit and Duncan Snidal, 101–39. New York: Oxford University Press, 2008. http://dx.doi.org/10.1093/oxfordhb/9780199219322.003.0006.

Kazhdan, Daniel. "Precautionary Pulp: Pulp Mills and the Evolving Dispute between International Tribunals over the Reach of the Precautionary Principle." *Ecology Law Quarterly* 38 (2011): 527–52.

Kelsen, Hans. *Pure Theory of Law*. 2nd ed. Berkeley: University of California Press, 1970.

Keohane, Robert O., and Joseph S. Nye. *Power and Interdependence: World Politics in Transition*. Boston: Little, Brown, 1977.

Killion, David. "Trans-Atlantic Ghost Busting: The Failed Attempt to Dispose of the Chesapeake 'Ghost Fleet' in the United Kingdom." *University of Richmond Law Review* 42 (2008): 731–52.

Krapohl, Sebastian, and Julia Dinkel. "From Finnish Pulp Mills and Blocked Bridges: The Escalation of Conflict and the Weakness of Judicialization in MERCOSUR." Paper presented at the European Consortium for Political Research General Conference, Reykjavík, 2011. http://ecpr.eu/Filestore/PaperProposal/bb2a7ab9-f8a2-4a30-8b85-e54f82b008ef.pdf.

Kratochwil, Friedrich. "Thrasymmachos Revisited: On the Relevance of Norms and the Study of Law for International Relations." *Journal of International Affairs* 37, no. 2 (1984): 343–56.

Kratochwil, Friedrich, and John Gerard Ruggie. "International Organization: A State of the Art on an Art of the State." *International Organization* 40, no. 4 (1986): 753–75. http://dx.doi.org/10.1017/S0020818300027363.

Kwiatkowska, Barbara. "The Ireland v. United Kingdom (Mox Plant) Case: Applying the Doctrine of Treaty Parallelism." *International Journal of Marine and Coastal Law* 18, no. 1 (2003): 1–58. http://dx.doi.org/10.1163/157180803X00016.

Langewiesche, William. "The Shipbreakers." *Atlantic Monthly* 286, no. 2 (2000): 31–49.

Lavranos, Nikolaos. "The Epilogue in the MOX Dispute: An End without Findings." *European Energy and Environmental Law Review* 18 (2009): 180–84.

———. "The Ospar Convention, the Aarhus Convention and EC Law: Normative and Institutional Fragmentation on the Right of Access to Environmental Information." In *Multi-Sourced Equivalent Norms in International Law*, edited by Tomer Broude and Yuval Shany, 143–89. Oxford: Bloomsbury, 2011.

Lee, Michael K. "The Uruguay Paper Pulp Mill Dispute: Highlighting the Growing Importance of NGOs and Public Protest in the Enforcement of International Environmental Law." *Sustainable Development Law and Policy* 7 (2006): 71–73.

Litfin, Karen T. "Sovereignty in World Ecopolitics." *Mershon International Studies Review* 51, no. 2 (1996): 167–204.

Luchi, Roberto, and Ariel Llorente. *Rules of Entanglement: The River Uruguay's Pulp Mills International Dispute, a Case Study*. IAE, Esculea de Dirección de Nogocios, Universidad Austral, 2008.

Luppi, Barbara, Francesco Parisi, and Shruti Rajagopalan. "The Rise and Fall of the Polluter-Pays Principle in Developing Countries." *International Review of Law and Economics* 32, no. 1 (2012): 135–44. http://dx.doi.org/10.1016/j.irle.2011.10.002.

Malamud, Carlos. "Pulp Mills Divide the River Plate." Elcano Royal Institute, 2006. http://www.realinstitutoelcano.org/analisis/944/944_Malamud_Pulp_Mills_Argentina_Uruguay.pdf.

Marsden, Simon. "MOX Plant and the Espoo Convention: Can Member State Disputes Concerning Mixed Environmental Agreements Be Resolved Outside EC Law?" *Review of European Community & International Environmental Law* 18, no. 3 (2009): 312–27. http://dx.doi.org/10.1111/j.1467-9388.2009.00652.x.

Martiniussen, Erik. "Final Decision Today: Radioactive Technetium-99 to Be Cleansed from Sellafield Discharges." *Bellona Report*, 21 April 2004. http://bellona.ru/bellona.org/english_import_area/energy/nuclear/sellafield/33433.

McClearn, Matthew. "Dark Voyage." *Canadian Business* 78, no. 20 (2005): 64–88.

McDorman, Ted L. "Access to Information under Article 9 of the Ospar Convention (Ireland v. United Kingdom)." *American Journal of International Law* 98, no. 2 (2004): 330–39. http://dx.doi.org/10.2307/3176735.

———. "Canada's Aggressive Fisheries Actions: Will They Improve the Climate for International Agreements?" *Canadian Foreign Policy* 2, no. 3 (1994): 5–28. http://dx.doi.org/10.1080/11926422.1994.9673039.

McDougal, Myres S. *Studies in World Public Order*. New Haven, CT: Yale University Press, 1960.

McDougal, Myres S., Harold D. Lasswell, and W. Michael Reisman. "The World Constitutive Process of Authoritative Decision." In *The Future of the International*

Legal Order, edited Cyril Edwin Black and Richard A. Falk, 73–154. Princeton, NJ: Princeton University Press, 1969.

Merkouris, Panos. "Case Concerning Pulp Mills on the River Uruguay (Argentina v. Uruguay): Of Environmental Impact Assessments and 'Phantom Experts.'" *Hague Justice Portal* (15 July 2010).

Mikelis, Nikos. "Introduction to the Hong Kong Convention and Its Requirements." Ship Recycling and Technology Transfer Workshop, Izmir, Turkey, 14–17 July 2010, 17–22.

Moen, Amy E. "Breaking Basel: The Elements of the Basel Convention and Its Application to Toxic Ships." *Marine Policy* 32, no. 6 (2008): 1053–62. http://dx.doi.org/10.1016/j.marpol.2008.03.002.

Morgenthau, Hans J., and Kenneth W. Thompson. *Politics among Nations: The Struggle for Power and Peace.* 6th ed. New York: Knopf, 1985.

Nadelson, Robert. "After MOX: The Contemporary Shipment of Radioactive Substances in the Law of the Sea." *International Journal of Marine and Coastal Law* 15, no. 2 (2000): 193–244. http://dx.doi.org/10.1163/157180800X00082.

Neuhold, Hanspeter, Winfried Lang, and Karl Zemanek. *Environmental Protection and International Law.* Boston: Graham & Trotman, 1991.

Onuf, Nicholas Greenwood. *World of Our Making: Rules and Rule in Social Theory and International Relations.* Columbia: University of South Carolina Press, 1989.

Orellana, Marcos A. "Shipbreaking and Le Clemenceau Row." *ASIL Insights* 10, no. 4 (2006).

Ormond, Thomas. "Hong Kong Convention and EU Ship Recycling Regulation: Can They Change Bad Industrial Practices Soon?" *Jean Monnet Working Paper Series* no. 5 (2013): 1–9. http://www.tradevenvironment.eu/uploads/Ormond_on_ship_recycling.pdf.

Ovodenko, Alexander, and Robert O. Keohane. "Institutional Diffusion in International Environmental Affairs." *International Affairs* 88, no. 3 (2012): 523–41. http://dx.doi.org/10.1111/j.1468-2346.2012.01087.x.

Pakkasvirta, Jussi. "From Pulp to Fiction?: Fray Bentos Pulp Investment Conflict through the Finnish Media." *Cooperation and Conflict* 43, no. 4 (2008): 421–46. http://dx.doi.org/10.1177/0010836708096883.

Parson, Edward A. *Protecting the Ozone Layer: Science and Strategy.* Oxford: Oxford University Press, 2003. http://dx.doi.org/10.1093/0195155491.001.0001.

Paul, Katie. "Exporting Responsibility: Shipbreaking in South Asia; International Trade in Hazardous Waste." *Environmental Policy and Law* 35, no. 4 (2004): 73–78.

Payne, Cymie R. "Pulp Mills on the River Uruguay: The International Court of Justice Recognizes Environmental Impact Assessment as a Duty under International Law," *ASIL Insights* 14, no. 9 (2010).

Pedrozo, Raul A.F. "Transport of Nuclear Cargoes by Sea." *Journal of Maritime Law and Commerce* 28 (1997): 207–36.

de la Plaza, Luis, and Sophie Sirtaine. "An Analysis of the 2002 Uruguayan Banking Crisis." In World Bank Policy Research Working Paper No. 3780. Washington, DC: World Bank, 2005. http://dx.doi.org/10.1596/1813-9450-3780.

Puder, Markus G. "The Rise of Regional Integration Law (RIL): Good News for International Environmental Law (IEL)?" *Georgetown International Environmental Law Review* 23 (2001): 199–210.

Puthucherril, Tony. *From Shipbreaking to Sustainable Ship Recycling: Evolution of a Legal Regime*. Leiden, Netherlands: Martinus Nijhoff, 2010. http://dx.doi.org/10.1163/ej.9789004174917.i-290.

Qadri, S. Tahir, ed. *Fire, Smoke, and Haze: The ASEAN Response Strategy*. Manila: Asian Development Bank, 2001.

Read, John E. "The Trail Smelter Dispute." *Canadian Journal of International Law* 1 (1963): 213–29.

Roberts, Anthea Elizabeth. "Traditional and Modern Approaches to Customary International Law: A Reconciliation." *American Journal of International Law* 95, no. 4 (2001): 757–91. http://dx.doi.org/10.2307/2674625.

Rosencranz, Armin, and Michael Jackson. "The Delhi Pollution Case: The Supreme Court of India and the Limits of Judicial Power." *Columbia Journal of Environmental Law* 28 (2003): 223–54.

Rubin, Alfred P. "Pollution by Analogy: The Trail Smelter Arbitration." *Oregon Law Review* 50 (1971): 259–82.

de Sadeleer, Nicolas. "The Polluter-Pays Principle in EU Law: Bold Case Law and Poor Harmonisation." *Pro Natura: Festskrift Til H. C. Bugge, Oslo, Universitetsforlaget* (2012): 405–19. http://www.tradevenvironment.eu/uploads/papers/de%20Sadeleer.pdf.

Schneider, Jan. *World Public Order of the Environment: Towards an International Ecological Law and Organization*. Toronto: University of Toronto Press, 1979.

Schwabach, Aaron. "From Schweizerhalle to Baia Mare: The Continuing Failure of International Law to Protect Europe's Rivers." *Virginia Environmental Law Journal* 19 (2000): 431–61.

Sharp, Mitchell. "Comments." *Canadian Yearbook of International Law. Annuaire canadien de Droit international* 8 (1970): 344–45.

———. "Comments." *Canadian Yearbook of International Law. Annuaire canadien de Droit international* 9 (1971): 284–85.

Slaughter, Anne-Marie, Andrew S. Tulumello, and Stepan Wood. "International Law and International Relations Theory: A New Generation of Interdisciplinary Scholarship." *American Journal of International Law* 92, no. 3 (1998): 367–97. http://dx.doi.org/10.2307/2997914.

Soroos, Marvin S. "The Turbot War: Resolution of an International Fishery Dispute." In *Conflict and the Environment*, edited by Nils Petter Gleditsch, 235–52. Dordrecht, Netherlands: Springer, 1997. http://dx.doi.org/10.1007/978-94-015-8947-5_15.

Springer, Allen. L. "The Canadian Turbot War with Spain: Unilateral State Action in Defense of Environmental Interests." *Journal of Environment & Development* 6, no. 1 (1997): 26–60. http://dx.doi.org/10.1177/107049659700600103.

———. "The 1997–98 Indonesian Forest Fires: Internationalizing a National Environmental Problem." In *International Environmental Cooperation: Politics and Diplomacy in Asia-Pacific*, edited by Paul Harris, 291–315. Boulder: University of Colorado Press, 2002.

———. "Towards a Meaningful Concept of Pollution in International Law." *International and Comparative Law Quarterly* 26, no. 3 (1977): 531–57. http://dx.doi.org/10.1093/iclqaj/26.3.531.

———. "United States Environmental Policy and International Law: Stockholm Principle 21 Revisited." In *International Environmental Diplomacy: The Management and Resolution of Transfrontier Environmental Problems*, edited by John C. Carroll, 45–66. Cambridge: Cambridge University Press, 1988.

Stec, Stephen, Alexios Antypas, Tonya Jansen, and Eszter Gulacsy. "Transboundary Environmental Governance and the Baia Mare Cyanide Spill." *Review of Central and East European Law* 27, no. 4 (2001): 639–91.

Stoett, Peter J. "Fishing for Norms: Foreign Policy and the Turbot War of 1995." In *Ethics and Security in Canadian Foreign Policy*, edited by Rosalind Irwin, 249–66. Vancouver: University of British Columbia Press, 2001.

Stone, Christopher D. *The Gnat Is Older Than Man: Global Environment and Human Agenda*. Princeton, NJ: Princeton University Press, 1993.

Syarif, Laode M. "Current Development of Indonesian Environmental Law." *IUCN Academy of Environmental Law e-Journal Issue* no. 1 (2010): 1–18.

Szakats, Alexander. "Cross Border Pollution: Private International Law Problems in Claiming Compensation." *Victoria University of Wellington Law Review* 32 (2000): 609–26.

Szusterman, Celia. "Pulp Friction: The Argentina-Uruguay Conflict," *openDemocracy*, 30 January 2008. https://www.opendemocracy.net/article/globalisation/the_great_divide_the_argentina_uruguay_pulp_mill_conflict.

Tan, Alan Khee-Jin. "Forest Fires of Indonesia: State Responsibility and International Liability." *International and Comparative Law Quarterly* 48, no. 4 (1999): 826–55.

Tanaka, Maki. "Lessons from the Protracted MOX Plant Dispute: A Proposed Protocol on Marine Environmental Impact Assessment to the United Nations Convention on the Law of the Sea." *Michigan Journal of International Law* 25, no. 2 (2004): 337–428.

Tay, Simon C. "Fires and Haze in Southeast Asia." In *Cross-Sectoral Partnerships in Enhancing Human Security*, edited by Pamela J. Noda, 53–80. Tokyo: Japan Center for International Exchange, 2002.

———. "South East Asian Forest Fires: Haze over ASEAN and International Environmental Law." *Review of European Community & International Environmental Law* 7, no. 2 (1998): 202–8. http://dx.doi.org/10.1111/1467-9388.00147.

———. "Southeast Asian Fires: The Challenge for International Environmental Law and Sustainable Development." *Georgetown International Environmental Law Review* 11 (1999): 241–305.

Utton, Albert E. "The Arctic Waters Pollution Prevention Act, and the Right of Self-Protection." In *International Environmental Law*, edited by Ludwik A. Teclaff and Albert E. Utton, 140–53. New York: Praeger, 1974.

Varkkey, Helen. "Malaysian Investors in the Indonesian Oil Palm Plantation Sector: Home State Facilitation and Transboundary Haze." *Asia Pacific Business Review* 19, no. 3 (2013): 381–401. http://dx.doi.org/10.1080/13602381.2012.748262.

———. "Patronage Politics, Plantation Fires and Transboundary Haze." *Environmental Hazards* 12, no. 3–4 (2013): 200–17. http://dx.doi.org/10.1080/17477891.2012.759524.

Walker, William. "Britain's Policies on Fissile Materials: The Next Steps." Special ISIS Report on the Future of UK Nuclear Weapons, Fissile Materials, Arms Control and Disarmament Policy, No. 2 (June 1997).

Walzer, Michael. *Just and Unjust Wars*. 4th ed. New York: Basic Books, 2006.

Wendt, Alexander. "Anarchy Is What States Make of It: The Social Construction of Power Politics." *International Organization* 46, no. 2 (1992): 391–425. http://dx.doi.org/10.1017/S0020818300027764.

Wolman, Andrew. "National Human Rights Commission and Asian Human Rights Norms." *Asian Journal of International Law* 3, no. 1 (2013): 77–99. http://dx.doi. org/10.1017/S2044251312000306.

Xue, Hanqin. *Transboundary Damage in International Law*. New York: Cambridge University Press, 2003. http://dx.doi.org/10.1017/CBO9780511494642.

Zengerling, Cathrin. *Greening International Jurisprudence: Environmental NGOs before International Courts, Tribunals, and Compliance Committees*. Leiden, Netherlands: Martinus Nijhoff, 2013. http://dx.doi.org/10.1163/9789004257313.

Documentary Bibliography

Cases

1900–1949

- 1924 Permanent Court of International Justice (PCIJ), "The Mavrommatis Palestine Concessions (Judgment of 30 August 1924)," *Permanent Court of International Justice* Series A, no. 2 (1924): 11.
- 1941 United Nations, "Trail Smelter Arbitration: United States, Canada (Final Decision, 16 April 1938, and 11 March 1941)," *Reports of International Arbitral Awards* 3 (1949): 1905–82.
- 1949 International Court of Justice (ICJ), "Corfu Channel Case (United Kingdom v. Albania) (Merits)," 9 April 1949, *ICJ Reports* (1949): 4, General List No. 1. http://www.icj-cij.org/docket/files/1/1645.pdf.

1950–1989

- 1957 "Lake Lanoux Arbitration (France v. Spain)," 16 November 1957, *Reports of International Arbitral Awards* 12 (1957): 281. http://www.ecolex.org/server2. php/libcat/docs/COU/Full/En/COU-143747E.pdf.
- 1974 ICJ, "Nuclear Tests (New Zealand v. France)," 20 December 1974, *ICJ Reports* (1974): 457, General List No. 59. http://www.icj-cij.org/docket/ files/59/6159.pdf.

1990–1999

- 1995 ICJ, "Fisheries Jurisdiction Case (Spain v. Canada) (Spain, Application Instituting Proceedings)," 28 March 1995. http://www.icj-cij.org/docket/ files/96/7197.pdf.
- 1995 ICJ, "Request for an Examination of the Situation in Accordance with Paragraph 63 of the Court's Judgment of 20 December 1974 in the Nuclear Tests: New Zealand v. France (Order of 22 September 1995)", *ICJ Reports* (1974): 288–308. http://www.icj-cij.org/docket/files/97/7555.pdf.
- 1997 ICJ, "Fisheries Jurisdiction Case (Spain v. Canada) (Jurisdiction of the Court)," 28 March 1998. http://www.icj-cij.org/docket/files/96/7533. pdf.
- 1997 ICJ, "Gabčíkovo-Nagymaros Project (Hungary/Slovakia) (Judgment), 25 September 1997," *ICJ Reports* (1997): 7, reprinted in *International Legal Materials* 37 (1998): 162. http://www.icj-cij.org/docket/files/92/7375.pdf.

2000–2009

- 2001 International Tribunal for the Law of the Sea (ITLOS), "MOX Plant Case: Ireland v. United Kingdom (Request for Provisional Measures and Statement of Case of Ireland)," Case No. 10, 9 November 2001. http://www.itlos.org/fileadmin/itlos/documents/cases/case_no_10/request_ireland_e.pdf.
- 2001 United Kingdom, Queen's Bench Division, "R (On the Application of Friends of Affairs and another," 15 November 2001, EWHC Admin 914, CO/402/20. http://www.lexisnexis.com/hottopics/lnacademic.
- 2001 ITLOS, "Ireland v. United Kingdom: MOX Plant Case (Order of 3 December 2001)," 3 December 2001. http://www.itlos.org/fileadmin/itlos/documents/cases/case_no_10/Order.03.12.01.E.pdf.
- 2003 Permanent Court of Arbitration (PCA), UNCLOS Annex VII Arbitral Tribunal, "Ireland v. United Kingdom: MOX Plant Case (Order No. 3)," 9 January 2003. http://www.pca-cpa.org/MOX%20Order%20no3a614.pdf?fil_id=81.
- 2003 PCA, OSPAR Arbitration, "Ireland v. United Kingdom: MOX Plant Case (Final Award)," 2 July 2003, http://www.pca-cpa.org/OSPAR%20Awarde17f.pdf?fil_id=447.
- 2003 India, Supreme Court, "Research Foundation v. Union of India, and Others," Writ Petition (Civil) 657 of 1995, 14 October 2003 Writ. http://www.elaw.org/content/india-research-foundation-v-union-india-others-wp-6571995-20031014-hazardous-wastes.
- 2006 France, Conseil d'État, "Association Ban Asbestos France, Association Greenpeace France, Comité Anti-amiante Jussieu, Association Nationale de Défense des Victimes de l'Amiante v. République Française ('Le Clemenceau') Conseil d'État (6ème et 1ère section réunies), Suspension Decision of 15 February 2006, N° 288801." http://archive.basel.int/ships/relevcaselaw.html.
- 2006 ICJ, "Case Concerning Pulp Mills on the River Uruguay: Argentina v. Uruguay (Request for Indication of Provisional Measures, Order of 13 July 2006)." http://www.icj-cij.org/docket/files/135/11235.pdf.
- 2007 ICJ, "Case Concerning Pulp Mills on the River Uruguay: Argentina v. Uruguay (Request for Indication of Provisional Measures, Order of 23 January 2007)." http://www.icj-cij.org/docket/files/135/13615.pdf.
- 2009 European Court of Human Rights, "Tatar v. Romania," 27 January 2009, No. 67021/01. http://hudoc.echr.coe.int/fre?i=003-2615810-2848789 http://hudoc.echr.coe.int/fre?i=003-2615810-2848789.

2010–Present

- 2010 ICJ, "Case Concerning Pulp Mills on the River Uruguay: Argentina v. Uruguay (Judgment of 20 April 2010)." http://www.icj-cij.org/docket/files/135/15877.pdf.
- 2010 ICJ, "Case Concerning Pulp Mills on the River Uruguay: Argentina v. Uruguay (Judgment of 20 April 2010, Separate Opinion of Judge Greenwood)." http://www.icj-cij.org/docket/files/135/15889.pdf.
- 2012 India, Supreme Court, "Research Foundation for Science, Technology and Natural Resource Policy v. Union of India & Ors.," I.A. Nos. 61 & 62 of 2012 in Written Petition C No. 657 of 1995, 30 July 2012, 14–15. http://www.supremelaw.in/2012/07/research-foundation-for-science.html.
- 2014 ICJ, "Whaling in the Antarctic: Australia v. Japan, New Zealand Intervening (Judgment of 31 March 2014)." http://www.icj-cij.org/docket/files/148/18136.pdf.

Conventions/Treaties

1900–1949

- 1909 United Kingdom and the United States, "Treaty Relating to Boundary Waters and Questions Arising Along the Boundary Between Canada and the United States," Washington, 11 January 1909 (in force 5 May 1910), in Charles Bevans, *Treaties and Other International Agreements of the United States* 1976–1949 12 (1949). http://www.ijc.org/en_/BWT.
- 1935 Canada and the United States, "Convention Relative to the Establishment of a Tribunal to Decide Question of Indemnity and Future Regime Arising from the Operation of Smelter at Trail, British Columbia," Ottawa, 15 April 1935, *U.S. Treaty Series*, No. 893.

1950–1969

- 1957 "Treaty Establishing the European Atomic Energy Community (EUR-ATOM)," Rome, 27 March 1957 (in force 1 January 1958). http://eur-lex.europa.eu/legal-content/EN/TXT/?uri=CELEX:12012A/TXT.
- 1960 "Convention on Third Party Liability in the Field of Nuclear Energy," Paris, 29 July 1960 (in force 10 April 1968), *United Nations Treaty Series*, 956: 251, *International Legal Materials* 28 (1989): 657. http://www.ecolex.org/server2.php/libcat/docs/TRE/Full/En/TRE-000435.txt.
- 1969 Brazil, Argentina, Bolivia, Paraguay, and Uruguay, "Treaty of the River Plate Basin," Brasilia, 23 April 1969 (in force 14 August 1970), *United Nations Treaty Series* no. 1250 (1973). http://www.internationalwaterlaw.org/documents/regionaldocs/La_Plata-1969.pdf.
- 1969 International Maritime Organization (IMO), "International Convention Relating to Intervention on the High Seas in Cases of Oil Pollution Casualties," Brussels, 29 November 1969 (in force 6 May 1975), *United Nations Treaty Series* vol. 970, no. 14049. https://treaties.un.org/doc/Publication/UNTS/Volume%20970/volume-970-I-14049-English.pdf.

1970–1979

- 1971 "Convention on International Liability for Damage Caused by Space Objects," New York, 29 November 1971 (in force 1 September 1972), *International Legal Materials* 10 (1971): 965. https://www.faa.gov/about/office_org/headquarters_offices/ast/media/Conv_International_Liab_Damage.pdf.
- 1972 IMO, "Convention on the Prevention of Pollution from Ships 73/78 (MARPOL)," London, 2 November 1973 (in force 12 October 1983). http://www.imo.org/en/KnowledgeCentre/ReferencesAndArchives/HistoryofMARPOL/Documents/MARPOL%201973%20-%20Final%20Act%20and%20Convention.pdf.
- 1972 IMO, "Convention on the Prevention of Marine Pollution by Dumping of Waste and Other Matter," London, 13 November 1972 (in force 30 August 1975), *United Nations Treaty Series* 1046 (1977): 138–218. https://treaties.un.org/doc/Publication/UNTS/Volume%201046/volume-1046-I-15749-English.pdf.
- 1973 "Convention on International Trade in Endangered Species (CITES)," Washington, 3 March 1973 (in force 1 July 1975). https://www.cites.org/eng/disc/text.php.

- 1973 United Nations Economic Commission for Europe (UNECE), "Convention on Long-Range Transboundary Air Pollution," Geneva, 13 November 1973 (in force 16 March 1983), in *International Legal Materials* 18 (1979): 1442. http://www.unece.org/fileadmin/DAM/env/lrtap/full%20text/1979.CLRTAP.e.pdf.
- 1975 Argentina and Uruguay, "Statute of the River Uruguay," Salto, 26 February 1975 (in force 18 September 1976), *United Nations Treaty Series* no. 21425 (1982): 347. http://www.internationalwaterlaw.org/documents/regionaldocs/Uruguay_River_Statute_1975.pdf.
- 1976 Association of Southeast Asian Nations (ASEAN), "Treaty of Amity and Cooperation," Bali, 24 February 1976 (in force 21 June 1976). http://cils.nus.edu.sg/rp/pdf/1976%20Treaty%20of%20Amity%20and%20Cooperation%20in%20Southeast%20Asia-pdf.pdf.
- 1978 "Convention on Future Multilateral Cooperation in the Northwest Atlantic Fisheries," Ottawa, 24 October 1978 (in force 1 January 1979). http://www.nafo.int/about/frames/convention.html.
- 1979 "Convention on the Protection of Migratory Species of Wild Animals (CMS)," Bonn, 23 June 1979 (in force 1 November 1983), *International Legal Materials* 11 (1979): 15. http://www.cms.int/en/convention-text.
- 1979 UNECE, "Convention on Long-Range Transboundary Air Pollution," Geneva, 13 November 1979 (in force 16 March 1983), *International Legal Materials* 18 (1979): 1442. http://www.unece.org/fileadmin/DAM/env/lrtap/full%20text/1979.CLRTAP.e.pdf.

1980–1989
- 1982 "United Nations Convention on the Law of the Sea," Montego Bay, 10 December 1982 (in force 16 November 1994), *International Legal Materials* 21 (1982): 1283. http://www.un.org/depts/los/convention_agreements/texts/unclos/unclos_e.pdf.
- 1985 "Convention for the Protection of the Ozone Layer," Vienna, 22 March 1985 (in force 22 September 1988), *United Nations Treaty Series* 1513: 323, *International Legal Materials* 26 (1987): 1529. http://www.unep.ch/ozone/pdfs/viennaconvention2002.pdf.
- 1985 ASEAN, "Agreement on Conservation of Nature and Natural Resources," Kuala Lumpur, 5 July 1985 (not yet in force). http://www.ecolex.org/server2.php/libcat/docs/TRE/Full/En/TRE-000820.txt.
- 1987 "Montreal Protocol on Substances That Deplete the Ozone Layer," Montreal, 16 September 1987 (in force 1 January 1989), *United Nations Treaty Series* 1522: 3, *International Legal Materials* 26 (1987): 1550. https://treaties.un.org/doc/Publication/UNTS/Volume%201522/volume-1522-I-26369-English.pdf.
- 1989 UNEP, "Convention on the Control of Transboundary Movements of Hazardous Waste and Their Disposal," Basel, 22 March 1989 (in force 5 May 1992). http://www.basel.int/Portals/4/Basel%20Convention/docs/text/BaselConventionText-e.pdf.

1990–1999
- 1991 UNECE, "Convention on Environmental Impact Assessment in a Transboundary Context," Espoo, 25 February 1991 (in force 10 September 1997), *United Nations Treaty Series* 1989: 310. http://www.unece.org/fileadmin/DAM/env/eia/documents/legaltexts/Espoo_Convention_authentic_ENG.pdf.

- 1991 Argentina, Brazil, Paraguay and Uruguay, "Treaty Establishing a Common Market," Asunción, 26 March 1991 (in force 29 November 1991), *International Legal Materials* 30 (1991): 1041–63. http://www.jstor.org/stable/20693593.
- 1992 UNECE, "Convention on the Transboundary Effect of International Accidents," Helsinki, 17 March 1992 (in force 19 April 2000). http://www.unece.org/fileadmin/DAM/env/documents/2013/TEIA/1321013_ENG_Web_New_ENG.pdf.
- 1992 United Nations, "United Nations Framework Convention on Climate Change," Rio de Janeiro, 9 May 1992 (in force 21 March 1994), *International Legal Materials* 31 (1992): 849. http://unfccc.int/files/essential_background/background_publications_htmlpdf/application/pdf/conveng.pdf.
- 1992 "Convention for the Protection of the Marine Environment of the North-East Atlantic," Paris, 22 September 1992 (in force 25 March 1998), http://sedac.ciesin.org/entri/texts/acrc/MEofNE.txt.html.
- 1994 "Convention on Cooperation for the Protection and Sustainable Use of the River Danube," Sofia, 29 June 1994 (in force 22 October 1998). http://ec.europa.eu/world/agreements/downloadFile.do?fullText=yes&treatyTransId=1406.
- 1994 International Atomic Energy Agency (IAEA), "Convention on Nuclear Safety," Vienna, 17 June 1994 (in force 24 October 1996). https://www.iaea.org/sites/default/files/infcirc449a1.pdf.
- 1995 United Nations General Assembly, "Agreement for the Implementation of the Provisions of the United Nations Convention on the Law of the Sea 10 December 1982 Relating to the Conservation and Management of Straddling Fish Stocks and Highly Migratory Fish Stocks," 4 August 1995 (in force 11 December 2001), *International Legal Materials* 34 (1995): 1542–91.
- 1996 IMO, "Protocol to the Convention on the Prevention of Marine Pollution by Dumping of Wastes and Other Matter," London, 7 November 1996 (in force 24 March 2006), *International Legal Materials* 36 (1997): 1. http://www.admiraltylawguide.com/conven/protodumping1996.html.
- 1998 UNECE, "Convention on Access to Information, Public Participation in Decision-Making and Access to Justice in Environmental Matters," Aarhus, 25 June 1998 (in force 30 October 2001). http://www.unece.org/fileadmin/DAM/env/pp/documents/cep43e.pdf.
- 1998 UNEP, "Convention on the Prior Informed Consent Procedure for Certain Hazardous Chemicals and Pesticides in International Trade," Rotterdam, 10 September 1998 (in force 24 February 2004). http://www.pic.int/TheConvention/Overview/TextoftheConvention/tabid/1048/language/en-US/Default.aspx.
- 1999 "Protocol on Liability and Compensation for Damage Resulting from Transboundary Movements of Hazardous Wastes and Their Disposal," Basel, 10 December 1999 (not yet in force), UN Doc. UNEP/CHW.1/WG/9/2. http://archive.basel.int/meetings/cop/cop5/docs/prot-e.pdf.

2000–Present
- 2001 UNEP, "Convention on Persistent Organic Pollutants," Stockholm, 22 May 2001 (in force 14 May 2004). http://chm.pops.int/TheConvention/Overview/TextoftheConvention/tabid/2232/Default.aspx.
- 2002 ASEAN, "Agreement on Transboundary Haze Pollution," Kuala Lumpur, 10 June 2002 (in force 25 November 2003). http://haze.asean.org/?wpfb_dl=32.

- 2003 UNECE, "The Protocol on Civil Liability and Compensation for Damage Caused by the Transboundary Effects of Industrial Accidents on Transboundary Waters," Kiev, 21 May 2003 (not yet in force). http://www.unece.org/fileadmin/DAM/env/civil-liability/documents/protocol_e.pdf.
- 2007 North Atlantic Fisheries Organization (NAFO), "Amendment to the Convention on Future Multilateral Cooperation in the Northwest Atlantic Fisheries," 28 September 2007 (not yet in force) (GC Doc 07/4). http://www.nafo.int/about/frames/convention.html.
- 2007 European Union (EU), "Consolidated Version of the Treaty on the Functioning of the European Union," signed 13 December 2007 (in force 1 December 2009), *Official Journal of the European Union* 115 (9 May 2008): 47, Doc. 2008/C 115/01. http://www.refworld.org/docid/4b17a07e2.html.
- 2009 IMO, "Hong Kong Convention for the Safe and Environmentally Sound Recycling of Ships," 19 May 2009, IMO Doc. SR/CONF/45. http://ec.europa.eu/environment/waste/ships/pdf/Convention.pdf.
- 2010 UNECE, "Protocol on Strategic Environmental Assessment to the Convention on Environmental Impact Assessment in a Transboundary Context," Kiev, 21 May 2003 (in force 11 July 2010). http://www.unece.org/fileadmin/DAM/env/eia/documents/legaltexts/protocolenglish.pdf.

National Governments, and International and Non-Governmental Organizations: Documents and Reports

1960–1969

- 1962 United Nations, General Assembly, "Permanent Sovereignty over Natural Resources," Res. 1803 (XVIII), 14 December 1962. http://www.un.org/ga/search/view_doc.asp?symbol=A/RES/1803%28XVII%29.
- 1966 International Law Association, "Helsinki Rules on the Uses of the Waters of International Rivers," *Report of the Fifty-Fifth Conference* (1966): 477–533.

1970–1989

- 1971 "Founex Report on Development and Environment: A Report Submitted by a Panel of Experts Convened by the Secretary General of the United Nations Conference on the Human Environment," Founex, Switzerland, 4–12 June 1971, in *International Conciliation* (January 1972), No. 586, 7–36.
- 1971 United Nations, Conference on the Human Environment, *Report of the United Nations Conference on the Human Environment*, Stockholm, 5–16 June 1972 (Doc A/Conf. 48/14), *International Legal Materials* 11 (1972): 1420. http://www.unep.org/Documents.Multilingual/Default.asp?documentid=97&articleid=1503.
- 1987 World Commission on Environment and Development, *Report of the World Commission on Environment and Development: Our Common Future* (Oxford: Oxford University Press, 1987).

1990–1999

- 1992 United Nations, General Assembly, "Rio Declaration on Environment and Development," in *Report of the United Nations Conference on Environment and Development*, Rio de Janeiro, 3–14 June 1992, Doc. A/CONF.151/26 (Vol. I),

Annex I, *International Legal Materials* 31 (1992): 874. http://www.unep.org/
Documents.Multilingual/Default.asp?DocumentID=78&ArticleID=1163.

- 1994 United Nations, General Assembly, "Draft Agreement for the Implementation of the Provisions of the United Nations Convention on the Law of the Sea 10 December 1982 Relating to the Conservation and Management of Straddling Fish Stocks and Highly Migratory Fish Stocks Prepared by the Chairman of the Conference," 1994 (Doc. A/Conf.164/22).
- 1995 ASEAN, "ASEAN Cooperation Plan on Transboundary Pollution," Singapore, June 1995.
- 1997 European Community, "Council Regulation No 120/97 of 20 January 1997 amending Regulation (EC) No 259/93 on the Supervision and Control of Shipments of Waste within, into and out of the European Community," *Official Journal* L 022 (24 January 1997): 0014-15.
- 1997 Indonesia, "Law Concerning Environmental Management (Law No. 23 of 1997)," 19 September 1997. http://faolex.fao.org/docs/html/ins13056.htm.
- 1997 ASEAN, "Regional Haze Action Plan," Singapore, 22–23 December 1997. http://haze.asean.org/?page_id=213.

2000–2009

- 2000 Organisation for Economic Co-operation and Development (OECD), "Guidelines for Multinational Enterprises: Revision 2000," (Paris: OECD, 2000). http://www.oecd.org/investment/mne/1922428.pdf.
- 2000 Hungary, Hungarian Ministry of Foreign Affairs, "Summary of the Environment Catastrophe Caused by the Cyanide Pollution to the River Tisza," 21 February 2000.
- 2000 UNEP, UNEP Office for the Coordination of Humanitarian Affairs (OCHA). "Cyanide Spill at Baia Mare," March 2000.
- 2000 Australia, Senate, "Corporate Code of Conduct Bill 2000- C2004b01333," 6 September 2000. http://www.comlaw.gov.au/Details/C2004B01333.
- 2000 European Union (EU), "Report of the International Task Force for Assessing the Baia Mare Accident, December 2000." http://viso.jrc.ec.europa.eu/pecomines_ext/docs/bmtf_report.pdf.
- 2002 UNEP, Conference of the Parties to the Basel Convention on the Control of Transboundary Movements of Hazardous Wastes and Their Disposal, "Technical Guidelines for the Sound Management of the Full and Partial Dismantling of Ships," sixth meeting, Geneva, 9–13 December 2002, U.N. Doc. UNEP/CHW.6/23 (8 August 2002). http://www.basel.int/Portals/4/Basel%20Convention/docs/meetings/sbc/workdoc/techgships-e.pdf.
- 2003 IMO, "Guidelines on Ship Recycling," 5 December 2003, IMO Doc. A 23/Res.962. https://www.transportstyrelsen.se/globalassets/global/sjofart/dokument/guidelines_on_ship_recycling_resolution_962.pdf.
- 2003 UNEP, Open-Ended Working Group of the Basel Convention on the Control of Transboundary Movements of Hazardous Wastes and Their Disposal (OEWG), "Report of the Open-ended Working Group of the Basel Convention on the Work of Its Second Session," Geneva, 20–24 October 2003, U.N. Doc. UNEP/CHW/OEWG/2/12 (16 December 2003), 17–18. http://www.basel.int/TheConvention/OpenendedWorkingGroup%280EWG%29/ReportsandDecisions/tabid/3413/Default.aspx.

- 2004 International Labor Organization (ILO), "Safety and Health in Ship-breaking: Guidelines for Asian Countries and Turkey," ILO Doc. GB.289/205 (March 2004). http://www.ilo.org/wcmsp5/groups/public/---ed_protect/---protrav/---safework/documents/normativeinstrument/wcms_107689.pdf.
- 2004 EU, "Directive 2004/35/CE of the European Parliament and of the Council of 21 April 2004 on Environmental Liability with Regard to the Prevention and Remedying of Environmental Damage," 21 April 2004, *Official Journal* L 143 (30 April 2004): 0056–75. http://eur-lex.europa.eu/legal-content/EN/TXT/?uri=CELEX:32004L0035.
- 2007 Republic of Ireland, Dáil Éireann, "Written Answers—Nuclear Debate," Vol. 635 (5 April 2007). http://debates.oireachtas.ie/dail/2007/04/05/00056.asp.
- 2009 IMO, *International Shipping and World Trade: Facts and Figures.* London: IMO Maritime Knowledge Centre, 2009.
- 2009 IMO, International Conference on the Safe and Environmentally Sound Recycling of Ships, "Statements by Delegations and Observers at the Closing Session of the Conference," Hong Kong, 11–15 May 2009, IMO Doc. SR/CONF/INF.8, 7. http://www.sjofartsverket.se/pages/19514/sr-conf-inf8.pdf.
- 2009 United Kingdom, Department of Energy and Climate Change, "UK Strategy for Radioactive Discharges" (July 2009). https://www.gov.uk/government/uploads/system/uploads/attachment_data/file/249884/uk_strategy_for_radioactive_discharges.pdf.

2010–Present
- 2011 UNEP, Basel Secretariat, "Note on Environmentally Sound Recycling of Ships," 11 July 2011, Doc. UNEP/CHW.10/18. http://archive.basel.int/meetings/cop/cop10/documents/18e.pdf.
- 2011 UNEP, "Report of the Conference of the Parties to the Basel Convention on the Control of Transboundary Movements of Hazardous Wastes and Their Disposal on Its Tenth Meeting," Cartagena, 17–21 October 2011, Doc. UNEP/CHW.10/28, 1 November 2011. http://archive.basel.int/meetings/cop/cop10/documents/28e.pdf.
- 2013 EU, "Regulation (EU) No. 1257/2013 of the European Parliament and of the Council of 20 November 2013 on Ship Recycling and Amending EC No. 103/2006 and Directive 2009/16/EC," *Official Journal of the European Union*, L330, 10 December 2013. http://eur-lex.europa.eu/legal-content/EN/TXT/PDF/?uri=CELEX:32013R1257&qid=1418667603088&from=EN.
- 2014 UNECE, Meeting of the Parties to the Convention on Environmental Impact Assessment in a Transboundary Context, "Report of the Implementation Committee on Its Thirtieth Session," 25–27 February 2014 [Doc. ECE/MP.EIA/IC/2014/2]. http://www.unece.org/fileadmin/DAM/env/documents/2014/EIA/IC/ece.mp.eia.ic.2014.2.as_resubmitted.pdf.